From Stonehenge to Samarkand

From Stonehenge to Samarkand

An Anthology of Archaeological Travel Writing

Brian Fagan

OXFORD
UNIVERSITY PRESS

OXFORD
UNIVERSITY PRESS

Oxford University Press, Inc., publishes works that further
Oxford University's objective of excellence
in research, scholarship, and education.

Oxford New York
Auckland Cape Town Dar es Salaam Hong Kong Karachi
Kuala Lumpur Madrid Melbourne Mexico City Nairobi
New Delhi Shanghai Taipei Toronto

With offices in
Argentina Austria Brazil Chile Czech Republic France Greece
Guatemala Hungary Italy Japan Poland Portugal Singapore
South Korea Switzerland Thailand Turkey Ukraine Vietnam

Published by Oxford University Press, Inc.
198 Madison Avenue, New York, New York 10016

ISBN-13: 978-0-7394-7975-9

Printed in the United States of America

Maps drawn by Mapping Specialists, Madison, Wisconsin

From Stonehenge to Samarkand

Contents

Maps and Timeline

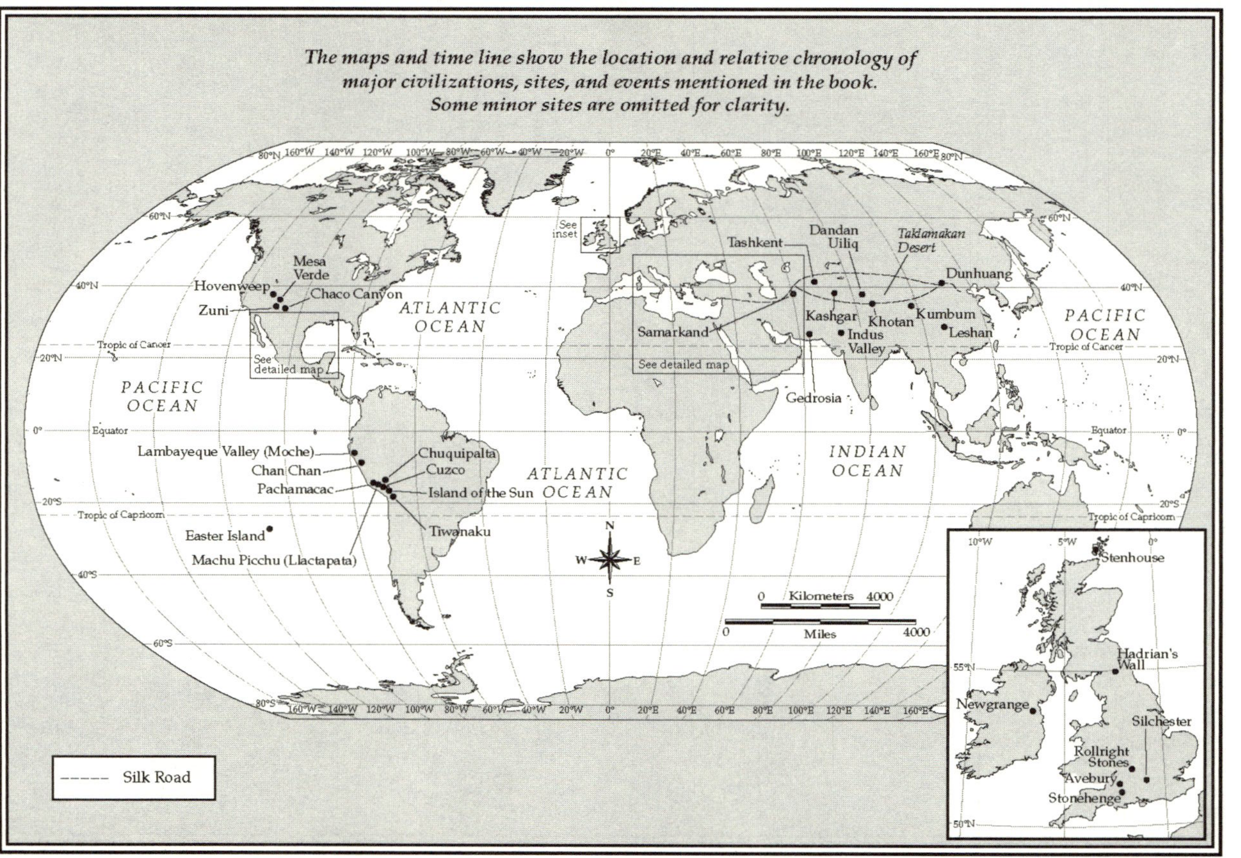
The maps and time line show the location and relative chronology of major civilizations, sites, and events mentioned in the book. Some minor sites are omitted for clarity.
Hovenweep
Mesa Verde
Chaco Canyon
Zuni
See detailed map
ATLANTIC OCEAN
PACIFIC OCEAN
Lambayeque Valley (Moche)
Chan Chan
Pachamacac
Chuquipalta
Cuzco
Island of the Sun
Tiwanaku
Easter Island
Machu Picchu (Llactapata)
ATLANTIC OCEAN
See inset
Tashkent
Samarkand
See detailed map
Dandan Uiliq
Taklamakan Desert
Dunhuang
Kashgar
Khotan
Kumbum
Leshan
Indus Valley
Gedrosia
INDIAN OCEAN
PACIFIC OCEAN
Tropic of Cancer
Equator
Tropic of Capricorn
N
W
E
S
0 Kilometers 4000
0 Miles 4000
Silk Road
Stenhouse
Hadrian's Wall
Newgrange
Silchester
Rollright Stones
Avebury
Stonehenge

FRANCE
Rhine R.
GERMANY
CZECH REP.
SLOVAKIA
SWITZ.
AUSTRIA
HUNGARY
Po R.
SLOV.
CROATIA
BOS. & HERZ.
SERB. & MONT.
ROMANIA
MOLDOVA
UKRAINE
Dnieper R.
Danube R.
BULGARIA
MACED.
ALBANIA
Adriatic Sea
ITALY
Rome
Herculaneum
Pompeii
Delphi
GREECE
Aegean Sea
Athens
Eleusis
Aegina
Sparta
Ephesus
Miletus
Halicarnissus
Mykonos
(Deios)
Sounion
Carthage
TUNISIA
Mediterranean Sea
Black Sea
Don R.
Volga R.
RUSSIA
GEORGIA
ARMENIA
AZERBAIJAN
TURKEY
CYPRUS
Caspian Sea
Aral Sea
KAZAKHSTAN
Kara Kum
UZBEKISTAN
Amu Darya
Samarkand
Bukhara
TURKMENISTAN
Mershed
Herat
AFGHANISTAN
IRAN
Isfahan
Persepolis
Shiraz
Nineveh
Tigris R.
Euphrates R.
SYRIA
Palmyra
IRAQ
Babylon
Ur
Baalbek
LEBANON
Bostra
ISRAEL
JORDAN
Petra
KUWAIT
Persian Gulf
Gulf of Oman
QATAR
U.A.E.
OMAN
SAUDI ARABIA
Tropic of Cancer
0 Kilometers 500
0 Miles 500
Arabian Sea
Red Sea
LIBYA
N
W
E
S
EGYPT
Giza
Memphis
Nile R.
Dendera
Valley of the Kings
Luxor (Thebes)
Aswan
Philae (Elephantine)
Abu Simbel
SUDAN
10°E
20°E
30°E
40°E
50°E
60°E
70°E
50°N
40°N
30°N
20°N

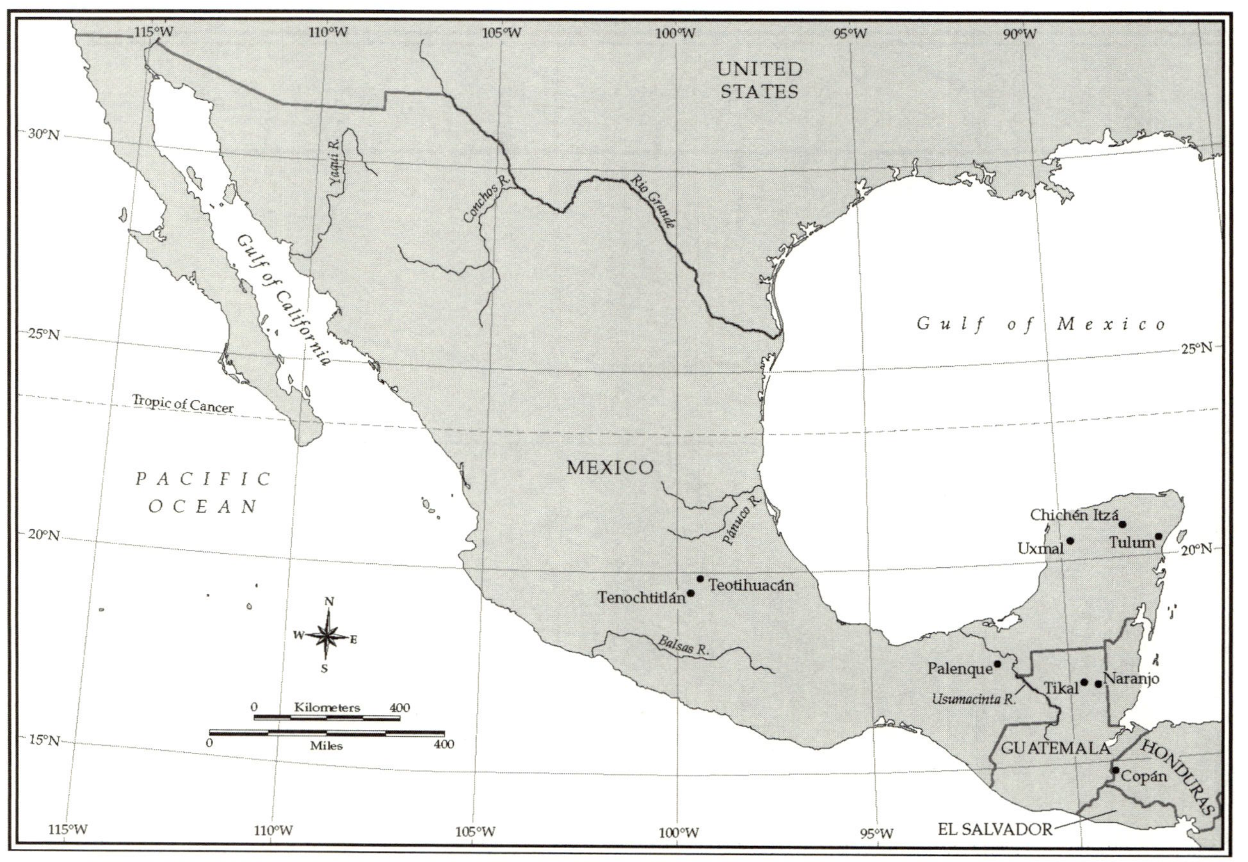
UNITED STATES
MEXICO
Gulf of Mexico
Gulf of California
PACIFIC OCEAN
Tropic of Cancer
Rio Grande
Conchos R.
Yaqui R.
Pánuco R.
Balsas R.
Usumacinta R.
Teotihuacán
Tenochtitlán
Chichén Itzá
Uxmal
Tulum
Palenque
Tikal
Naranjo
Copán
GUATEMALA
HONDURAS
EL SALVADOR
N
W
E
S
0 Kilometers 400
0 Miles 400
30°N
25°N
20°N
15°N
115°W
110°W
105°W
100°W
95°W
90°W

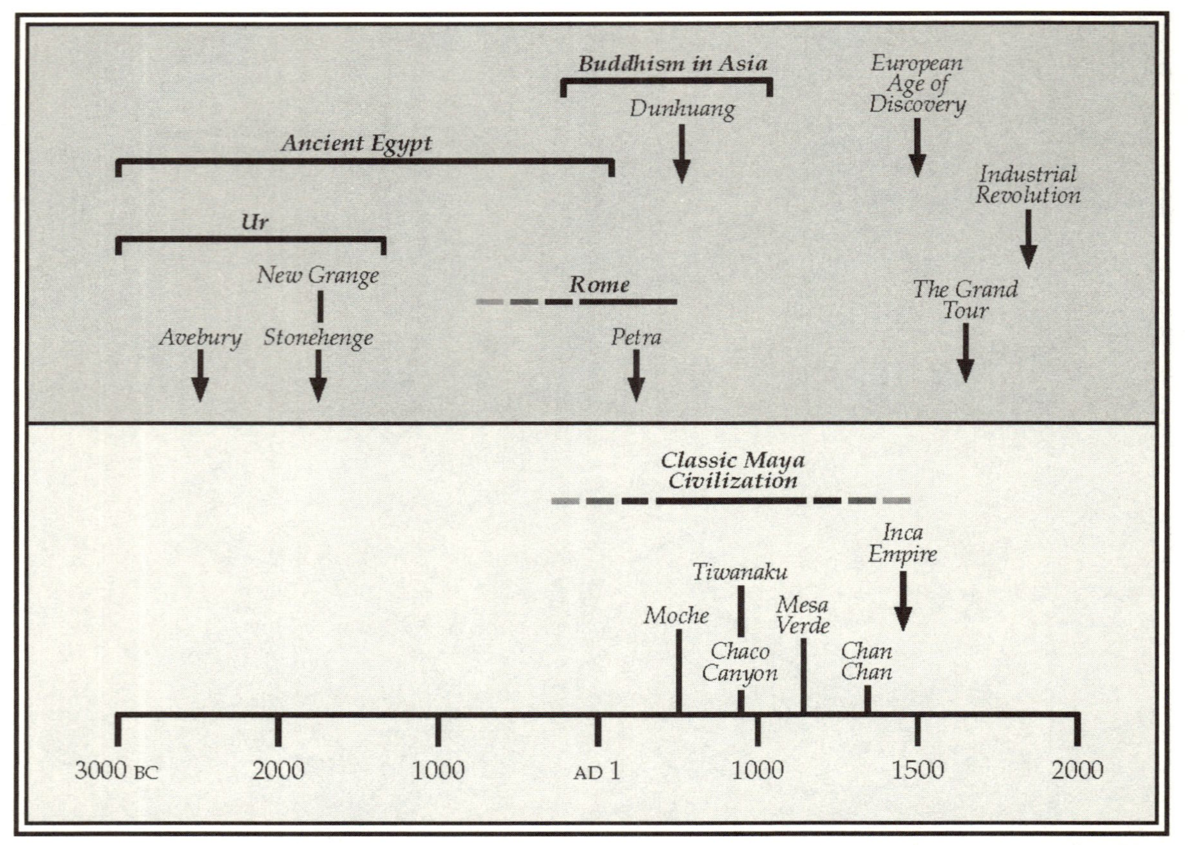
Buddhism in Asia
Dunhuang
European Age of Discovery
Ancient Egypt
Industrial Revolution
Ur
New Grange
Rome
The Grand Tour
Avebury
Stonehenge
Petra
Classic Maya Civilization
Inca Empire
Tiwanaku
Moche
Mesa Verde
Chaco Canyon
Chan Chan
3000 BC
2000
1000
AD 1
1000
1500
2000

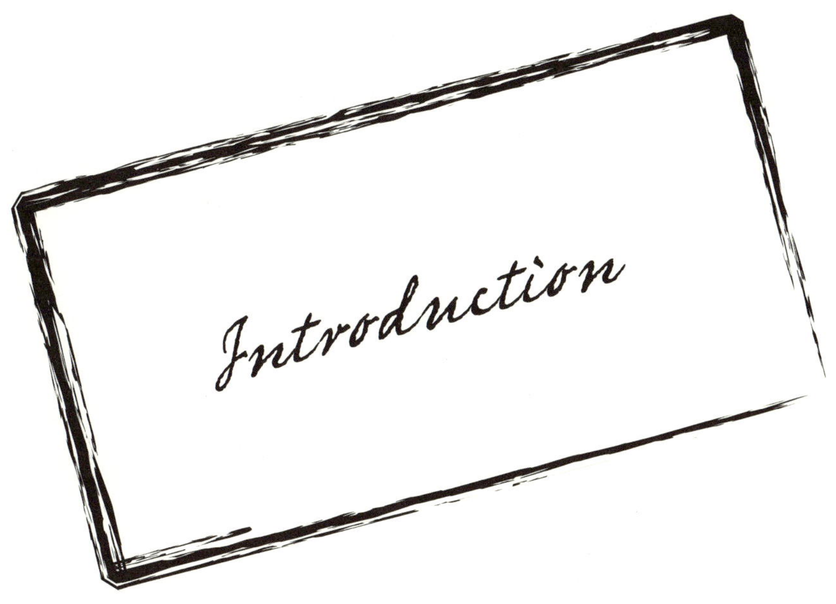

My name is Ozymandias, king of kings:
"Look on my works, ye Mighty, and
despair!"
Nothing beside remains. Round the decay
Of that colossal wreck, boundless and bare
The lone and level sands stretch far away.

PERCY BYSSHE SHELLEY
Ozymandias (1817)

Introduction

In 1846, the French novelist Gustave Flaubert wrote to a friend, "Yesterday I saw some ruins, beloved ruins of my youth which I knew already. . . . I thought again about them and about the dead whom I had never known and on whom my feet trampled. I love above all the sight of vegetation resting upon old ruins; this embrace of nature, coming swiftly to bury the work of man the moment his hand is no longer there to defend it."[1] A fascination with the ruins of the past, with archaeological sites, spectacular and unspectacular, has been part of Western consciousness for more than two thousand years.[2] The antiquarian, depicted as an often strangely dressed eccentric, was the butt of popular jokes two centuries ago. But an interest in antiquity, in the monuments and artifacts of the past, extended far beyond narrow antiquarian circles. The history of archaeology as an emerging science is as much entwined with stirring tales of adventure and discovery as it is with travelers' tales. The archaeological traveler was a commonplace long before the English adventurer Austen Henry Layard excavated at Nineveh in the 1840s, before the Germans introduced scientific excavation at Olympia, Greece, in the 1870s, and before Thomas Cook organized steamship tours up the Nile in the late nineteenth century. The so-called grand tour from northern Europe to Italy introduced the wealthy and well connected of the British gentry to the glories of ancient Rome before the seventeenth century. Less affluent travelers, who could not afford the grand tour, marveled at Stonehenge's burial mounds and nearby Avebury's stone circles instead. The mass-market archaeological travel of today has deep roots in an earlier curiosity about the past—roots from a time when Greece was still a remote land and Mesopotamia was "the land between the rivers," the geographical equivalent of outer space.

From Stonehenge to Samarkand is a vicarious archaeological journey that begins with the gossipy Herodotus, the Greek historian and traveler of the fifth century B.C., who puzzled over the Egyptian pyramids and the complex process of mummification. We then visit the leisurely world of the antiquarian travelers, who grappled with the mysterious origins of Avebury and Stonehenge, where the Druid-obsessed William Stukeley dined atop one of the trilithons in the early eighteenth century. At the time, Christian dogma held that the world was only six thousand years old, as dated by the Old Testament genealogies. Next, the grand tour takes us to Mediterranean lands, to the Roman Forum, and on to Herculaneum and Pompeii, where the most privileged visitors descended into excavations that searched buried houses for their sculpture. Soon Pompeii was a popular attraction, where the imaginations of visitors soared far beyond the cares of an ever-faster-moving industrial world to a simpler past.

Greece entered the consciousness of the archaeological traveler in the late eighteenth century, after Lord Elgin's scandalous rape of the Parthenon for the marbles that bear his name. General Napoleon Bonaparte's Egyptian campaign brought a small army of savants to the Nile in 1798. When the war ended, a steady stream of visitors began to travel by boat up the Nile. The first serious archaeological tourism developed with the arrival of the steamship, the railroad, and the Suez Canal in the late nineteenth century. By then, the ruins of Nineveh, Babylon, and Persepolis were familiar, if still exotic, territory to the archaeological traveler. So were Maya ruins and the remnants of Inca civilization, described by the naturalist Alexander von Humboldt in 1801 and by the American diplomat and journalist Ephraim Squier, who visited both the highlands and the lowlands of Peru in 1863. Another American, the traveler and self-styled archaeologist Hiram Bingham, journeyed to the last major unknown Inca site, Machu Picchu, in 1912.

Archaeological travel changed profoundly during the first half of the twentieth century. By then, Egypt, Greece, and the Holy Land were familiar stamping grounds. But to venture further east was to venture into much less familiar archaeological landscapes, even if spectacular temples like Angkor Wat and Anuradhapura in Sri Lanka were on the map thanks to travels by missionaries, colonial administrators, and the occasional bold archaeologist exploring far from the beaten track. A steady trickle of young Europeans, often Britons, traveled deep into central Asia in search of the past between the 1920s and the 1950s, among them the cynical and somewhat eccentric Robert Byron, who became obsessed with brick mortuary towers in the outer reaches of what is now Iran. The travels of these young people were not as hazardous as those of their contemporary, the archaeologist Aurel Stein, for they—unlike Stein—never ventured into regions as remote as the territory he covered along central Asia's Silk Road. Nevertheless, Byron and others left a fascinating chronicle of archaeological sites long before the invention of the jumbo jet, the guidebook, and the global package tour.

Our traveling forebears were often expert observers, and not averse to clothing the past and its ruins in ethereal dress. The past has always unleashed the romantic in visitors. The eighteenth-century antiquary William Stukeley was an unashamed idealist who clothed archaeological sites and ruins in an aura of mystery and legend. He wrote of ancient priests, of a savage humankind, of places like Stonehenge that were still wild and unkempt and set in rural landscapes. Stukeley and his contemporaries saw archaeological sites as evocative places apart from their scientific value—something that does not necessarily appeal to the scientist. As the art historian Christopher Woodward remarks, "archaeologists will argue that flowers and ivy on a ruin are just Picturesque fluff, curlicues to amuse an artist's pencil."[3] Woodward points out that that any archaeological site has two values: an objective value as a material artifact, and a subjective value as an inspiration to artists and, I would add, to the visitor who has curiosity and imagination. Writes Woodward, "You can uproot that alder tree . . . erect more fences, spray more weed-killer, excavate and polish. You will preserve every single brick for posterity, and analyze the occasional discovery of an ornamental fragment in a learned publication. You will have a great many bricks, but nothing more." Indeed, visit Ephesus, the Parthenon, the Roman Forum, or Angkor Wat, and the guides will bombard you with facts and dates, with descriptions of architectural styles, with names of gods and goddesses. Guiding is now serious business. Every Greek guide is currently trained for over three years on how to guide, and they do it very well. But they rightly describe scientific findings, so that their work is often devoid of emotion and imagination—the very stock-in-trade of the perceptive archaeological traveler who desires so much more from his or her visit.

"Unscientific!" you say. Of course, for the past is far more than a deserted, sanitized ruin to be catalogued and analyzed. Many writers have reminded us that the past is foreign territory, far removed from our world, a place inhabited by science and our imaginations—and it is our curiosity, our lively minds, and evocative experience that bring it to life for us to enjoy.

Think for a moment of ancient Rome, for centuries an irresistible lure to the artist, the poet, the traveler, and the writer. The Protestant cemetery bears testimony to them—the poets John Keats and Percy Bysshe Shelley, and many others, wealthy and poor, famous and long-forgotten. With

Christopher Woodward's book as my guide, I visited Shelley's grave, where there is only a plain, undecorated slab, which Woodward calls "still shining water reflecting clouds and sunlight." The slab invokes profound thought, careful reflection—far more so than the elaborately decorated monuments nearby. There is something special here, in a cemetery where lush vegetation embraces the tombs, where you get a sense of returning to the earth, of renewal, of planting and harvest and the endless cycle of human life—birth, growth, maturity, and death. Shelley's gravestone evokes a man who valued the past as a reflection of the present. Ever since the morning that I visited Shelley's grave, I have thought of archaeological sites as mirrors that reflect the past, not only in a scientific way, but in such a way that we think of the site as living history. *From Stonehenge to Samarkand* is a book about the mirrors of the past and how they affected both adventurer and tourist.

There is nothing new in this idea. When François René, Vicomte de Chateaubriand, visited the Roman Colosseum in 1801, he was writing a book, *The Genius of Christianity* (published the following year), that argued for the revival of Christianity in France after the Revolution. During his trip, he learned that the hermit who had occasionally sounded his bell in the silent ruins had died: "It is thus we are warned at each step of our nothingness; man goes on to meditate on the ruins of empires; he forgets that he is himself a ruin still more unsteady, and that he will fall before these remains do."[4] Ruins have long been a metaphor for death and resurrection, a reminder that the faithful will decay before achieving eternal life. In a sense ruins are memento mori, so much so that when Pope Pius II introduced, in 1462, the very first legislation to protect classical antiquities from destruction, he specifically mentioned their "exemplary frailty."

As numerous extracts in this book attest, the past comes down to us in many ways, and occasionally at the most unexpected moments. Many years ago, I climbed high among the seats of the great amphitheater at Epidauros, Greece. I sat in the deserted tiers, savoring the warmth of a spring afternoon as the shadows lengthened. The scent of eucalyptus wafted on the soft breeze. A German professor with a group of his students arrived. They sat in the lower seats as he stood midstage and recited dramatic stanzas from Euripides' play *Ion*. The soft Greek cascaded and rolled across the serried amphitheater. The professor was delighted when his students joined in the chorus. Even individual syllables caressed my ears as I sat spellbound. I imagined the theater crammed with spectators, hot, sweating, excited, wooed to silence by the familiar verses, swaying to the chorus and its refrains. Then the spell was broken. A package tour group arrived and swarmed the small stage. The professor gathered his charges and the amphitheater fell silent once more.

I believe that the only limit to your enjoyment as a traveler seeking the past is your imagination. Today, however, new impediments to your enjoyment are the crowds that are drawn to a "hit list" of attractions.

Chateaubriand was not the first or the only traveler to have elevated thoughts of ancient monuments, both as symbols of human mortality and also as proof of the triumph of Christianity over pagan beliefs and empires. Earlier travelers had dwelt on human imperfections, on our short-lived existence in the Great Chain of Being. "All flesh is as grass, it withereth," preached the Scriptures, this before the soul escaped and returned to God. The Jesuit Robert Southwell, in his *Triumphs over Death* (1596), compared death to demolishing a decrepit structure in order to build a new house. "Withdraw your eies from the ruine of this cottage, & caste them upon the majestie of the second building," he wrote.[5] When the Last Trumpet sounded on the Day of Judgment, then all human structures, whether cathedrals, palaces, or just humble dwellings, would collapse into dust. Ruins reminded our predecessors, as they remind us, of the fleeting nature of human achievement and existence. We may not derive powerful religious metaphors from them today, but they do offer us a historical precedent, serving as reminders that civilizations rise and fall, that our own industrial civilization is, in the larger context of time, a transitory phenomenon.

We look at the past through mirrors—ancient monuments and ruins—sometimes for a glimpse of the future, sometimes for pure aesthetic pleasure, but today usually out of historical curiosity or simply because we are told that they are "worth seeing." No longer do we think of ruins in terms of the Last Judgment or as part of a picturesque landscape, although you can still experience the latter by visiting great-house gardens in England or France. Today, archaeological sites that are visited on even a minor scale are inventoried and fenced off to prevent vandalism or damage caused by rapidly increasing numbers of visitors. I vividly remember walking among Stonehenge's weathered stone circles in the late 1950s, and remember the outcry when gravel was laid among the circles to prevent erosion of the soil caused by the thousands of people who flocked there. Today you can visit the interior of the site only after applying for a special permit and then obtaining it in person from English Heritage, the organization responsible for Stonehenge and other monuments. Your visit takes place before opening hours at 10 A.M., when the public is permitted to walk around along a tarmac pathway set well clear of the circles.

No longer can you wander freely through the Parthenon's columns or in the stacked dwellings of the Cliff Palace at Mesa Verde. Access to the pharaohs' tombs in the Valley of the Kings is carefully controlled, with each visitor allowed to see just two or three sepulchers. Even so, the numbers of visitors to monuments and ruins overwhelm authorities worldwide. At Petra and Angkor Wat, you can still explore unfettered by restrictions, but the accumulated damage is obvious, and it is only a matter of time before these places, too, are managed with carefully controlled access. With so many people anxious to see them, the world's major archaeological sites are quickly becoming another commodity, to be marketed as part of a highly competitive market for the tourist dollar.

One cannot enjoy the past as our forebears did. There are simply too many of us trying to do so. Yet the potential for letting your imagination run riot survives, if you are prepared to forsake the crowds, make careful preparations, and throw away the guidebook once you know the history and the science—what the archaeologists have discovered. Then you can imagine the footsteps of the Roman legionary, the pine-scented copal incense (made from the dried resin of the copal tree) and drums of a Maya ceremonial, the pounding of mortar and pestle in a southwestern pueblo as the women prepare the evening meal. This, to me, is what archaeology and archaeological travel are all about—the enjoyment of the past as part of living in our own world. This enjoyment is a transitory thing, something potentially given to all of us, to be experienced anew, and in different ways, by each generation. I count myself lucky to have walked alone under the hot African sun through Olduvai Gorge in Tanzania, one of the true cradles of humanity; to have stood alone on the earthen ramparts of the Iron Age fortress at Maiden Castle in southern England; and to have wandered, solitary, through the overgrown plazas of barely investigated Maya cities in the Yucatán. Experiencing the past is a strangely personal thing that adds a special dimension to one's life.

I wonder what the archaeological traveler of the future will see and experience. Today, archaeology is under siege from developers, from disruption by deep plowing and mining, from looters and mass tourism, to the point that the past is in danger of being loved to death by a fascinated and devoted public. Will the travelers of tomorrow be able to wander unrestricted along Hadrian's Wall or climb paths through the fortress at Mycenae as they can today? Or will the realities of ever-growing crowds and the demands of conservation demand ever more regulation and sanitation of archaeological sites, perhaps even the construction of precise replicas specifically for tourists? One only hopes that the visitor of the future will have the opportunities that we have to explore the past with imagination in full train.

There is more to our common cultural heritage than scientifically arranged assemblages of columns and marble boulders, stone foundations, or Disney-like replicas that pretend to take one back to a past complete with noises and smells. In the 1950s, the English writer Rose Macaulay wrote to a friend, "I am living in a ruinous world of crumbling walls, green jungle drowning temples and places in Mexico and Ceylon, friezes and broken columns sunk in the blue seas, with crabs scuttling about among them. Such visions of beauty are haunting, like pleasure."[6] At the time, Macaulay was writing her *Pleasure of Ruins* as an essay on the cycles of destruction and revival in history; it was an essay that stemmed from her despondency over the London Blitz in 1940–1941, when she lost her home. "Ruins must be a fantasy, veiled by the mind's dark imaginings," she wrote at the end of her book. May we never lose the fantasy, the opportunity to exercise our imaginations in search of the past. Otherwise, archaeological travel of the future will become a mere pursuit of the material, of sterile monuments and meaningless temples—something no true archaeological traveler desires.

Fortunately, travel writing is still a thriving genre, even if archaeology does not necessarily figure much in the literary equation. Surprisingly few travel writers include any sustained accounts of archaeological sites in their narratives, probably because most of the better-known locations are now well traveled and accessible even to package tourists, who can be wafted in comfort on a cushion of air at 40,000 feet (12,000 meters) to the remotest parts of central Asia. Also, many writers lack the scientific background in archaeology needed to unravel the complexities of little-known sites. Only a few writers venture further afield, and then almost invariably in search of a little-known site, like, for example, an Inca palace high in the Andes rumored to be spectacular. Most archaeological travel is now a routine carried out according to a strict schedule. The last time I was at Ephesus in Turkey, my group had precisely 90 minutes to explore the whole site. The first time I was there, we spent six hours and had the ancient city almost to ourselves. On the plus side, a tourist who once considered going to the Parthenon a grand adventure can now visit almost any important archaeological site in the world, simply by taking an airliner, bus, or cruise ship.

Good archaeological travel writing is an interesting mix of the prosaic and the romantic, the scientific and the evocative. What comes across most of all is a pervasive sense of wonderment, of surprise and delight. First impressions are all-important, even if you are not contemplating ruins as a symbol of Divine Wrath. First impressions have produced some memorable writing, few of them as vivid as the American traveler John Lloyd Stephens's lyrical description of the Maya city at Copán. As he describes troops of monkeys moving through the dry branches overhead, it is as if we are at his side, sweating profusely, swatting mosquitoes at every turn. Few writers achieve this height of vivid archaeological writing, but there are enough to have made the compilation of this book a genuine pleasure. *From Stonehenge to Samarkand* offers a varied menu of a lesser-known genre of travel writing in the hope that it will tempt you, too, to travel in search of a still-living past.

Chapter One
Beginnings

The ghosts of Nineveh and Babylon, those mighty cities gone down into the immensities of the desert, have haunted men's minds with a sense of fearful hugeness.

Rose Macaulay[1]
The Pleasure of Ruins

CHAPTER ONE

Beginnings

The intoxicating fascination of archaeology and ancient ruins comes not from a melancholy romanticism brought on by shattered towers and collapsing walls, but from what the English novelist and traveler Rose Macaulay called "the soaring of the imagination into the high empyrean where huge episodes are tangled with myths and dreams; it is the stunning impact of world history on its amazed heirs. . . . It is less ruin-worship than the worship of a tremendous past."[2] Macaulay herself was an indefatigable traveler in search of the ghosts of the past. She looked at far more than the serried columns of the Parthenon in Athens or the ruins of Roman Palmyra. Her travels took her to sites that required imagination as well as some specialized knowledge. "Nineveh and Babylon . . . are, in fact, little more than mounds."

Macaulay was not the first to articulate this. The nineteenth-century English archaeologist Austen Henry Layard wrote of the "stern, shapeless mound rising like a hill from the scorched plain, the stupendous mass of brickwork occasionally laid bare by winter rains."[3] He was an archaeologist of energy and vast imagination, intoxicated with the grandeur of the Assyrian bas-reliefs on Nineveh's palace walls—human figures, gods, kings, warriors, human-headed lions.

Nineveh captivated the Victorians. "Is not Nineveh most delightful and prodigious?" wrote one young lady to her brother in India. "Papa says nothing so truly thrilling has happened in excavations since they found Pompeii."[4] Layard and others wrote books about the mighty palaces that once dazzled the ancient world. Inevitably, the tourists came to wander through the tunnels that Layard's workers had carved into the city's mounds. Inevitably, too, many of them succumbed to fever, recovering to remember an exotic underground world they had seen in their delirium. Today, you must rely on your restless imagination amid bare heaps of earth, desert on every side. You inescapably remember the words of the Old Testament prophet Zephaniah as you tread on twenty centuries of Assyrian history: "And he will stretch out his hand against the north, and destroy Assyria, and will make Nineveh a desolation, and dry like a wilderness. . . . How is she become a desolation, a place for beasts to lie down in!"[5]

The Desolation of Babylon

The biblical prophets had no interest in powerful cities, except when they fell into ruin. Zephaniah would certainly have disapproved of the archaeologists who dig into Nineveh, and of the German excavator Robert Koldeway, who reconstructed ancient Babylon from dusty oblivion, from being a place where the "wild beasts of the desert" lay. At Nineveh, the seers triumphed, but elsewhere their dire predictions came to nothing. The Persian king Cyrus did not destroy Babylon and all its wickedness in 539: instead, he embellished it and turned it into a great Persian city. When the Greek traveler and historian Herodotus visited Babylon fifty years later, he described its salient features and the myth of Queen Semiramis:

Once he had subdued the rest of the continent, Cyrus launched a strike against the Assyrians. Now, among all the many important cities in Assyria, the most famous and well fortified—and the place where the royal palace was located after the devastation of Ninus—was Babylon. Here is a description of the city. It is situated on a huge plain, and the length of each of its sides (it forms a square) is 120 stades; altogether, then, the circumference of the city is 480 stades long. So much for its size. Its design differs from that of any other city in the known world. First there is a wide, deep moat, full of water, surrounding the entire city. Then there is a defensive wall 50 royal cubits thick and 200 cubits high (a royal cubit is three fingers longer than an ordinary one).

I had better add an explanation of where the earth that was dug out of the moat was used and a description of the construction of the wall. The earth that the excavation of the moat yielded was being made into bricks even while the digging was going on. Whenever they had moulded enough bricks, they fired them in kilns. Then, using a mortar of hot bitumen and inserting a course of reed mats every thirty layers of bricks, they built first the banks of the moat and then, by the same method, the wall itself. Along the edges of the top of the wall they built, facing one another, one-room buildings which were separated by gaps wide enough for a four-horse chariot to drive through. The wall contains a hundred gates, of solid bronze, with bronze posts and lintels too. Now, there is another place eight days' journey away from Babylon called Is, where there is an insignificant river (also called Is) which is a tributary of the Euphrates. This River Is produces, along with its water, plenty of lumps of bitumen, and the bitumen which was used for the wall of the city of Babylon was fetched from there.

So that is how Babylon's defensive wall was built. The city has two districts, because a river—the Euphrates—divides the city down the middle. The

Euphrates is a wide, deep, and fast-flowing river which rises in Armenia and issues into the Red Sea. Each wall, then, curves when it reaches the river and from there angles back along each bank of the river as a low wall of fired brick. The city itself is packed with three-storeyed and four-storeyed houses and criss-crossed by straight streets, some running right through the city and others at right angles to them going down to the river. At the end of each of these transverse streets there are postern gates set into the wall which runs beside the river: one gate for each alleyway. As well as being bronze (like the other gates) these postern gates also afford access to the river.

This wall is a breastplate, then, but another wall runs along inside this first one. It too surrounds the city, and although it is not much weaker than the first one, it is less thick. In the centre of one of the two districts of the city stands the royal palace, surrounded by a tall, strong wall, and in the centre of the other there is a bronze-gated sanctuary to Zeus as Bel, still standing in my day and forming a square with each side two stades long. In the middle of the sanctuary has been built a solid tower, a stade long and the same in width, which supports another tower, which in turn supports another, and so on: there are eight towers in all. A stairway has been constructed to wind its way up the outside of all the towers; halfway up the stairway there is a shelter with benches to rest on, where people making the ascent can sit and catch their breath. In the last tower there is a huge temple. The temple contains a large couch, which is adorned with fine coverings and has a golden table standing beside it, but there are no statues at all standing there. No one is allowed to spend the night there except a single local woman who (according to the Chaldeans, who are the priests of Bel) has been selected from among all the local women by the god.

The Chaldeans also say that the god comes in person to the temple and rests on the couch; I do not believe this story myself, although it is exactly the same as what happens in Thebes (that is, Egyptian Thebes), according to the Egyptians. The parallel even extends to the fact that a woman sleeps in the temple of Zeus at Thebes as well, and it is said that neither of these women has intercourse with any man. The same goes for the prophetess of the god at Patara in Lycia, when there is one. I mean, an oracle is not a constant feature of the place, but when there is a prophetess there, she spends every night shut up inside the temple with the god.

Lower down in the Babylonian sanctuary there is also another temple, where there is a large golden statue of a seated Zeus, with a large golden table beside him; the base of the statue and the throne on which he is seated are both golden too. As the Chaldeans told it, eight hundred talents of gold went into the making of these pieces. Outside the temple there is a golden altar, and also another large altar, which is used for sacrificing the pick of the flocks, while they are allowed to sacrifice only unweaned creatures on the golden altar. On the larger altar the Chaldeans also burn a thousand talents of frankincense each year during the festival of this god. At the time of Cyrus' conquest this precinct also contained a statue of solid gold, twelve cubits high. I did not see it myself, but I am repeating what the Chaldeans say. Darius the son of Hystaspes had designs on this statue, but did not have the effrontery to take it; however, his son Xerxes did take it, as well as killing the priest who was telling him not to touch it. Anyway, this is how the sanctuary has been decorated, apart from numerous private votive offerings.

The design and ornamentation of the walls and sanctuaries of Babylon were the work of a number of Babylonian kings . . . but also of two women. Five generations separated these two queens. The one who ruled first was called Semiramis, and the remarkable dykes on the plain were her work. Before then, the river had used to flood the whole plain.

The second of these two queens was called Nitocris. She was a more intelligent ruler than her predecessor. Apart from the monuments she left to posterity, which I am going to describe, she also noticed the size and restlessness of the Median empire, saw that other places, including Ninus, had been taken by them, and took all the precautions she possibly could. The first precaution she took was to alter the course of the River Euphrates (the river which flows through the middle of Babylon). Up until then the river had flowed in a straight line, but she had channels dug above the city which made its course so very crooked that it actually flows past one of the Assyrian villages—called Ardericca—at three points. Even today, anyone travelling from our sea to Babylon will come to this village three times, on three separate days, as he sails down the Euphrates.

This was quite a feat she accomplished. Another one was to have an embankment built along both sides of the river; this is well worth seeing for its bulk and height. Some way north of Babylon, she had a lake excavated next to the river and not far away from it; she had it dug down to the water level at each point, and it was broad enough to have a perimeter of 420 stades. She had all the earth that was excavated from this site used for the embankments by the river. Once the lake had been excavated, she had a pavement built around it, made out of stones brought from elsewhere.

The reason for both of these projects—diverting the river and creating by means of the excavation an area of nothing but marshland—was to reduce the speed of the river by having it spend its current against numerous curves, and to force anyone sailing to Babylon to take a meandering course followed by a lengthy circuit of the lake. These works of hers were carried out in the part of the country where there were passes and the shortest route from Media, in order to prevent the Medes mingling with her people and gathering information about her affairs.

So she gave the city this thorough defensive system, and then, with that basis in place, added the following projects. Since the city was divided by the river into two districts, whenever anyone wanted to cross from one district to the other in the time of earlier rulers, they had to be ferried across, which was a nuisance, I am sure. She took care of this problem too. The excavation of the basin for the lake gave her the opportunity to leave another monument to posterity as well, from the same project. She quarried huge long stones, and when the stones were ready and the lake site had been excavated, she completely diverted the river into the excavated site. While it was filling up, the old river bed dried out. This gave her the time to build up the banks of the river in the city and the stairs from the postern gates to the riverside with fired bricks in the same way as in the construction of the defensive wall. She also used the quarried stones to build a bridge, more or less in the centre of the city, and she joined the stones together with braces of iron and lead. During the day squared-off planks of wood used to be laid on it, so that the Babylonians could walk across on them, but at night these planks would be removed so that people did not cross over and steal from one another. When the excavated lake had been filled by the river and the bridge had been completed down to the last detail, she let the Euphrates flow out of the lake and back to its original bed. So in becoming a marsh the excavated site was thought to serve a useful purpose, and at the same time the Babylonians gained a bridge.[6]

Alexander the Great came to Babylon a century after Herodotus had been there, and he found much to admire, although the Greek geographer Strabo tells us that much of Babylon lay buried in detritus that would have taken ten thousand workmen two months to clear. Soon afterward, Babylon was reduced to earthen mounds, mountains of confused debris, to the puzzlement of occasional visitors.

But, Rose Macaulay insists, Babylon has its rewards:

The view over the undulating, ruin-strewn desert, with its shifting colours in the changing light, the long city site lying along the palm-fringed Euphrates, the waters of Babylon; the knowledge that among and underneath the mounds lies the jumbled debris that was three thousand years of the greatest city of the world . . . should be enough for the romantic ruin-fancier. . . . Travelers no longer think they see the Tower of Babel rising among the lesser ruins; but still they can . . . unite themselves with the triumph of Alexander riding into Babylon, his conquered capital, seeing above him the mighty walls, the pinnacles and palaces, the hanging gardens rising in tiers above the city."[7]

Herein lies the appeal of archaeological travel—the quest not for tangible ruins, although their settings often provoke admiration, but for sparking the imagination in search of the past. Generations of archaeologists have investigated the pyramids of Giza in Egypt, with (at first) gunpowder, with high-tech scientific methods, and with often brilliant detective work. All these tactics were far in the future when Herodotus was at Giza 2,500 years ago. Ancient Egyptian civilization was a recent memory, and many of its beliefs and customs still intact. But the pyramids were already a mystery, deeply intriguing to a perennially curious traveler like Herodotus. His account of Giza recalls the wildest stories of tour guides, and all the fascinated curiosity of a gullible sightseer. He was, after all, the first archaeological tourist.

1-1 The scale of the pyramids at Giza, a staggering reality even to modern tourists, is what most impressed Herodotus when he ventured into Egypt in the fifth century B.C.

Herodotus at the Pyramids

Legions of classical travelers visited ruined cities, temples, and burial places. To such visitors, the silent pillars, walls, and fortifications were physical reminders of a quite recent past, often of known history like the Persian wars or the glories of Pericles's Athens. Egypt was another matter—exotic, off the beaten track, with ruins as ancient as civilization itself. Then as now, the ancient Egyptians exercised a powerful fascination for the visitor, but none spent more time there—or were more gullible when there—than Herodotus.

Herodotus of Halicarnassus (now Bodrum on the western Turkish coast) was born in about 484 B.C. We know little of his life, for he does not appear to have witnessed first-hand any of the events described in his *Histories*. He may have taken part in political struggles against the Persian-appointed tyrant Lygdamis, and was exiled from his home city for the rest of his life. The man commonly known as the "Father of History" comes down to us only through the nine books of his great work. We learn from its pages that he traveled widely through the eastern Mediterranean world. He appears to have died in the 420s, apparently when less than sixty years old.

The *Histories* may have originated as recitations or readings about things Herodotus discovered on his travels, delivered in Athens and other cities. While in Athens, he might have encountered such luminaries as the playwrights Euripides and Sophocles, the statesman Pericles, and a young aristocrat, Thucydides, who went on to write an analytical history of the Peloponnesian War between Athens and Sparta. Between them, Herodotus and the austere Athenian Thucydides created the intellectual discipline of history as we know it today.

Herodotus tells us in his first sentence that his purpose is to "prevent the traces of human events from being erased by time." The nine books of his *Histories* are part travelogue, part history and myth, and part sheer gossipy storytelling. The Persian wars are the backdrop for a fascinating description of the known world as it was in Herodotus's lifetime. The itinerant historian accumulated an enormous mass of information, which he linked together by using the device of inheritance from one generation to the next. Individuals like the Persian monarch Xerxes appear as actors on the stage, but they dance to policies and traditions set by their predecessors—for example, the Persian tradition of imperial conquest. The result is a seemingly rambling work, one whose author is little more than a charming, if garrulous, raconteur. But this description does Herodotus an injustice, for his writings reflect not an attempt to create a disciplined historian's narrative like that of Thucydides, but an attempt to lay out the human condition as he saw it during his travels, in all its bewildering complexity. He did not expect his readers to believe everything that he reported. "I am obliged to record the things I am told, but I am certainly not required to believe them," he remarks in the midst of his account of the Persian wars. Herodotus is both our tour guide and our proxy observer, in a world where almost every aspect of human knowledge passed from one generation to the next by word of mouth—with all the inherent unreliability that entails.

The *Histories* are a mosaic of historical narrative and dozens of well-told stories, which, in themselves, become much-loved gems, repeated again and again by those who enjoy exploring the books—and "exploring" is truly the word. No one reads Herodotus from cover to cover. He enlightens and entertains, but leaves us to draw our own conclusions. Herodotus is at his best in Egypt, where he talked to priests, observed mummification, and described the breeding habits of Egyptian cats. We learn about crocodiles and Nile boats, about the inundation and the deeds of pharaohs. And, in perhaps his most famous narrative, we visit the pyramids of Giza, then, as now, one of the great monuments of early civilization.

The Old Kingdom pharaohs embarked on a spurt of pyramid building near Memphis after 2650 B.C. This orgy of funerary construction culminated in the pyramids of Giza. In 2528 B.C., Pharaoh Khufu built the Great Pyramid, one of what are now called the "seven wonders of the ancient world." The Great Pyramid covers 13.1 acres (5.3 hectares) and is 481 feet (146 meters) high. The Great Pyramid, like the pyramids of Khufu's successors Khafre and Menkaure, was a symbolic ladder to heaven for the king to ascend to his rightful place in the sky alongside the sun god Ra. Each pyramid was part of an elaborate complex of queen's tombs, mortuary temples, and causeways, all designed to ensure the pharaoh's immortality.

Herodotus was the first traveler to leave an account of Khufu's pyramid:

> The priests said that up to the reign of King Rhampsinitus Egyptian society was stable and the country was very prosperous, but that under their next king, Cheops, it was reduced to a completely awful condition. He closed down all the sanctuaries, stopped people performing sacrifices, and also commanded all the Egyptians to work for him. Some had the job of hauling blocks of stone from the quarries in the Arabian mountain range as far as the Nile, where they were transported across the river in boats and then passed on to others, whom he assigned to haul them from there to the Libyan mountains. They worked in gangs of 100,000 men for three months at a time. They said that it took ten years of hard labour for the people to construct the causeway along which they hauled the blocks of stone, which I would think involved not much less work than building the pyramid, since the road is five stades long, ten fathoms wide, and eight fathoms high at its highest point, and is made of polished stone, with figures carved on it. So they spent ten years over this road and the underground rooms which Cheops had constructed as his sepulchral chambers in the hill on which the pyramids stand, which he turned into an island by bringing water from the Nile there along a canal. The actual pyramid took twenty years to build. Each of its sides, which form a square, is eight plethra long, and the pyramid is eight plethra high as well. It is made of polished blocks of stone, fitted together perfectly; none of the blocks is less than thirty feet long.
>
> The pyramid was built up like a flight of stairs (others use the image of staggered battlements or altar steps). When that first stage of the construction process was over, they used appliances made out of short pieces of wood to lift the remaining blocks of stone up the sides. First they would raise a block of stone from the ground on to the first tier, and when the stone had been raised up to that point, it was put on to a different device which was positioned on the first level, and from there it was hauled up to the second level on another device. Either there were the same number of devices as there were tiers, or alternatively, if the

device was a single manageable unit, they transferred the same one from level to level once they had removed the stone from it. I have mentioned two alternative methods, because that is exactly how the information was given to me. Anyway, they finished off the topmost parts of the pyramid first, then the ones just under it, and ended with the ground levels and the lowest ones.

There is a notice in Egyptian script on the pyramid about how much was spent on radishes, onions, and garlic for the labourers, and if my memory serves me well, the translator reading the notice to me said that the total cost was sixteen hundred talents of silver. If that is so, how much more must have been spent, in all likelihood, on iron for the tools, and on food and clothing for the work-force, considering how much time, as I mentioned, was spent building the pyramid? And then, I suppose, there was also the not inconsiderable amount of time spent quarrying the stone and bringing it to the site and excavating the underground chambers.

Cheops was such a bad man that when he was short of money he installed his own daughter in a room with instructions to charge a certain amount of money (I was not told exactly how much) for her favours. She did what her father had told her to do, but she also had the idea of leaving behind her own personal memorial, so she asked each of the men who came in to her to give her a single block of stone in the work-site. I was told that the middle pyramid of the group of three was built from these blocks of stone—the one which stands in front of the large one and the sides of whose base are one and a half plethra long.

The Egyptians said that after a reign of fifty years Cheops died and the kingdom passed to his brother Chephren. He carried on in the same manner as his brother, and not least in the sense that he too built a pyramid, although it did not reach the size of his brother's. I know because in fact I measured them both myself. There are no underground chambers in Chephren's pyramid, nor does a channel come flowing into it from the Nile, as in the case of the other one, where a conduit was built so that the Nile would encircle an island on which, they say, Cheops himself is buried. The bottom layer of Chephren's pyramid was made out of patterned Ethiopian stone and the whole thing is the same size as the other pyramid, but forty feet less tall. Both of them stand on the same hill, which is about a hundred feet high. They said that Chephren's reign lasted fifty-six years.

So by their own reckoning, this terrible period in Egypt lasted 106 years, and the sanctuaries, locked for all these years, were never opened. The Egyptians loathe Chephren and Cheops so much that they really do not like to mention their names. Instead, they say the pyramids belonged to a shepherd called Philitis, who at this time used to graze his flocks on the same land.

The priests said that the next king of Egypt was Mycerinus the son of Cheops, and that he disapproved of what his father had done. He not only reopened the sanctuaries and let the people, who had been ground down to a state of total misery, return to their work and their sacrifices, but he was also the fairest of all the kings in judging their legal cases. Because of this they speak more highly of Mycerinus than they do of any other Egyptian king.[8]

The Colossi of Memnon

Herodotus is the best known of the earliest archaeological travelers, although it really is a misnomer to label him an antiquarian. His interests were omnivorous, gossipy, and almost butterfly-like as he jumped from one topic to another. There were many other classical writers who took an interest in the monuments of antiquity, writers like Hecateus of Miletus, who traveled clockwise around the Mediterranean and Black seas from the Strait of Gibraltar, ending up in Morocco in the early fifth century B.C. The historian Diodorus Siculus visited Egypt in the first century. So did the geographer Strabo in the A.D. 20s, when his patron was a prefect there.

During the heyday of the Roman Empire, Egypt was a prosperous and stable province, one of Rome's major granaries. But the Egyptians always remained aloof from their masters, worshiping their age-old gods, cultivating their fields as they always had, perpetuating many institutions of earlier times. A distinctive way of life continued to flourish quietly, surrounded by the lasting monuments of what the Romans assumed was the earliest of all civilizations. The institutions of civilization, notably innovations in medicine and science, had stemmed from ancient Egypt, whose pyramids and temples were a symbol of thousands of years of stable government. Egypt was a benevolent destination for the leisured Roman tourist, who boarded ship at galley ports in southern Italy for a six-day passage to Alexandria, or crossed to Carthage in North Africa and then traveled to the Nile by coast road. The galleys ran like clockwork to Alexandria. Expert teachers in philosophy, medicine, and other subjects awaited those anxious to sample Egypt's ancient wisdom. The less-cultured visitor could spend time savoring the city's fleshpots before taking a boat up the Nile.[9]

Most people traveled to Egypt to learn about history and geography, to widen their philosophical horizons. They followed a well-beaten path—to Memphis, capital of the pharaohs, to the pyramids, to Thebes with the temples of the sun god Amun, and to the Valley of the Kings, already known to be the burial place of Egypt's most powerful rulers. The journey ended at the lovely Temple of Isis on the Island of Philae, close to the First Cataract. The island was the "island of the time [of Re]," of creation, close to Elephantine Island, where the ram god Khnum presided over the Nile's life-giving waters that nourished Egypt's fields.

Like so many visitors through the ages, Roman tourists scratched graffiti on pyramid and temple. The Romans saw the Giza pyramids with their limestone casing stones intact, and they scratched their names on the

1-2 According to Pliny, the local inhabitants of Giza worshiped the massive Sphinx as a deity.

stones. Subsequently, medieval contractors removed nearly all of the stones to build the Citadel in Cairo. The earliest known Giza inscription dates to A.D. 1475, but we know from the travels of the German monk Rudolph von Suchem, who visited the pyramids in 1336, that earlier inscriptions did exist. Pliny the Elder came to Giza during the first century and was one of the first Roman authors to describe the Sphinx. "It impresses one by its stillness and silence, and is the local divinity of the inhabitants of the surrounding district," he declared.[10] Pliny liked ruins. Of the fallen Colossus of Rhodes—a statue of Helius the sun god and one of the seven wonders of the ancient world—he remarked: "Great cavities gape in the broken limbs, and inside them one can see stones of great size, which were used to weight the Colossus down." He added colorfully: "Few people can make their arms meet around the thumb."[11]

Back in Egypt, some visitors inscribed their names by torchlight on the walls of royal tombs in the Valley of the Kings. Nearby stood the vast seated statues of the pharaoh Amenophis III, statues known to everyone as the Colossi of Memnon, which once stood in front of the king's now-vanished mortuary temple. The Greeks had identified the statues with the mythical King Memnon of Ethiopia, son of the Dawn, who had assisted the Trojans against Achilles and the Greeks. An earthquake damaged both statues in 27 B.C., but this did not prevent the northern figure of the pair from emitting a bell-like sound as the sun rose. Tourists flocked to hear the daily performance, many of them scratching their names on the huge quartzite feet. Strabo suspected that the local priests had installed a secret mechanism to cause the sound. In fact, the early-morning warmth of the sun made the stones expand. In A.D. 130, none other than the emperor Hadrian visited the Colossi. The Colossi remained silent on the first day, but sounded off on the second to the delight of the imperial party. Julia Balbilla, a poetess in Hadrian's retinue, wrote on the statue:

> By Julia Balbilla, when Hadrian Augustus heard Memnon: I had been told that Memnon the Egyptian, warmed by the ray of the sun, spoke from his Theban stone. And when he saw Hadrian, king of all, before the rays of the sun, he greeted him as best he could. But when Titan, driving through the sky with his white horses, held the second measure of the hours in shadow, Memnon again uttered a sharp-toned cry as of bronze being struck: in greeting he also uttered a third call. Then the lord Hadrian himself also offered ample greetings to Memnon and on the monument left for posterity verses marking all that he had seen and all he had heard. And it was made clear to all that the gods loved him. [November 20, 130.][12]

Three-quarters of a century later, the Colossi made the fatal mistake of not performing for Emperor Septimus Severus. He tried to placate the god by restoring the head and torso, but this was an act that silenced the statue forever.

The Roman interest in Egypt stemmed from plain intellectual curiosity about the cradle of civilization. The monuments themselves became objects of pilgrimage, notably the Temple of Isis at Philae just below the First Cataract, the southernmost frontier of ancient Egypt. An Alexandrian visitor inscribed on its walls, "Whoever prays to Isis at Philae becomes happy, rich, and long lived."[13]

The Romans were not archaeologists, although they did collect Greek statuary and Egyptian obelisks to adorn their homes and public places. For the most part, their interest in the past was casually philosophical. The Roman author Plutarch had a passionate interest in religious antiquities, was a priest at Delphi, and traveled to Egypt. But ancient ruins like Delphi or the pyramids were mere backdrops to other concerns—the writing of history, philosophical argument, investigating the frontiers of the known world. All the classical writers with an interest in antiquity lived in a world surrounded by what they called "barbarians": fierce

Germanic tribes, the Picts of the far north, the nomadic Scythians who used human skulls as drinking vessels—these peoples and many others, like the Garamantes of the Sahara Desert, pressed on the boundaries of the civilized Mediterranean world. Chaos always threatened order, and this was a much greater concern to writers of the day than the silent ruins of their forebears.

As for the past itself, it was the stuff of legend and speculation, well summarized by the Greek writer Hesiod as early as the late eighth century B.C. In his poem *Works and Days*, he wrote how the gods, "who live on Mount Olympus," first fashioned a "golden race of mortal men." They feasted and lived a life of ease. When they died out, the deities created a "lesser, silver race of men, unlike the gold in stature or in mind." Then "Zeus, the father, made a race of bronze, sprung from the ash tree . . . strange and full of power." Finally, after a brief interlude of demi-heroes, Zeus fashioned the race of iron, the present inhabitants of the earth. "Now, by day, men work and grieve unceasingly, by night they waste away and die." Hesiod himself lamented his fate: "I wish I were not of this race, that I had died before, or had not been born."[14] In a somewhat similar vein, a Chinese compilation of A.D. 52 wrote of ages of stone, bronze, and iron, perhaps a folk memory of much earlier societies, but certainly not an archaeological observation. These were but philosophical musings, which persisted in one form or another right through classical times—the myth of a "golden age," a sense of passing time well expressed by the Roman poet Lucretius:

> Thus the sum of things is ever being renewed, and mortals live dependent one upon another. Some races increase, others diminish, and in a short space the generations of living creatures are changed and like runners hand on the torch of life.[15]

For centuries after the decline of the Roman Empire, the great monuments of antiquity lay neglected and crumbling, occasionally the object of casual curiosity, but normally just ignored. It was not until the initial stirrings of the Renaissance that archaeological travel began in earnest, in the hands of a new breed of tourist—the antiquarian.

> Thither I summoned some of the country people, and over a pot and a pipe, fished out what I could from their discourse, as we sat surveying the corn growing on the spot.... The most charming sight that can be imagined is the perfect vestigial of a temple, as easily discernible in the corn as on paper.
>
> WILLIAM STUKELEY[1]

CHAPTER TWO

The Antiquarians

"Time we may comprehend," wrote the English physician Sir Thomas Browne in 1643. "'Tis but five days older than ourselves."[2] Browne's view of the past encompassed the Greeks and Romans and a humankind created by God in the Old Testament. Also in the seventeenth century, Archbishop James Ussher of Armagh in Ireland used the long genealogies in the Scriptures to calculate that the world had been created on the evening of October 22, 4004 B.C. Thus, according to Christian dogma, the entire span of human existence was a mere six thousand years.

After the collapse of the Roman Empire, the study of the past fell into oblivion. Babylon reverted to desert; Petra slumbered in its secluded canyon. Ancient ruins of any kind were a curiosity, often thought to be the work of giants. With the Renaissance came a renewed interest in classical learning and in the remains of ancient civilizations. Thomas Browne and his English contemporaries were steeped in knowledge of ancient Greece and Rome. The Renaissance was an age of collectors and scholars, of acquisitive cardinals and nobles who flocked to Mediterranean lands and returned laden with antiquities for their private collections and for what were then known as "cabinets of curiosities." Soon, a stream of young travelers followed in their footsteps to Italy, taking what became known as the "grand tour" as part of their education (see Chapter 3). Such often frivolous travelers became the first archaeological tourists, but not necessarily the most perceptive.

"The Backward-looking Curiosity"

By 1550, it was fashionable to be an antiquary, a collector or student of ancient things. But only the wealthiest traveler could afford a grand tour and could pay for classical treasures. The less affluent indulged their passion for the past at home, collecting Roman coins and inscriptions and, above all, traveling the countryside in pursuit of what the English schoolmaster William Camden (1551–1623) called "the backward-looking curiosity." This open-ended inquisitiveness took Camden and his contemporaries to eroded burial mounds on windy uplands, to ancient fortifications in Denmark, and to the mysterious stone circles known as Stonehenge.

Stonehenge was the most famous of all curiosities, a place where—in the words of Henry of Huntingdon, a twelfth-century author—"stones of wonderful size have been erected after the manner of doorways. . . . No one can conceive how such great stones have been so raised aloft, or why they were built there."[3] Henry was an archdeacon at Lincoln Cathedral, commissioned by his bishop, Alexander of Blois, to write a short account of Britain and its marvels. Stonehenge was an obvious choice for the marvels section of a British history that was a curious mingling of classical allusions and historical events. In Henry's version of history, Brutus, great-grandson of Aeneas of Troy, had led a band of Trojans on a long sea voyage to a northern land called Albion. There they settled on the coast and in the interior; Brutus became the first king of the Britons. As for Stonehenge—and we should assume that Henry went there—it remained unexplained.

While on a visit to the monastery of Bec in Normandy, Henry came across another British history, the *Historia Regium Britannia* by Geoffrey of Monmouth, which included an account of the building of Stonehenge as a memorial to British lords murdered in a Saxon massacre.[4] The magician Merlin is called in, dismantles a "stone construction" on Mount Killaraus in Ireland, and erects a stone circle around the burials of the lords at Stonehenge. Like the rest of Monmouth's *Historia*, this passage was a curious mixture of history, translation, and just plain mythology—exactly what his audience wanted: adventure, chivalry, and suspense mixed with a healthy dose of patriotism. Here is a translation of the section about the construction of Stonehenge in Geoffrey's *Chronicle of England*, printed by William Caxton in 1480 from a French manuscript:

And whan the kyng of Irland that was callyd guillomez herd telle that stranngers were arryed in his londe he assembled a grete power & fought agenst hem, but he and his folke were discomfyted. The Britons went byfore till they come to the mounte of kylyon and clymed onto the mount. But whan they sawe the stones & the maner how they stoode they had great meuiayle & sayd bitwene hem that noman shold remeue for no strength ne engyne so huge they were & so long, but Merlyn thurgh hys crafte and queyntise remeued hem & brought hem in to his shippes & come ageyene in to this land. And Merlyn sette the stones there that the kynge wold bane hem and sette hem in the same manner that they stoden in irland. & When the kyng sawe that it was made he thanked Merlyn and richely him rewarded at his own wylie & that place lete caile Stonhenge for evermore.[5]

Stirring stuff, and influential—Merlin remained part of the tapestry of legend that surrounded Stonehenge until at least the eighteenth century, especially in the theater. Numerous fables also surrounded the stone circles, including one contending that they were artificial, built of a form of concrete, and erected by giants. A later antiquarian, John Aubrey, was to remark in 1685 that "the errour runnes from generation to generation concerning Stonenheng, that the stones there are artificiall."[6]

William Camden and *Britannia*

Stonehenge, burial mounds, occasional finds of bronze artifacts in plowed fields, and flaked stone axes that seemed to be human-made and much earlier than 4,000 B.C.: there was ample material in England to kindle the traveler's sense of wonder. The first true archaeological travelers were antiquarians, consumed with a passionate and omnivorous inquisitiveness about the countryside and its natural wonders and oddities. The antiquarians' long tradition of leisured travel and observation founded the tradition of archae-

2-1 William Camden, shown here in an engraving from 1691, was the epitome of antiquarians turned explorers, and he helped make archaeological tourism the widespread cultural phenomenon it is today.

ological tourism as we know it today, a tradition remarkable for its acute observation and unbridled speculation.

One of the first of these men, and arguably the greatest, was William Camden (1551–1623), a teacher at Westminster School in London, and Clarenceux King of Arms in the College of Heralds, an important and prestigious institution at a time when heraldry was a profoundly serious and often deeply political enterprise. Camden was an inveterate traveler, no mean achievement in an England where most roads were little more than muddy tracks. Unlike other travelers, he spent a great deal of time studying antiquities, which he was well aware other people thought a complete waste of time. He remarked, "In the study of Antiquity . . . there is a sweet food of the mind well benefiting such as are of honest and noble disposition."[7] In 1586, at the age of thirty-five, Camden produced his masterwork *Britannia*, the first guide to the antiquities of Britain. *Britannia* was an omnivorous work, a walkabout, as it were, of Britain, where everything was grist to the author's mill—county boundaries, towns, markets, archaeological sites, folklore, and geography. It is a testament to its merit that *Britannia* remained in print through successive editions for two hundred years.

Camden's primary interest was mapping Roman Britain, but his interests were eclectic. Everything from Roman ruins to Saxon churches, to say nothing of prehistoric circles and burial mounds, was grist to his antiquarian mill. He wrote of Stonehenge that "in the time of King Henrie the Eighth, there was found neer this place a table of metal, as it had beene tinne and lead commixt, inscribed with many letters, but in so strange a Character that neither Sir Thomas Eliot, nor master Lily, Schoolmaster of Pauls, could read it. Had it been preserved, something happily might have been discovered as concerning *Stonehenge* which now lieth obscured."[8] The metal table is almost certainly a myth, preserved in local folklore for many generations, perhaps as a result of the discovery of a richly decorated prehistoric grave in a burial mound.

William Camden lived in an era when archaeology did not exist. Even the most learned of antiquarians operated in a fog of ignorance and unexplained phenomena. Places like Stonehenge—in fact, everything or nearly everything pre-Roman—could be described only in the context of a mythic history, larded with classical heroes and circumscribed by the six thousand years of human existence proclaimed by the Scriptures. In a quest for knowledge, Camden himself rode the highways and byways of England, collecting topographic information, local folklore, and tales of giants and unexplained phenomena. To him, the past was yet another curiosity, but one that looked backward. Camden was a pioneer and apparently a loner, less sociable than later travelers. Some of his successors went so far as to send out questionnaires to landowners. "Are there any ancient *Sepulchres* hereabout of Men of *Gigantik stature, Roman generals,* and *others* of ancient times?" asked one such document.[9] The responses told of burial mounds, of stone circles, and of artifacts plowed up in the fields, but threw no light on the objects' origins. In William Camden's day, the past was a foreign country, a world totally alien to those who explored it.

Camden was a careful observer, as sober in his interpretations as one could be in an era when the past seemed like a closed book. Silbury Hill is a large, artificial hill near Avebury in southern England, 130 feet (40 meters) high and covering 5.4 acres (2.2 hectares). The hill stands like a benign carbuncle in the heart of the Wiltshire countryside, something quite unlike any of the other numerous prehistoric earthworks and burial mounds that stand out on the nearby landscape.[10] Thanks to a 229-foot (70-meter) tunnel that the archaeologist Richard Atkinson dug to the center of the mound in 1968, we know that construction began in 2200 B.C. and unfolded in three stages. Atkinson's meticulous investigation revealed how the builders laid out a circle on a low hillock, deposited gravel inside it, and followed this with a layer of sod. The sods were so well preserved that ants and anthills survived in them, sufficient to tell us that they were cut in late summer, just as the ants grew wings. But after all this effort, and the dissection of the entire building process, we have absolutely no idea why the builders elected to construct such a stupendous monument—and this with the panoply of modern archaeology and history at our fingertips. William Camden had none of these scientific artifacts, just his perceptive antiquarian eye and an inveterate traveler's insatiable thirst for knowledge. Here's what he wrote in *Britannia*:

> Here Selbury, a round hill, riseth to a considerable height, and seemeth by the fashion of it, and by the sliding down of the earth about it, to be cast up by men's hands. Of this sort there are many to be seen in this County, round and copped, which are call'd Burrows or Barrows, perhaps raised in memory of the Soldiers there slain. For bones are found in them; and I have read that it was a custom among the Northern People, that every soldier escaping alive out of Battel, was to bring his Helmet full of earth toward the raising of Monuments for their slain Fellows. Tho' I rather think this Selbury-hill to be placed instead of a boundary, if not by the Romans, yet by the Saxons, as well as the ditch call'd Wodensdike, seeing there were frequent battels in this country between the Mercians and the West Saxons about their limits; and Boetius, and the Writers that treat about Surveying, tell us, that such heaps were often raised for Landmarks.[11]

Like Stonehenge, or Hadrian's Wall in northern England—perhaps the ultimate Roman frontier statement—Silbury Hill stands out on the landscape for the visitor to admire and climb. Camden was the first archaeological traveler to marvel not only at pyramids and other unmistakable monuments, but also at the most inconspicuous of archaeological sites. When Camden visited the site of the Roman town at Silchester (Calleva Atrebatum), some 10 miles (16 kilometers) west of the modern town of Reading in south-central England, he happened to be there at a dry time in late summer. He expected to see little, but was delighted to find the ancient streets highlighted in the rows of corn:

> But now age has eras'd the very tracks of it; and to teach us that Cities dye as well as men, it is at this day a corn-field, wherein when the corn is grown up, one may observe the draughts of streets crossing one another, (for where they have gone the corn is thinner) and such crossings they commonly call *St. Augustine's cross.* Nothing now remains, but some ruinous walls of a tower, of a square form, and cemented with a sort of sand extremely binding. One would imagine this had been the *Acropolis,* it looks down from so great a height upon the wet plains in Thanet, which the Ocean, withdrawing itself by little and little, has quite left. But the plot of the City, now plow'd, has often cast up the marks of it's Antiquity, gold and silver coyns of the Romans.[12]

Calleva Atrebatum, once a native British town founded by the indigenous inhabitants, was almost entirely constructed of wood, and it burned down in a disastrous fire in the third century, leaving virtually nothing on the surface. The local people were well aware of what they called "the crossings," but it took an antiquarian visitor to interpret the crossings' meaning as streets.

Camden was widely admired in his own day, and he corresponded frequently with an informal network of clergymen, fellow antiquarians, and landowners as he tracked down inscriptions and pieced together history. He took a remarkable joy in the past, a passion for leisured discovery that was to be the mark of later travelers. In the 1600 edition of *Britannia*, he described the ten Roman altars at Stenhouse in Scotland, which he visited with his fellow antiquary Sir John Cotton. Camden was fulsome in his praise of Cotton in the new edition:

> a singular lover of antiquity, what time as he and I together, of an affectionate love to illustrate our native country, made a survey of these coasts in the yeare of our redemption in 1599, not without the sweet food and contentment of our mindes. . . . He . . . most diligently preserveth these inscriptions, which by others that are unskilfull and unlettered be straight waies defaced, broken, and converted to other uses to exceeding great prejudice and detriment of antiquity.[13]

The constant lament over unthinking destruction resonates down the centuries, and is still an only too familiar lament today. Destruction was widespread in Camden's day and accelerated as villagers robbed castles, monasteries, and ancient stone circles for stones for building. But the ravages of Camden's time pale in significance compared to modern-day industrial development, which has done more damage to archaeological sites in the past half century than all the other depredations on the past wrought since Camden's time.

John Aubrey and Edward Llwyd

In 1649, the antiquarian and country squire John Aubrey (1626–1697) rode into the middle of Avebury's stone circles while out fox hunting. The self-promoting Aubrey tells us that he was "wonderfully surprized at the sight of these vast stones of which I had never heard before."[14] An ambitious man, Aubrey was anxious for royal preferment, so the "surprize" may not have been a first-time discovery. He returned to Avebury to sketch and explore to such effect that King Charles II read Aubrey's descriptions, announced his intention to visit the site, and instructed Aubrey to dig for human bones. The squire never excavated at Avebury, but he did complete the first plane table survey of the earthworks and stone circles, recording the position of many stones that have since vanished at quarrymens' hands. (A plane table is a portable surveying instrument consisting of a drawing board and a ruler mounted on a tripod; it is used to sight and map topographical details.) Charles II, true to his

2–2 When John Aubrey visited Avebury, he was struck by its age; he determined that the circles must have been pre-Roman.

word, did visit the site with Aubrey in 1663 and climbed nearby Silbury Hill.

Like most intellectuals of his day, Aubrey was interested in everything from archaeology to natural history to classical mythology. He traveled widely, sketching numerous ancient monuments for his masterwork *Monumenta Britannica*, which languished in Oxford's Bodleian Library until it finally saw publication in the twentieth century. "Surely my stars compelled me to be an antiquary," he wrote. "I have had the strongest luck at it, that things drop into my mouth."[15] He lived during a period when the Scriptures were the source of most history and all wisdom, but realized that Avebury's circles dated to pre-Roman times. The site intoxicated him, not least because it remained less well known than Stonehenge. "It does as much exceede in greatness the so renowned Stonehenge, as a cathedral doeth a parish church."[16] Who, then, were its builders? He drew on the Scriptures, on Julius Caesar's description of Britain in 55 B.C., and on what little was known of native Americans:

> Let us imagine then what kind of countrie this was in the time of the Ancient Britons. By the nature of the soil, which is a sour woodsere land, very natural for the production of oakes especially, one may conclude that this North Divison was a shady dismal wood; and the inhabitants almost as savage as the Beasts whose skins were their only rayment. The language British, which for the honour of it was in those days spoken from arcades to Italie and Spain. The Boats of the Avon (which signifies River) were basketts of twigges covered with an oxe skin; which the poore people in Wales use to this day. They call them curricles. Within this Shire I believe that there were several Reguli which often made war upon another; and the great ditches which run on the Plaines and elsewhere so many miles (not unlikely) their boundaries; and with all served for defence against the incursions of their enemies, as the Pict's wall, Offa's Ditch; and that in China, to compare things small to great. Their religion is at large described by Caesar. Their priests were Druids some of their temples I pretend to have restored, as Avbury, Stonehenge, etc as also British sepulchres. Their way of fighting is lively sett down by Caesar. Their camps with their way of meeting I have sett down in another place. They knew the use of iron. . . . They were two or three degrees I suppose less savage than the Americans. . . . The Romans subdued and civilized them.[17]

Aubrey's friend Edward Llwyd (pronounced "th-lew-id"; 1660–1709) was another polymath, who became keeper of the Ashmolean Museum in Oxford, a veritable cabinet of curiosities founded by another antiquarian, Elias Ashmole. Llwyd traveled extensively through the British Isles, studying languages and folklore and visiting archaeological sites in a search for Britain's past. In 1699 he visited Ireland as part of a project to

2-3 The entrance to the tomb passage in New Grange, Ireland, is marked by a large curbstone inscribed with spirals. Called the "Entrance Stone," it has been dated to 3200 B.C.

write an account of the archaeology and natural history of the Celtic regions of the British Isles and France. While there, he explored the prehistoric mound at New Grange in the Boyne Valley, one of the most spectacular megalithic monuments in Europe. He wrote of his visit to his friend Dr. Tancred Robinson in a letter subsequently published in the *Philosophical Transactions of the Royal Society* of London:

We continued not above three days at Dublin, when we steer'd our course toward the Giants Causeway. The most remarkable curiosity we saw by the way, was a stately Mount at a place called New Grange near Drogheda; having a number of huge stones pitch'd on end round about it, and a single one on the top. The gentleman of the village (one Mr. Charles Campbel) observing that under the green turf this mount was wholly composed of stones, and having occasion for some, employ'd his servants to carry off a considerable parcel of them; till they came at last to a very broad flat stone, rudely carved, and placed edgewise at the bottom of the mount. This they discover'd to be the door of a cave, which had a long entry leading into it. At the first entering we were forced to creep; but still as we went on, the pillars on each side of us were higher and higher; and coming into the cave, we found it about 20 foot high. In this cave, on each hand of us was a cell or apartment, and another went on streight forward opposite to the entry. In those on each hand was a very broad shallow bason of stone, situated at the edge. The bason in the right hand apartment stood in another; that on the left hand was single; and in the apartment straight forward there was none at all. We observed that water dropt into the right hand bason, tho' it had rained but little in many days; and suspected that the lower bason was intended to preserve the superfluous liquor of the upper whether this water were sacred, (or whether it was for Blood in Sacrifice) that none might come to the ground. The great pillars round this cave, supporting the mount, were not at all hewn or wrought; but were such rude stones as those of Abury in Wiltshire, and rather more rude than those of Stonehenge: but those about the basons, and some elsewhere, had such barbarous sculpture (viz. spiral like a snake, but without distinction of head and tail) as the fore-mentioned stone at the entry of the cave. . . . They found several bones in the cave, and part of a Stags (or else Elks) head, and some other things, which I omit, because the labourers differ'd in their account of them. A gold coin of the Emperor Valentinian, being found near the top of this mount, might bespeak it Roman; but that the rude carving at the entry and in the cave seems to denote it a barbarous monument. So, the coin proving it ancienter than any Invasion of the Ostmans or Danes; and the carving and rude sculpture, barbarous; it should follow, that it was some place of sacrifice or burial of the ancient Irish.[18]

William Stukeley and Stonehenge

Barbarians, human sacrifice, rude carving: Llwyd and his contemporaries traveled in an archaeological fog. The discipline of archaeology as we know it did not exist; archaeological excavations were unknown, and any scientific inquiry was shackled with the chains of theological dogma. Visitors to Stonehenge or New Grange fumbled in the dark—occasionally quite literally—and let their imaginations roam. Ancient British, Danes, wild Irish, and, above all, Druids were all grist to the visitor's mill.

The Druids were a favorite; they were thought of as a priesthood of ancient Britons who had long hair, were encountered by Julius Caesar, and were subsequently written into antiquarian lore. They worshipped in forested groves and practiced bizarre rites. From there, it was but a short intellectual stretch to connect them with Avebury, New Grange, and Stonehenge. The Druids persist today in strange midsummer rituals at Stonehenge, conducted each midsummer's day by modern-day Druids.

William Stukeley (1687–1765) was a quintessential eighteenth-century antiquarian—curious, eccentric, and probably a delightfully erratic travel companion. But there was more to Stukeley than a lively curiosity. He could write well and imaginatively, as he did of the Rollright Stones: he wrote that they were "the greatest Antiquity we have yet seen . . . corroded like wormeaten wood by the harsh Jaws of Time, . . . a very noble, rustic sight and strike an odd terror upon the spectators and admiration at the design of 'em."[19] Yet he was also a much more scientific traveler than most

2-4 After his first visit to the ancient and weathered monument of Stonehenge, William Stukeley later wrote, "There is enough of every part to preserve the idea of the whole."

of his contemporaries. He made the first survey of Stonehenge and mapped Avebury, walking the surrounding landscape, where he observed burial mounds and ancient roads. Stukeley spent the summers from 1721 through 1724 at Stonehenge, putting together "a most accurate description" of Stonehenge with "nice plans and perspectives." He and his company even dined atop one of the trilithons, where he found space enough for "a steady head and nimble heels to dance a minuet."[20] Clearly the weathered stone circles had a profound effect on him, as he wrote in *Stonehenge: A Temple Restored to the British Druids* (1740):

Stonehenge stands not upon the very summit of a hill, but pretty near it, and for more than three quarters of the circuit you ascend to it very gently from lower ground. A half mile distance, the appearance of it is stately and awful, really august. As you advance nearer, especially up the avenue, which is to the north-east of it, (of which side is now most perfect) the greatness of its contour fills the eye in an astonishing manner. . . .

As you enter the building, whether on foot or horseback and cast your eyes around, upon the yawning ruins, you are struck into an exstatic *reverie*, which none can describe, and they only can be sensible of it, that feel it. Other buildings fall by piece meal, but here a single stone is a ruin and lies like the haughty carcase of *Goliath*. Yet there is as much of it undemolished, as enables us sufficiently to recover its form, when it was in its most perfect state. There is enough of every part to preserve the idea of the whole. . . . When we advance further, the dark part of the ponderous imposts over our heads, the chasm of sky between the jams of the cell, the odd construction of the whole, and the greatness of every part surprises. . . . If you look upon the perfect part, you fancy intire quarries mounted up into the air: if on the rude havock below, you see as it were the bowels of a mountain turn'd inside outwards. . . .

Nothing in nature could be of a more simple idea than this vast circle of stones, and its crown-work or *corona* at top; and yet its effect is truly majestic and venerable, which is the main requisite in sacred structures. A single stone is a thing worthy of admiration, but the boldness and relievo of whole *compages*, can only be right apprehended, from view of the original. . . . The whole system of jointing in this building is very curious, and seems to be the oldest and only specimen of this kind of work in the world. There is nothing, that I know of, comes in competition with it, but the celebrated ruins at *Persepolis*.[21]

Stukeley lamented the ongoing destruction of the stone circles by "rude and sacrilegious hands" as he contemplated the landscape surrounding Stonehenge and the burial mounds lying close by where other destructive forces were at work:

There are the nearest barrows planted with rabbets, which do so much damage too at *Stonehenge*, and threaten no less the ruin of the whole. . . . But they are really no more than family burying-places, set near this temple, for the same reason as we bury in church-yards and consecrated ground.[22]

Stukeley began his great work on Stonehenge with feelings of wonder and what he called "exstacy":

A serious view of this magnificent wonder, is apt to put a thinking and judicious person into a kind of exstacy, when he views the struggle between art and nature, the grandeur of the art that hides itself, and seems unartful. For tho' the contrivance that put this massy frame together, must have been exquisite, yet the founders endeavour'd to hide it, by the seeming rudeness of the work. The bulk of the constituent parts is so very great, that the mortices and tenons must have been prepar'd to an extreme nicety, and, like the fabric of *Solomon's* temple, every stone tally'd; and neither axes and hammers were heard upon the whole structure. . . . Yet 'tis highly entertaining to consider the judicious carelessness therein, really the grand gusto, like a great master in drawing, secure of the effect: a true masterpiece. Every thing proper, bold, astonishing. The lights and shades adapted with inconceivable justness. Notwithstanding the monstrous size of the work, and every part of it; 'tis far from appearing heavy: 'tis compos'd of several species of work, and the proportions of the dissimilar parts recommend the whole, and it pleases like a magical spell. . . . And we that can only view it in its ruins, the less regret those ruins, that, if possible, add to its solemn majesty.[23]

But who built Stonehenge? Stukeley attributed the circles to the ancient Britons and specifically to their priests, the Druids. In later life, Stukeley became increasingly eccentric and Druid-obsessed; his observations about ancient priests at Stonehenge echo down the generations. As the modern-day Stonehenge expert Christopher Chippindale remarks: "Stonehenge has never fully recovered from the Reverend Stukeley's vision."[24]

Stukeley visited sites the length and breadth of England, including Avebury, the Rollright Stones, Roman Bath and Verulamium, and numerous prehistoric burial mounds. One of his favorites was Hadrian's Wall in northern England, the most famous frontier defense work in the Roman Empire. He described his reaction to the wall in his *Itinerarium Curiosum*:

The amazing scene of Roman grandeur in Britain which I beheld this journey, the more it occurred with pleasure to my own imagination, the more I despaired of conveying it to the reader in a proper light by a rehearsal. It is easy for some nations to magnify trifles and in words gild over inconsiderable transactions till they swell to the appearance of an history; and some moderns have gone great lengths that way; but if in any people action has outdone the capacity of rhetoric, or in any place they have left historians far behind in their valour and military performances, it was in our own country; and we are as much surprised in finding such infinite reliques of theirs here, as that we have no history of them that speaks with any particularity of the last 300 years that the Romans dwelt in Britain, and rendered it perfectly provincial. The learned memoirs are very short; and it is well they were guided with such a spirit, as left monuments sufficient to supply that defect, when handled as they deserve; though I have no hope of coming up to that yet I hold myself obliged to preserve, as well as I can, the memory of such things as I saw; which, added to what future times will discover, will revive the Roman glory among us, and may serve to invite noble minds to endeavour to that merit and public-spiritedness which shine through all their actions. This tribute at least we owe them, and they deserve it at our hands, to preserve their remains.[25]

William Stukeley epitomized the eighteenth-century antiquarian—curious, often gullible, and omnivorous in his interests. He was one of many travelers of modest means who went in search of the past by simply riding out close to home. But there were others, notably the wealthy and well connected, who could afford the considerable expense of traveling abroad. They became the first archaeological tourists in Mediterranean lands, and we will meet them in Chapter 3.

> Every step I take in Italy, I am more and more sensible of the obligation I have to my father in allowing me to undertake the Grand Tour. . . . How amply is a traveler rewarded by the pleasure and knowledge he finds in almost every place.
>
> EDWARD GIBBON, 1764[1]

CHAPTER THREE

The Grand Tour

While many English archaeological travelers visited Avebury, Stonehenge, and other monuments at home, the more affluent traveled the classical lands. By the eighteenth century, the so-called "grand tour," a leisurely journey through Europe, became an essential part of a gentleman's education. Typically, the oldest son of a well-off family went abroad to complete his education, often with a tutor both to instruct and to keep an eye on his charge: "If a young man is wild, and must run after women and bad company, it is better he should do so abroad."[2] At first these tours were a form of education for courtiers and career diplomats, meant to train a young gentleman to take his place in a world where mere patriotism was not enough. But they soon became a kind of finishing school for the aristocracy. "Sir," pronounced Dr. Samuel Johnson, "a man who has not been to Italy is always conscious of an inferiority, from his not having seen what it is expected a man should see. The grand object of travelling is to see the shores of the Mediterranean."[3]

An Excursion to Acquire Taste

Until the late sixteenth century, the journey through Europe was both dangerous and uncomfortable, thanks to bandits, smallpox epidemics, robbers, and appalling conditions on the road. There was also a danger of being seized by the Inquisition as a Protestant, especially at Easter, when the authorities watched for those who failed to take the sacrament. In 1592 and 1595, the pope complained at the number of English heretics who traveled to Venice. Travel for pleasure was by this time fashionable. By 1700, the grand tour had become the ideal way of imparting taste and knowledge into the minds of ignorant youths who would otherwise indulge in unbridled debauchery.

3-1 In his painting *Planning the Grand Tour*, the artist Max Volkhart (1848–1935) romanticized the eighteenth-century cultural phenomenon that fueled an interest in archaeological travel.

There were bound to be numerous hazards and mishaps along the way for the long sightseer. Guidebooks provided (usually inaccurate) maps and directions to hotels along the post routes. *The Gentleman's Pocket Companion for Travelling into Foreign Parts*, first published in 1722, laid out a delicious, if hazardous, scenario of what could happen at an inn. The dialogue is among a tourist, an innkeeper, and a chambermaid, and is conducted in French, German, and Italian:

"God keep you from misfortune, my host!"
"You are welcome, Gentlemen!"
"Shall we be well lodged with you for this night?"
"Yes, very well, Sir."
"Have you good stable, good hay, good oats, good litter, good wine?"
"The best. . . ."
[The Tourist alights with his companions and enters the inn where he drinks too heavily with his meal.]
"By your leaves, Gentlemen, I find myself somewhat indispos'd."

"Sir, if you are not well, go take your rest, your chamber is ready. Joan, make a good fire in his chamber, and let him want for nothing."

"Sweetheart, is my bed made? Is it good, clean, warm?"

"Yes, Sir, it is a good featherbed. The sheets are very clean."

"Pull off my stockings, and warm my bed, for I am much out of order. I shake like a leaf in a tree. Warm a Napkin for my head and bind it well. Gently, you bind it too hard. Bring my pillow, and cover me well; draw the curtains, and pin them together. Where is the chamber-pot? Where is the privy?"

"Follow me and I will show you the way. Go strait up and you will find it on your right hand; if you see it not you will soon smell it. Sir, do you want anything else?"

"Yes, my dear, put out the candle and come nearer to me."

"I will put it out when I am out of the room; what is your will? Are you not well enough yet?"

"My head lies too low, raise up the bolster a little. I cannot lie so low. My dear, give me a kiss, I should sleep the better."

"You are not sick since you talk of kissing. I would rather die than kiss a man in his bed, or any other place. Take your rest in God's name. God give you a good night and good rest."

"I thank you, fair maid."[4]

Romantic episodes aside, these young men, and sometimes young women, roistered and visited art galleries, passed through Florence, Venice, Rome, and Naples, admired the Roman Colosseum, and collected paintings and classical statuary for their country houses back in England. An intense interest in classical antiquities among Britain's elite led to the founding in 1732 of the Society of Dilettanti, a social club that met once a month and drank toasts to "Grecian taste and Roman spirit." Many members had taken the grand tour and encouraged a "taste for those objects which had contributed so much to their entertainment abroad." The society was a quintessential Enlightenment enterprise—a search for antiquity. The members visited foreign lands, explored them, and sketched ancient monuments. They sent talented artists to record art and architecture in Italy, Greece, and elsewhere. The Dilettanti were sociable, wealthy men, who believed that the classical world informed their own world and had left it a priceless legacy of art, architecture, philosophy, and poetry.

The Attractions of Naples

By the mid-eighteenth century, the routine of the grand tour was well established, complete with an extensive literature penned by cosmopolitan visitors. Naples in particular became a favorite destination; Naples, the city that had once been the summer residence for Rome's elite, with its lavish villas and fish ponds by the bay. The informed visitor made a pilgrimage to Virgil's tomb, where it was fashionable to read passages of the *Aeneid* in Latin before the sepulcher. Two centuries ago, the setting of the tomb was bucolic, so it was an ideal place to contemplate the glories of ancient Rome. Today, an idyll of this type is impossible. The tomb lies close to a traffic-clogged road tunnel. From Virgil's tomb, the traveler took a carriage back into Naples, a city in a paradisiacal setting, but dirty, crowded, and disorderly. The city was said to be "inhabited by devils," the noisy, barefooted inhabitants, who were notably villainous. The Italians, and especially the Neapolitans, became stereotypes. Complained Pietro Napoli-Signorelli of Naples,

> "When one sees travel writers repeating always the same things by copying their predecessors without further examination, one has good grounds to suspect that they compile their books before seeing Italy and that they then descend here to verify, if they can, that which is outrageous, for the rest not caring to scrutinize the evident truth when it does not fit with what they read before crossing the Alps."[5]

But this "devilish" destination did not want in popularity. John Evelyn traveled as far south as Naples in 1645 and declared in his diary that there was nothing worth seeing elsewhere. "From the reports of divers experienced and curious persons, I had been assured that there was little more to be seen in the rest of the civil world, after France, Flanders, and the Low Countries, but plain and prodigious barbarism." As late as 1776, Voltaire remarked that Spain was "a country of which we know no more than of the most savage parts of Africa, and it is not worth the trouble of being known."[6] Italy was still one of the favorite destinations of the archaeological traveler.

At first the grand tour was a general educational experience, but, by the eighteenth century, its educational value was mainly confined to knowledge of the ancient world. What had begun during the Renaissance as a tenuous network, involving hazardous travel over long distances transcending significant political and religious boundaries, had now become much more consolidated and formalized. Large communities of foreigners stayed the winter in Rome and Naples; learned travelers received warm welcomes in salons across Europe. A resident population of painters, musicians, and guides served visitors from many countries to whom the grand tour was part of a cosmopolitan experience. The grand tour was now an established industry. The traveler passed from inn to inn where horses were changed, and everywhere, knowledgeable *ciceroni* guided tourists from site to site; painters attended them; sculptors were at hand to make copies of ancient works. An explosion of guidebooks published in the eighteenth century—and mostly copied one from the other—brought a stultifying uniformity to the visitor's experience. Nevertheless, the grand tour, with its moments of contemplation at Virgil's tomb and other sites, brought a physical reality to the ancient world only imagined while reading Latin texts at home. The guidebooks used by travelers were often copied from, or modeled on, Joseph-Jérôme Lefrançais Lalanne's *Voyage of a Frenchman in Italy*, first published in Paris and Venice in 1769 after the author's 1765–1766 visit to Italy. Lalanne's book combined practical directions with descriptions of monuments and translations of inscriptions. There was even an essay on the different kinds of cheese available in various Italian cities. This book and others like it were the precursors of modern travel guides.

Naples was the climax of the grand tour, with Roman baths, Virgil's tomb, and the smoldering Vesuvius nearby, as well as paintings, church interiors, and convents. In the evening, one went to the opera. Naples's setting when seen from the hills above the bay was stunning, and is no less so today. The city itself was a theater of contrasts, between classical beauty and the misery and poverty of most of the inhabitants. Eighteenth-century Naples was the most populous city in Europe after Paris and London. The rich lived in luxurious palaces, the poor in abject misery. Ferdinando Galiani, a Neapolitan who often watched travelers, wrote contemptuously to a friend of the foreign tourist:

> They come to a city in which the government, its characteristics, and the political system are the only interesting things which merit study, and yet they do nothing but see a few bricks and bits of marble at Pozzuoli and Portici, a few smouldering rocks at the Sofatara and the Vesuvius, a day at San Martinoi, a night at the theatre, and in eight days they have dispatched with everything. In this way they inform themselves of a city of four hundred thousand souls, which is unique in Italy and perhaps in the world.[7]

The Rome of the Grand Tour

In comparison, Rome came as somewhat of an anticlimax. Charles Dickens thought that it looked like smoke-mantled London. Rome was a dusty city, washed only by the occasional heavy rain. Tourists would witness processing flagellants whipping themselves through the streets, and attend the ceremony of the washing of the Apostles' feet by Christ in the form of the pope, who cleansed those of twelve carefully selected elderly pilgrims. The pontiff received many visitors, and they prostrated themselves before him to kiss his toe. And finally there were the Capuchin catacombs with skeletons still in their habits.

A visitor interested in antiquities was well advised to employ an expert guide. When John Wilkes (1727–1797), a member of Parliament expelled from Britain for seditious libel, came to Rome in 1765, he was fortunate to retain Johann Joachim Winckelmann, the German antiquarian who was superintendent of antiquities in Rome and librarian to Cardinal Albani, a prominent collector of antiquities. Winckelmann was an expert on classical art, and he was passionately interested in the excavations at the buried Roman towns of Herculaneum and Pompeii. Excavations at Herculaneum had begun under the Spanish engineer Rocque Joaquin de Alcubierre in 1738; excavating was then a process involving tunneling and gunpowder. Work began at Pompeii a decade later. The excavators were little more than treasure hunters, but their rich finds were strictly controlled by the king of the Two Sicilies in Naples. Only the most distinguished visitors could descend into the dark tunnels. The monarch forbade Winckelmann access to the excavations. The persistent German was eventually permitted to visit some of the excavations in 1762; his reputation was such that even his enemies recognized his scholarship. Winckelmann studied statuary placement—such as the placement of household gods—in Herculaneum's residences, and he wrote his masterpiece *History of the Art of Antiquity* in 1767, based in large part on the finds from Herculaneum and Pompeii. Wilkes described him as a "gentleman of exquisite taste and sound learning."[8]

Winkelmann had not got on well with a less interested tourist, Frederick Calvert, sixth Lord Baltimore, whom he had met a few years earlier:

> My Lord is an original and deserves to be written up. He thinks he has too much brain and that it would be better if God had substituted brawn for a third part of it. He has wearied of everything in the world, we went through the Villa Borghese in ten minutes. . . . Nothing pleased him but St. Peter's and the Apollo Belvedere. . . . He finally got so unbearable that I told him what I thought of him and shall have no more to do with him. He has £30,000 sterling of annual rent which he does not know how to enjoy. . . . His retinue consists of a young and pretty English girl but he is looking for a male travelling companion; he will have difficulty finding one.[9]

Few guides were as knowledgeable as Winkelmann, but those who were could show the visitor remarkable things—things that were less conspicu-

3-2 Visitors to the Roman Forum today can easily see and access the most impressive of the ruins, but they are not permitted to damage or remove ancient artifacts—as they could when Johann Joachim Winckelmann was giving tours.

ous than they are today, buried as they were under many meters of occupational debris from later centuries. Boswell was shocked to find that the Colosseum was home to a hermit and that parts of it were "full of dung." But there was much to see—arches and columns, villas, baths, and temples. In 1764, Edward Gibbon received inspiration for his great work, *History of the Decline and Fall of the Roman Empire*, while wandering through the Forum:

> After a sleepless night, I trod, with a lofty step, the ruins of the Forum; each memorable spot where Romulus stood or Tully spoke, or Caesar fell, was at once present to my eye; and several days of intoxication were lost or enjoyed before I could descend to a cool and minute investigation . . .
>
> It was on the fifteenth of October in the gloom of the evening, as I sat musing on the Capitol, while the barefoot fryars were chanting their litanies in the temple of Jupiter, that I conceived the first thought of my history. My original plan was confined to the decay of the city; my reading and reflection pointed to that aim; but several years elapsed, and several avocations intervened before I grappled with the decline and fall of the Roman Empire.[10]

A visitor could spend weeks wandering through churches and archaeological sites in and around the city, or he could do what one English gentleman did, who saw "very little utility" in antiquities. He spent six weeks in Rome, then hired a post chaise and four horses and devoted two hectic days to what other visitors had seen in six weeks—and he is said not to have missed a thing. The Reverend John Chetwode Eustace, on the other hand, was entranced by Rome. In 1812, he described a visit to the dilapidated Colosseum and its environs:

> But the glories of the Forum are now fled for ever; its temples are fallen; its sanctuaries have crumbled into dust; its colonnades encumber its pavements, now buried under their remains. The walls of the Rostra stripped of their ornaments and doomed to eternal silence, a few shattered porticos, and here and there an insulated column standing in the midst of broken shafts, vast fragments of marble capitals and cornices heaped together in masses, remind the traveler that the field which he now traverses was once the Roman Forum. . . . When Rome began to revive, and architecture arose from its ruins, every rich and powerful citizen wished to have, not a commodious dwelling merely, but a palace. The Coliseum was an immense quarry at hand; the common people stole, the grandees obtained permission to carry off its materials, till the interior was dismantled, and the exterior half stripped of its ornaments. It is difficult to say where this system of depredation, so sacrilegious in the opinion of the antiquary, would have stopped, had not Benedict XIV, a pontiff of great judgment, erected a cross in the centre of the arena, and declared the place sacred, out of respect to the blood of the many martyrs who were butchered there during the persecutions. This declaration, if issued two or three centuries ago, would have preserved the Coliseum entire; it can now only protect its remains, and transmit them, in their present state to posterity.[11]

But Naples, not Rome, persisted as the real draw, and was said by many to be more beautiful than London or Paris, and to be a place with a stimulating vitality and warm winters. "Naples is a paradise," wrote the German philosopher Goethe in 1786; "in it everyone lives in a sort of intoxicating self-forgetfulness."[12] Numerous English tourists spent months in the town, attending the opera and theater, which were as much a social happening as a performance. Wealthy expatriates held court in their villas, among them Sir William Hamilton, the British minister in Naples from 1764 to 1800. Sir William is remembered today as the husband of Horatio Nelson's mistress Emma, but he was famous in his lifetime as an avid collector of antiquities. In just seven years he amassed 730 ancient Greek vases and more than 6,000 coins and other artifacts, which he sold to the British Museum. His lavish folio volumes about his collection encouraged a generation of artists.

3-3 An aerial photograph of the coast of Naples reveals why many traveling to southern Italy in the eighteenth century considered it to be paradise.

Pompeii and Herculaneum

On August 24, A.D. 79, a huge fountain of ash, rocks, and smoke burst from Vesuvius and buried the Roman towns of Pompeii and Herculaneum under ash and pumice. Herculaneum vanished from sight. Only the eaves of the tallest buildings remained aboveground at Pompeii. Soon grassy mounds covered the two forgotten towns.

Sixteen centuries later, in 1709, a peasant digging a well found some fragments of sculpted marble and sold them to a dealer. A local prince heard of the discovery and arranged for workers to be lowered into the well and then dig horizontally. Fighting noxious gases, they recovered more sculpture. The well had penetrated into the heart of Herculaneum's theater. Rocque Joaquin de Alcubierre used gunpowder to blast down through about 60 feet of rock-hard volcanic debris. Then his diggers tunneled horizontally into underground galleries, recovering jewelry, statues of eminent Herculaneans, and artifacts from a rich buried city.

Rumors of the discovery soon spread across Europe. Yet only a few distinguished visitors were allowed into the mile or more of tunnels to examine the theater, marble-columned houses, and frescoed rooms by the light of smoking torches. Everything portable went into the king's personal museum at Portici, near Naples. The only reliable source of information on the excavations was Johann Joachim Winckelmann, who placed Herculaneum's art in the context of Greek mythology and tried to produce order from chaos. His great book *History of the Art of Antiquity* appeared in 1764. Unfortunately, Winkelmann was murdered before he could confirm his findings with his own excavations, and the chaotic treasure hunting continued for the rest of the century. William Hamilton witnessed the looting and complained bitterly to the king, but to no avail. During the Napoleonic Wars of the early nineteenth century, when France ruled Italy, French excavators stripped buildings of their contents, and left them to decay.

Generations of visitors visited Herculaneum and Pompeii during these treasure-hunting days. They would see the rooms where the finds were repaired and would study collections of statuary in Naples. The two buried cities exercised a profound influence on public taste, triggering a frenzied renaissance in interior design, furniture, and pottery. Some of Sheraton and Hepplewhite's furniture used classical motifs uncovered in the excavations. Sheraton even called one of his chairs "the Herculaneum."

A visit to the excavations was a highlight for late eighteenth- and nineteenth-century tourists. By Victorian times, a typical tour was well organized; witness the experience of Hippolyte Taine, a distinguished French scholar, in 1864. He had a passion for how ancient societies functioned, so he looked beyond the ruins and imagined the lives of the people who once lived in Pompeii's houses:

> All these streets are narrow; the greater portion are mere lanes, over which one strides with ease. Generally there is room only for a cart, and ruts are still visible: from time to time wide stones afford a crossing like a bridge. These details indicate other customs than our own; there was evidently no great traffic as in our cities, nothing like our heavily-loaded vehicles, and fast-trotting fanciful carriages. Their carts transported grain, oil, and provisions: much of the transportation was done on the arm and by slaves: the rich travelled about in litters. They possessed fewer and different conveniences. One prominent trait of antique civilisation is the absence of industrial pursuits. All supplies, utensils, and tissues, everything that machines and free labour now produce in such enormous quantities for everybody and at every price, were wanting to them. It was the slave who turned the mill-wheel: man devoted himself to the beautiful, and not to the useful; producing but little, he could consume but little. Life was necessarily simple, and philosophers and legislators were well aware of this; if they enjoined temperance it was not through pedantic motives, but because luxury was visibly incompatible with the social state of things. A few thousands of proud, brave, temperate

men, with only half a shirt and a mantle apiece, who delighted in the view of a hill with a group of beautiful temples and statues, who entertained themselves with public business, and passed their days in the gymnasium, at the forum, in the baths and the theatre, who washed and anointed themselves with oil, and were content with things as they stood, such was the city of antiquity. When their necessities and refinements get to be immoderate, the slave who only has his arms no longer suffices. For the establishment of vast complicated organisations like our modern communities, for example, the equality and security of a limited monarchy, in which order and the acquisition of wealth is the common end of all, there was no basis; when Rome desired to create it the cities were crushed out, the exhausted slaves had disappeared, the spring to set it in motion was broken, and all perished.

This becomes clearer on entering the houses—those of Cornelius Rufus, Marcus Lucretius, the Casa Nuova, and the house of Sallust. They are small, and the apartments are yet smaller. They are designed expressly for enjoying cool air and to sleep in; man passed his days elsewhere—in the forum, in the baths, and at the theatre. Private life, so important to us, was then much curtailed; the essential thing was public life. There is no trace of chimneys, and certainly there were but few articles of furniture. The walls are painted in red and black, a contrast which produces a pleasing effect in a semi-obscurity; arabesques of a charming airiness abound everywhere—Neptune and Apollo building the walls of Troy, a Triumph of Hercules, exquisite little cupids, dancing females apparently flying through the air, young girls inclining against columns, and Ariadne discovered by Bacchus. What vigour, what ingenuousness in all these youthful forms! Sometimes the panel contains only a graceful sinuous border, and in its centre a griffin. The subjects are merely indicated, corresponding to our painted wall-papers; but what a difference! Pompeii is an antique St. Germain or Fontainebleau, by which one easily sees the gulf separating the old and the new worlds.

Almost everywhere in the centre of the house is a garden like a large saloon, and in the middle of this a marble basin, a fountain flowing into it, and the whole enclosed within a portico of columns. What could be more charming, and simple, and better disposed for the warm hours of the day? With green leaves visible between two white columns, red tiles against the blue of the sky, the murmuring water sparkling among flowers like a jet of liquid pearls; and those shadows of porticoes intersected by the powerful light; is there a more congenial place for the body to grow freely, for healthy meditation, and to enjoy, without ostentation or affectation, all that is most beautiful in nature and in life? Some of these fountains bear lion's heads, and sprightly statuettes of children, with lizards, dogs, and fauns grouped around their margins. In the most capacious of all these houses, that of Diomed, orange and lemon trees, similar, probably, to those of ancient days, are putting forth their fresh green buds; a fishpool gleams brightly, and a small colonnade encloses a summer dining-room, the whole embraced within the square of a grand portico. The more the imagination dwells on the social economy of antiquity, the more beautiful it seems, and the more conformable to the climate and the nature of man. The women had their *gynaeceum* in the rear behind the court and portico, a secluded retreat with no external communication, and entirely separated from public life. They were not very active in their small apartments; they indulged in indolent repose, like Italian ladies of the present day, or employed themselves on woollen fabrics, awaiting a father's or husband's return from the business and converse of men. Wandering eyes passed carelessly over obscure walls, dimly discerning, not pictures, as in our day, plastering them, not archaeological curiosities, and works of a different art and country; but figures repeating and beautifying ordinary attitudes, such as retiring to and arising from bed, the siesta, and various avocations; goddesses surrounding Paris, a Fortune, slender and elegant, like the females of Primaticcio, or a Deidamia frightened and falling backward on a chair. Habits, customs, occupations, dress, and monuments, all issue from one and a unique source; the human plant grew but on one stalk, which stalk had never been grafted.[13]

Today, Pompeii is a madhouse of packaged tours during the summer season, where one swims through the crowds and sometimes fights to see the most famous buildings. But there still is much that resonates with Taine's experience of a century and a half ago, when visiting Pompeii was much more of an adventure. And at Pompeii, unlike at many other sites, one can conjure up images of what life must have been like in this once-prosperous town.

3-4 Despite constant crowds (remarkably absent in this photograph), Pompeii is a veritable time capsule for today's visitors, who continue to be amazed by the extent to which this ancient town remains intact.

Wastrels and "Macaronis"

Taine visited Pompeii after the fad of the grand tour had passed into history, but his experience mirrored that of generations of young gentlemen who traveled to Italy to widen their experience and gain a leavening of culture. Some returned as wastrels, "meet only to keep a tennis court." One seventeenth-century gentleman, Sir William Trumbull, admitted that the grand tour taught him little "besides the language, partly from my youth and the warmth of my temper, partly from lazynesse and debauchery."[14] Many of the young men were indeed adolescents, no more than sixteen to eighteen, at a time when most tourists were under twenty-one. Influential thinkers inveighed against the youth of the grand tour participants: "I never liked young travelers," said Gibbon. "They go too raw to make any great remarks." Most of them met few influential foreigners and spent all their time with their own kind. They were seen as unattractive visitors: ignorant, petulant, rash, and profligate, most of them accompanied by incompetent tutors. One troublesome son wrote to his father from Italy, "Pray, Sir, let me come home; for I cannot find that one is a jot better for seeing all these outlandish places and people."[15]

The more vapid returnees were called "macaronis," idle and effete youths with elaborate clothes who "wenched without passion." But a minority in fact returned with a lifelong interest in antiquities and the past. They formed the Society of Dilettanti and its successor the Traveller's Club, which was founded in 1819 after the disruptions of the Napoleonic Wars and was meant for gentlemen with wider interests who had traveled at least 500 miles (800 kilometers) from London. These men brought a cosmopolitan influence home with them, an intellectual curiosity and an appreciation of beauty that extended many peoples' sources of pleasure through art, architecture, and antiquities.

By the time the nineteenth century began, the French Revolution and the Napoleonic Wars had brought the grand tour to an end. By the 1830s, railroad tracks were laid across Europe. Thirty years later, Rome was only sixty hours from London, and one could go round the entire world in less time than it took to travel from London to Rome in the 1760s. But travel had changed as well, moving away from the familiar highways of the grand tour to slightly more remote, exotic places, like Lord Byron's Greece and Napoleon Bonaparte's Egypt.

CHAPTER FOUR
Greece Bespoiled

Place me on Sunium's marble steep,
Where nothing save the waves and I
May hear our mutual murmurs sweep;
There, swan-like, let me sing and die.

BYRON[1]
Don Juan

CHAPTER FOUR

Greece Bespoiled

The grand tour took the young and wealthy to Rome and Naples, but not as far as Greece, which had sunk into oblivion under its Byzantine emperors, who began to rule in A.D. 527. For seven hundred years Greece remained masked in obscurity as Crusaders, Venetians, and then Turks established princedoms and trading posts there. The Turks entered Athens in 1455 and turned the Parthenon and Acropolis into a fortress, transforming Greece into a rundown province of the Ottoman Empire. Worse yet, the ravages of wind, rain, and earthquake, of villagers seeking building stone and mortar, buried and eroded the ancient Greek temples and sculptures. Only a handful of intrepid artists and antiquarians came from Europe to sketch and collect before 1800, for Greek art and architecture were still little known or admired in the West, overshadowed as they were by the fashion for things Roman that dominated eighteenth-century taste. A small group of English connoisseurs financed the artists James Stuart and Nicholas Revett on a mission to record Greek art and architecture in 1755, and the first book in their multivolume *Antiquities of Athens* appeared in 1762. This, and other works, stimulated antiquarian interest, but in spite of such publications, few travelers ventured far off the familiar Italian track.

The Parthenon was, of course, well known, but places like the oracle at Delphi, the temple of Poseidon at Sounion—at the time a pirates' nest—and Olympia were little visited. In 1766, however, Richard Chandler, an Oxford academic, did visit Olympia, under the sponsorship of the Society of Dilettanti. The journey took him through overgrown fields of cotton shrubs, thistles, and licorice. Chandler had high expectations, but found himself in an insect-infested field of ruins:

> Early in the morning we crossed a shallow brook, and commenced our survey of the spot before us with a degree of expectation from which our disappointment

on finding it almost naked received a considerable addition. The ruin, which we had seen in evening, we found to be the walls of the cell of a very large temple, standing many feet high and well-built, its stones all injured . . . From a massive capital remaining it was collected that the edifice had been of the Doric order. At a distance before it was a deep hollow, with stagnant water and brick-work, where, it is imagined, was the Stadium. Round about are scattered remnants of brick-buildings, and the vestiges of stone walls. The site is by the road-side, in a green valley, between two ranges of even summits, pleasantly wooded.[2]

The Parthenon and Eleusis

By 1800, barely a dozen archaeological travelers had visited Greece, despite occasional sketches and architectural drawings of the temple of Minerva—as the Parthenon was then called. Athens itself was little more than a large village surrounding the Parthenon, girded with modern Turkish fortifications. As a further complication, the Turkish governor of Athens, Hadji Ali Haseki, was a ferocious despot who made it difficult for foreigners to acquire antiquities of any kind. Nevertheless, a French antiquarian and collector, Louis François Sebastian Fauvel (1753–1838),

4-1 A carte-de-visite portrait of Lord Elgin taken around 1830, roughly fifteen years after he sold the Elgin marbles to the British Museum.

managed to identify many forgotten sites and to steal numerous antiquities out from under the noses of the authorities. "Take everything you can," he wrote, "miss no occasion to pillage in Athens and the surrounding territory everything that is pillageable; spare neither the dead nor the living."[3] By 1803, several avaricious collectors had descended on Greece, among them the Earl of Elgin, British ambassador to the Sublime Porte in Constantinople. Elgin saw his role as a cultural ambassador as well as a political ambassador—as one who would improve the taste of his fellow Englishmen by procuring the finest specimens of Greek sculpture.

Elgin's name is forever associated with the so-called Elgin marbles, crafted by the sculptor Phidias on the pediments of the Parthenon. On the west gable, Athena stood confronting Poseidon as they fight for Attica, their chariots drawn up before them. When Elgin arrived with a team of artists and technicians in 1800, the marbles were already in a sorry state. He obtained a *firman*, or permit, from the sultan of Constantinople to record the Parthenon freely and to remove sculptures from the Acropolis. After prolonged difficulties, Elgin succeeded in removing the sculptures that now bear his name and sold them in 1816 to the British Museum for £35,000, a huge sum at the time. The controversy over his dastardly deed (or heroic deed—it depends on who you talk to) continues to this day.[4]

The years after the Napoleonic Wars brought more visitors, many of whom inscribed their names on the Parthenon. Even then, the numbers were small, perhaps no more than two hundred between 1800 and 1830, excluding military personnel. Many of the visitors were sober, observant travelers of considerable learning, who came to see and, if possible, acquire. Among them was Dr. Edward Daniel Clarke (1769–1822), professor of mineralogy at Cambridge University, who traveled to Greece in 1799 as the tutor to an amiable young man, John Cripps. The two men were the first grand tourists to reach Constantinople and Greece, where they spent much time buying the ancient silver coins that adorned many women's caps. They were not alone in their interest in coins: one French collector, the consular official E. M. Cousinéry, acquired between 1810 and 1821 four coin collections totaling 26,000 coins, which he sold to the highest bidders upon returning to Paris.

Clarke and Cripps were among the few travelers who visited Eleusis, one of the great sanctuaries of antiquity, the place where Demeter was said to have paused in her search for Persephone, who had been carried to the underworld by Pluto. When Demeter, in grief, shut herself up in a temple and refused to allow seeds to sprout, famine threatened humanity. Zeus allowed Persephone to visit the earth for part of each year so that Demeter

4-2 Although worn by time, this detail—which shows Athena (left) and Hephaestus—from Phidias's east frieze of the Parthenon in Athens (c. 438–432 B.C.) exemplifies the type of classical art that Lord Elgin found so valuable.

would cause fruit and crops to grow abundantly. The performance of the mysteries of Eleusis was one of the great rituals of the ancient Greek world, celebrated in secret into the Christian era. By 1800, the sanctuary was but a jumble of stones near a small village. Here, the upper part of a statue, said to be that of Demeter, stood in a fragmentary state, regarded by the locals with great veneration. Clarke and Cripps greatly admired the statue, which weighed over 2 tons (1.8 tonnes), and decided to take it to England. They were lucky to obtain a *firman* from the governor of Athens with the help of the gifted Italian artist Giovanni Lusieri, who was at the time working for Lord Elgin. But their troubles had hardly begun, as Clarke later wrote:

The difficulties to be encountered were not trivial; we carried with us from Athens but few implements: a rope of twisted herbs, and some large nails, were all that the city afforded, as likely to aid the operation. Neither a wheeled carriage, nor blocks, nor pulleys, nor even a saw, could be procured. Fortunately, we found at *Eleusis* several large poles, an axe, and a small saw about six inches in length, such as cutlers sometimes adapt to the handle of a pocket knife. With these we began to work. The stoutest of the poles were cut, and pieces were nailed in a triangular form, having transverse beams at the vertex and base. Weak as our machine was, it acquired considerable strength by the weight of the *Statue*, when placed up upon the transverse beams. With the remainder of the poles were made rollers, over which the triangular frame might move. The rope was then fastened to each extremity of the transverse beams. This simple contrivance succeeded, when perhaps more complicated machinery might have failed: and an amass of marble weighing near two tons was moved over the brow of the hill or *Acropolis of Eleusis*, and from thence to the sea in about nine hours.

An hundred peasants were collected from the village and neighbourhood of *Eleusis* and near fifty boys. The peasants were ranged, forty on each side, to work at the ropes; some being employed, with levers, to raise the machine, when rocks

> or large stones opposed its progress. The boys who were not strong enough to work at the ropes and levers were engaged in taking up the rollers as fast as the machine left them and in placing these again in the front.
>
> But the superstition of the inhabitants of *Eleusis*, respecting an idol which they all regarded as the protectress of their fields, was not the least obstacle to be overcome. In the evening, soon after our arrival with the firman, an accident happened which had nearly put an end to the undertaking. While the inhabitants were conversing with the *Tchohadar* [in the Turkish army of the day, a sergeant and guard commander], as to the means of its removal, an ox, loosed from its yoke, came and placed itself before the Statue, and after butting with its horns for some time against the marble, ran off with considerable speed, bellowing, into the Plain of *Eleusis*. Instantly a general murmur prevailed; and several women joining in the clamour, it was with difficulty any proposal could be made. *They had been always, they said, famous for their corn and the fertility of the land would cease when the Statue was removed. . . .*
>
> The people had assembled and stood around the *Statue*; but no one among them ventured to begin the work. They believed that the arm of any person would fall off who should dare to touch the marble, or to disturb its position. . . . Presently however the Priest of *Eleusis*, partly induced by entreaty and partly terrified by the menaces of the *Tchohadar*, put on his canonical vestments, as for a ceremony of high mass, and descending into the hollow where the *Statue* remained upright . . . gave the first blow with a pickaxe for the removal of the soil, that the people might be convinced no calamity could befall the labourers.[5]

Clarke and Cripps moved the statue on rollers to the nearby harbor, where they were lucky to be able to engage a merchant ship to load it using the ship's on-board derrick. Eventually, the statue and Clarke's enormous archaeological, geological, and natural history collections almost reached England, only to be wrecked off the Sussex coast. Fortunately, the ship ran aground near Cripps's home. His father was able to save the statue and seventy-six cases of antiquities and other specimens—more than 1,000 Greek coins, 6,000 exotic plant specimens, and a large collection of minerals, insects, and drawings. The statue was presented to Cambridge University and displayed prominently. Clarke insisted that it was Demeter, publishing an artist's reconstruction of her as a seated goddess. But experts soon determined that the statue was a mere caryatid, crafted in Roman times. A better-preserved sister is now in the Eleusis museum in Greece.

Charles Cockerell and Friends at Aphaia

In 1810, Charles Robert Cockerell (1788–1863), son of a wealthy architect, arrived in Athens with a friend, John Foster. They, as well as two other young men, crossed to the island of Aegina in an open boat to sketch and paint, despite the pirates who infested the islands in the Saronic Gulf. Their destination was the sanctuary of Aphaia high above the ocean, a romantic temple with scattered marbles and lonely columns that could be seen from the coasts of both Attica and Argolis. The young *milordi* (as English visitors were called) settled in to camp at the ruins for two weeks, feasting on fish, partridges, and lambs purchased from the local villagers. On their second day, they uncovered the first of many sculptures, including the head of a helmeted warrior, soon identified by classical art experts as having been carved before the marbles on the Parthenon.

Cockerell realized the value of the Aegina marbles at once and bought them from the islanders for £40. A bidding war started almost immediately, pitting the British, the French, and the Germans against one another. The final sale, won by Prince Ludwig of Bavaria, was advertised in newspapers across Europe. Heavily restored in the 1820s, the marbles are now in Munich. Today, it is hard to imagine what Cockerell and his friends experienced, but the young traveler's account of his weeks on Aegina gives a wonderful impression of archaeological tourism nearly two centuries ago. The temple of Aphaia is now a major tourist attraction overrun with thousands of visitors during the summer months, with regular ferries running to it from Athens. Cockerell's story comes from his son Samuel Pepys Cockerell's *Travels in Southern Europe and the Levant* (1903), which was based on Charles's diaries.

I told you we were going to make a tour in the Morea, but before doing so we determined to see the remains of the temple at Aegina, opposite Athens, a three hours' sail. Our party was to be Haller, Linckh, Foster, and myself. At the moment of our starting an absurd incident occurred. There had been for some time a smouldering war between our servants and our janissary [bodyguard, usually a soldier]. When the latter heard that he was not to go with us, it broke out into a blaze. He said it was because the servants had been undermining his character, which they equally angrily denied. But he was in a fury, went home, got drunk, and then came out into the street and fired off his pistols, bawling out that no one but he was the legitimate protector of the English. For fear he should hurt some one with his shooting, I went out to him and expostulated. He was very drunk, and professed to love us greatly and that he would defend us against six or seven or even eight Turks; but as for the servants, "Why, my soul," he said, "have they thus treated me?" I contrived, however, to prevent his loading his pistols again, and as he worked the wine off, calm was at length restored; but the whole affair delayed us so long that we did not walk down to the Piraeus till night. As we were sailing out of the port in our open boat we overtook the ship with Lord Byron on board. Passing under her stern we sang a favourite song of his, on which he looked out of the windows and invited us in. There we drank a glass of port with him, Colonel Travers, and two of the English officers, and talked of the three English frigates that had attacked five Turkish ones and a sloop of war off Corfu, and had taken and burnt three of them. We did not stay long, but bade them "bon voyage" and slipped over the side. We slept very well in the boat, and next morning reached Aegina. The port is very picturesque. We went on at once from the town to the Temple of Jupiter, which stands at some distance above it; and having got together workmen to help us in turning stones, etc., we pitched our tents for ourselves, and took possession of a cave at the northeast angle of the platform on which the temple stands—which had once been, perhaps, the cave of a sacred oracle—as a lodging for the servants and the janissary. The seas hereabouts are still infested with pirates, as they always have been. One of the workmen pointed me out the pirate boats off Sunium, which is one of their favourite haunts, and which one can see from the temple platform. But they never molested us during the twenty days and nights we camped out there, for our party, with servants and janissary, was too strong to be meddled with. We got our provisions and labourers from the town, our fuel was the wild thyme, there were abundance of partridges to eat, and we bought kids of the shepherds; and when work was over for the day, there was a grand roasting of them over a blazing fire with an accompaniment of native music, singing and dancing. On the platform was growing a crop of barley, but on the actual ruins and fallen fragments of the temple itself no great amount of vegetable earth had collected, so that without very much labour we were able to

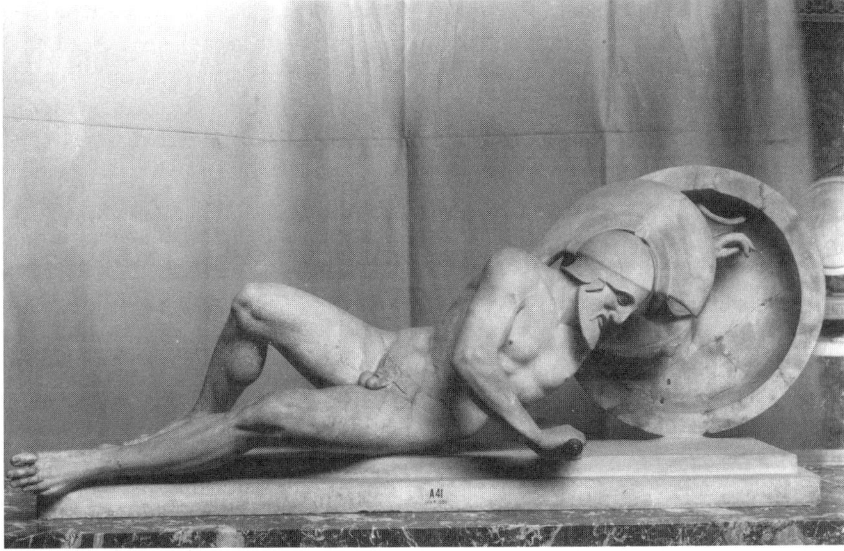

4-3 This figure of a fallen warrior, from the east pediment of the temple of Aphaia at Aegina, c. 490 B.C., is the type of marble statue that Charles Robert Cockerell was so delighted to discover.

find and examine all the stones necessary for a complete architectural analysis and restoration. At the end of a few days we had learnt all we could wish to know of the construction, from the stylobate to the tiles, and had done all we came to do.

But meanwhile a startling incident had occurred which wrought us all to the highest pitch of excitement. On the second day one of the excavators, working in the interior portico, struck on a piece of Carian marble which, as the building itself is of stone, arrested his attention. It turned out to be the head of a helmeted warrior, perfect in every feature. It lay with the face turned upwards, and as the features came out by degrees you can imagine nothing like the state of rapture and excitement to which we were wrought. Here was an altogether new interest, which set us to work with a will. Soon another head was turned up, then a leg and a foot, and finally, to make a long story short, we found under the fallen portions of the tympanum and the cornice of the eastern and western pediments no less than sixteen statues and thirteen heads, legs, arms, etc. [another account says seventeen and fragments of at least ten more], all in the highest preservation, not three feet below the surface of the ground. It seems incredible, considering the number of travellers who have visited the temple, that they should have remained so long undisturbed.

It is evident that they were brought down with the pediment on the top of them by an earthquake, and all got broken in the fall; but we have found all the pieces and have now put together, as I say, sixteen entire figures.

The unusual bustle about the temple rapidly increased as the news of our operations spread. Many more men than we wanted began to congregate round us and gave me a good deal of trouble. Greek workmen have pretty ways. They bring you bunches of roses in the morning with pretty wishes for your good health; but they can be uncommonly insolent when there is no janissary to keep them in order. Once while Foster, being away at Athens, had taken the janissary with him, I had the greatest pother with them. A number that I did not want would hang about the diggings, now and then taking a hand themselves, but generally interfering with those who were labouring, and preventing any orderly and businesslike work. So at last I had to speak to them. I said we only required ten men, who should each receive one piastre per day, and that that was all I had to spend; and if more than ten chose to work, no matter how many they might be, there would still be only the ten piastres to divide amongst them. They must settle amongst themselves what they would choose to do. Upon this what did the idlers do? One of them produced a fiddle; they settled into a ring and were preparing to dance. This was more than I could put up with. We should get no work done at all. So I interfered and stopped it, declaring that only those who worked, and worked hard, should get paid anything whatever. This threat was made more efficacious by my evident anger, and gradually the superfluous men left us in peace, and we got to work again.

It was not to be expected that we should be allowed to carry away what we had found without opposition. However much people may neglect their own possessions, as soon as they see them coveted by others they begin to value them. The primates of the island came to us in a body and read a statement made by the council of the island in which they begged us to desist from our operations, for that heaven only knew what misfortunes might not fall on the island in general, and the immediately surrounding land in particular, if we continued them. Such a rubbishy pretence of superstitious fear was obviously a mere excuse to extort money, and as we felt that it was only fair that we should pay, we sent our dragoman [guide] with them to the village to treat about the sum; and meanwhile a boat which we had ordered from Athens having arrived, we embarked the marbles without delay and sent them off under the care of Foster and Linckh, with the janissary, to the Piraeus, and from thence they were carried up to Athens by night to avoid exciting attention. Haller and I remained to carry on the digging, which we did with all possible vigour. The marbles being gone, the primates came to be easier to deal with. We completed our bargain with them to pay them 800 piastres, about 40L, for the antiquities we had found, with leave to continue the digging till we had explored the whole site. Altogether it took us sixteen days of very hard work, for besides watching and directing and generally managing the workmen, we had done a good deal of digging and handling of the marbles ourselves; all heads and specially delicate parts we were obliged to take out of the ground ourselves for fear of the workmen ruining them. On the whole we have been fortunate. Very few have been broken by carelessness. Besides all this, which was outside our own real business, we had been taking measurements and making careful drawings of every part and arrangement of

4-4 Although the Parthenon, and indeed all of the Acropolis, remained unprotected for centuries, enough of it remains standing to convey an impression of the importance of this building to the Greeks who constructed it.

the architecture till every detail of the construction and, as far as we could fathom it, of the art of the building itself was clearly understood by us. Meanwhile, after one or two days' absence, Foster and Linckh came back; and it then occurred to us that the receipt for the 800 piastres had only been given to the names of Foster and myself (who had paid it), and Linckh and Haller desired that theirs should be added. Linckh therefore went off to the town to get the matter rectified. But this was not so easy. The lawyer was a crafty rogue, and pretending to be drunk as soon as he had got back the receipt into his hands, refused to give it up, and did not do so until after a great deal of persuasion and threatening. When we fell in with him at dinner two days later he met us with the air of the most candid unconcern. It was at the table of a certain [Ottoman official] who had been sent from Constantinople to receive the rayah [poll] tax. Linckh had met him in the town when he went about the receipt, and the [official] had paid us a visit at the temple next day and dined with us, eating and especially drinking a great deal. A compliment he paid us was to drink our healths firing off a pistol. I had to do the same in return. The man had been to England, and even to Oxford, and had come back with an odd jumble of ideas which amused us but are not worth repeating. Next day, as I have said, we dined with him and the rogue of a lawyer. He was very hospitable. Dinner consisted mainly of a whole lamb, off which with his fingers he tore entire limbs and threw them into our plates, which we, equally with our fingers, a la Turque, ate as best we could. We finished the evening with the Albanian dance, and walked up home to our tent.[6]

Today, we are horrified at the cavalier way in which Cockerell, Elgin, and many others removed priceless works of art from temple and sanctuary. But in those days, Greece was a remote, little-traveled land, its temples overgrown and neglected except as a source of building stone or as makeshift fortifications and storerooms. Travelers were left to their own devices, enduring flea-ridden lodgings, steep mountain tracks, insects, and suspicious local people who had suffered under Turkish rule for centuries. In those days, *milordi* traveled freely through the countryside accompanied by a Turkish janissary and large quantities of baggage in ways that were unimaginable in brigand-infested Italy. But they regarded the Greeks with indifference, despite receiving many kindnesses, and treated the archaeological sites as a source of potential wealth. Lord Byron criticized the popular mindset of the time when he wrote,

Where is the human being that ever conferred a benefit on Greece or Greeks? They are to be grateful to the Turks for their fetters and to the Franks for their broken promises and lying counsels. They are to be grateful to the artist who engraves their ruins and to the antiquary who carries them away; to the traveler whose janissary flogs them and to the scribbler whose journal abuses them. This is the amount of their obligations to foreigners.[7]

And we, we shall die, and Islam will wither away, and the Englishman straining far over to hold his beloved India will plant a firm foot on the banks of the Nile and sit in the seats of the Faithful, and still that sleepless rock will lie watching and watching the works of the new busy race with those same sad earnest eyes, and the same tranquil mien everlasting. You dare not mock at the Sphynx.

A. W. KINGLAKE[I]

CHAPTER FIVE

Pharaohs and Pyramids

The Nile slashes through the eastern Sahara Desert like an arrow, a stalk of green amid some of the most arid landscape on earth. Each summer, floodwaters from deep in tropical Africa inundate the floodplain, depositing fertile silt and nourishing growing crops, enabling an Egyptian civilization to endure for five thousand years. Along the river's banks, pharaohs, considered to be living gods, created a palimpsest of pyramids, rock-cut tombs, and temples that have fascinated the traveler since Herodotus's day.

Egypt was the land of Ra, the sun god, whose golden rays shone day after day in an unchanging chronicle of human existence and immortality—birth, life, and death. Ra's rays shine between the serried pillars of Karnak's Hypostyle Hall, darken the jagged contours of the Valley of Kings in deep shadow, project the steep slopes of the pyramids of Giza over the surrounding desert. Ancient Egyptian ruins cast a profound spell over the visitor, especially in the days before Egyptologists measured the ruins and recorded their secrets. They were desolate, unfamiliar, their gods irrevocably gone, the hieroglyphs on the walls unintelligible except to a privileged few—and that only after about 1830, when Jean François Champollion's decipherment came into common use. But the sense of time and history these monuments conveyed was, and still is, pervasive. The figures on temple and tomb walls expose the habits, fantasies, and beliefs of thirty dynasties. Even today, there is an underlying sense of permanence along the Nile. The pharaohs have vanished, succeeded by caliphs, pashas, colonial overlords, and presidents, but life along the Nile still follows a timeless routine of planting and harvest, of life and death.

Napoleon's Donkeys

The traveler has been part of this timeless landscape for more than two thousand years. We have already encountered Roman tourists at the

5-1 The pyramids of Giza have a close association with the sun god Ra; they represent sun rays by which the dead pharaoh ascended to the heavens to take his place at Ra's side.

Colossi of Memnon. Christian pilgrims on their way to Jerusalem passed through, too, although travel was difficult for the faithful in what was now Islamic territory. The founding in London of the Levant Company in 1581, originally to foster trade with Turkey—among other things, trade in coffee—brought more visitors, some of them in search of *mumiya*, pounded-up Egyptian mummy, considered to be a powerful aphrodisiac. By the end of the eighteenth century, at least twenty Englishmen had carved their names on the Great Pyramid; French maps depicted the Nile at least superficially as far south as the First Cataract. Then, in 1798, General Napoleon Bonaparte invaded Egypt, bringing with him 167 scientists to explore both the modern country and its rich history.

Napoleon's "donkeys," so named by his soldiers because they were deemed useless, were a remarkably talented group, headed by Vivant Denon (1747–1825), an artist and diplomat with a taste for antiquities. There were agronomists and cartographers, antiquarians and geologists, mainly young men who worked together in a spirit of remarkable harmony at the newly founded French Institute in Cairo. They pored over the trilingual Rosetta Stone, traveled with regiments, sketched and collected. When they ran out of pencils, they melted down lead bullets to continue taking notes. Years later, they produced one of the great works of archaeological writing, the multivolume *Description de l'Egypte*, published between 1809 and 1828. The magnificent illustrations in this publishing masterpiece brought ancient Egypt to life for the learned world and caused a sensation in Europe.

Denon himself beat his colleagues to the punch with the publication of his *Travels in Upper and Lower Egypt*, first printed in French, then in English in 1802. His travels with the army took him as far south as Philae by the First Cataract, where he waxed lyrical over the temple of Isis:

After passing the cataracts, the rocks grow loftier, and on their summit rocks of granite are heaped up, appearing to cluster together, and to hang in equipoise, on purpose to produce the most picturesque effects. Through these rough and rugged forms the eye all at once discovers the magnificent monuments of the island of Philae, which form a brilliant contrast, and one of the most singular surprises the traveler can meet with. The Nile here makes a bend, as if to come and visit this enchanting island, where the monuments are only separated by tufts of palm-trees or rocks that appear to be left merely to contrast the forms of nature with the magnificence of art, and to collect, in one rich spot, every thing that is most beautiful and impressive."[2]

The army cleared out the inhabitants who were rash enough to fire on the visitors, and Denon had a few hours to wander among the temples. In the end, he paid six visits to this enchanted spot between 1798 and 1804.

Champollion Visits the Nile

The end of the Napoleonic Wars brought more visitors to the Nile, among them numerous adventurers and tomb robbers, lusting for fame and fortune. One such individual, the circus performer turned antiquities collector Giovanni Belzoni (1778–1823), spent three years amassing a large collection of Egyptian antiquities. His finds, which he exhibited in London to enthusiastic crowds, included the sarcophagus of the New Kingdom pharaoh Seti I. The French consul Bernardino Drovetti (1776–1852) vied with Belzoni in a bitter rivalry over places to dig and sold three collections in Europe.[3] The depredations of these two men and many others like them were incalculable, and were fueled by the insatiable appetite in Europe for mummies, papyri, and other Egyptian antiquities.

Other visitors came to see, to marvel, and to collect, on an extension of the grand tour. Among these were two English sea captains, Charles Irby and James Mangles, who helped Belzoni clear the entrance of the temple of Abu Simbel above the First Cataract in 1817.[4] They did so with the expectation of encountering great riches, but found, to their disappointment, that the chambers were bare. Five years earlier, the Swiss traveler Johann Ludwig Burckhardt (1784–1817), one of the immortals of exploration, had approached the temple's façade of seated pharaohs from the high ground above them. At first he was not impressed, but when he turned upstream a little way he realized the full extent of the figures. He wrote, "On the wall of the rock, in the centre of the four statues, is the figure of the hawk-headed Osiris, surmounted by a globe; beneath which, I suspect, could the sand be cleared away, a vast temple would be discovered of which the above colossal figures would probably serve as ornaments." The single exposed head had "a most expressive, youthful countenance, approaching nearer to the Grecian model of beauty than that of any ancient Egyptian figure I have seen."[5]

Five years later, Champollion deciphered hieroglyphic writing by using royal names and the Greek inscription on the Rosetta Stone, but it was a decade before his achievement was widely accepted. In 1828, Champollion spent seventeen months in Egypt at the head of a joint French and Tuscan expedition, a fascinating experience for all concerned, for they were the first to read the inscriptions on the walls of the great temples and to understand their significance. Champollion's party traveled in two boats, pausing to record inscriptions and tomb paintings. Their most electrifying moment came at the temple of Hathor at Dendera, where, unable to restrain themselves, the young men rushed ashore from their moored sailing boats on a brilliantly moonlit night and stormed the temple in a wild state of excitement:

> The moonlight was magnificent. . . . [A]lone and without our guides, but armed to the teeth, we set off across the fields. . . . We walked like this, singing the most recent opera marches. . . . I will not try to describe the impression which the great propylon and especially the portico of the great temple made on us. . . . It is grace and majesty brought together in the highest degree.[6]

For two glorious hours the travelers wandered through the moonlit temple, drunk with enthusiasm and rapture, before returning to their boats at three in the morning.

The First Tourists

For all the destruction dealt by Europeans, a handful of visitors came with more serious objectives, to sketch and record what they saw. Among them was the Englishman John Gardner Wilkinson (1797–1875), destined to become one of Egyptology's seminal figures. He arrived in Alexandria in 1821 and adopted a Turkish lifestyle, wearing Turkish dress and keeping a mistress. He traveled widely, living for months on end in a tomb on the west bank of the Nile opposite Luxor. Wilkinson's illustrated *Manners and Customs of the Ancient Egyptians* appeared in 1837 and brought the ancient Egyptians to life for the general public as never before. Thousands of readers purchased it at railroad bookstores.

By 1820, Napoleon, and later the pasha of Egypt, Muhammad Ali, had made Upper Egypt more secure. Muhammad Ali controlled the country as far upstream as the Second Cataract, making it possible for Europeans to travel deep into what is now Sudan. Soon there were guidebooks, like Jean Jacques Rifaud's *Tableau de l'Égypte, de la Nubie, et des lieux circonvoisins* (Guidebook to Egypt, Nubia, and Surrounding Attractions), published in 1830. This guidebook led the traveler from Alexandria to the Second Cataract, complete with side trips, an Arabic vocabulary, and essays on geography and the local people. Rifaud's guide was superficial at best and was soon superseded by more ambitious works like John Gardner Wilkinson's *Handbook for Travellers in Egypt*, published by the London publisher John Murray in 1847 as one of a series of popular guides. Wilkinson recommended allowing at least three months for a journey to the Second Cataract and back. One traveled by means of a *dahabiyya*, a Nile sailing vessel that sailed upstream with the prevailing north winds and floated downstream with the current. Wilkinson urged the traveler to sink the boat first to rid it of "rats and other noxious inhabitants." A wise visitor shipped out with a chicken coop and a plentiful supply of biscuits as provisions for the journey.

"Far more beautiful than I had expected"

Egypt rapidly became more accessible. Consular records tell us that at least sixty-five Americans visited Alexandria and Cairo between 1832 and 1842. Benjamin Disraeli came to the Nile in 1831 and rhapsodized over the charms of Cairo's narrow streets and mosques. On January 1, 1836, "with a fair wind and the star-spangled banner made for [him] by an Arab tailor," a young American, John Lloyd Stephens, accompanied only by an experienced Italian traveler, Paolo Nuozzo, set sail up the Nile in a rented felucca (Nile sailing vessel). He took his time and made his way into pyramid and tomb, finding Ancient Egypt "beautiful, far more beautiful than I had expected." Egypt turned the young Stephens into a passionate explorer of the past, one soon to achieve fame for exploring Petra and then introducing an astonished world to the glories of Maya civilization (see Chapter 9). Already, at Dendera and Thebes, we see his literary gifts in full flow. He explored the temple of Dendera after walking through green fields of lucerne. He was enraptured by the carvings of Osiris, Isis, and other gods that were repeated dozens of times on the walls:

The temple of Dendera is one of the finest specimens of the arts in Egypt, and the best preserved of any on the Nile. It stands about a mile from the river, on the edge of the desert, and coming up, may be seen at a great distance. The temples of the Egyptians, like the chapels in Catholic countries, in many instances stand in such positions as to arrest the attention of the passer-by; and the Egyptian boatman, long before he reached it, might see the open doors of the temple of Dendera, reminding him of his duty to the gods of his country. I will not attempt any description of this beautiful temple; its great dimensions, its magnificent propylon or gateway, portico, and columns; the sculptured figures on the walls; the spirit of the devices, and their admirable execution, the winged globe and the sacred vulture, the hawk and the ibis, Isis, Osiris, and Horus, gods, goddesses, priests and women; harps, altars, and people clapping their hands, and the whole interior covered with hieroglyphics and paintings, in some places, after a lapse of more than two thousand years, in colors fresh as if the work of yesterday.

It was the first temple I had seen in Egypt; and although I ought not perhaps to say so, I was disappointed. I found it beautiful, far more beautiful than I had expected; but look at it as I would, wander around as I would, the ruins of the Acropolis at Athens rose before me; the severe and stately form of the Parthenon; the beautiful fragment of the temple of Minerva, and the rich Corinthian columns of the temple of Jupiter came upon me with a clearness and vividness I could not have conceived. The temple was more than half buried in the sand. The Arabs have built their huts within and around it, range upon range, until they reached and almost covered the tops of the temple. . . .

Nor is this the worst affliction of the traveler at Dendera. He sees there other ruins, more lamentable than the encroachments of the desert and the burial in the sand, worse than the building and ruin of successive Arab villages; he sees wanton destruction by the barbarous hand of man. The beautiful columns, upon which the skillful and industrious Egyptian artist had labored with his chisel for months, and perhaps for years, which were then looked upon with religious reverence, and ever since with admiration, have been dashed into a thousand pieces, to build bridges and forts for the great modern reformer.

We also owe to Stephens a vivid description of the tomb of the pharaoh Seti I (r. 1291–1278 B.C.), discovered by Giovanni Belzoni in the Valley of the Kings in 1817:

The entrance is by a narrow door; a simple excavation in the side of the mountain, without device or ornament. The entrance hall, which is extremely beautiful, is twenty-seven feet long and twenty-five broad, having at the end a large door opening into another chamber, twenty-eight feet by twenty-five, the walls covered with figures drawn in outline, but perfect as if recently done. Descending a large staircase and passing through a beautiful corridor, Belzoni came to another staircase, at the foot of which he entered another apartment, twenty-four feet by thirteen, and so ornamented with sculptures and paintings that he called it the Hall of Beauty. The sides of all the chambers and corridors are covered with sculpture and paintings; the colors appearing fresher as the visitor advances towards the interior of the tomb; and the walls of this chamber are covered with the figures of Egyptian gods and goddesses, seeming to hover round and guard the remains of the honored dead.

Farther on is a large hall, twenty-eight feet long and twenty-seven broad, supported by two rows of square pillars, which Belzoni called the Hall of Pillars; and beyond this is the entry to a large saloon with a vaulted roof, thirty-two feet in length and twenty-seven in breadth. Opening from this were several other chambers of different dimensions, one of them unfinished, and one forty-three feet long by seventeen feet, six inches wide; in which he found the mummy of a bull; but in the center of the grand saloon was a sarcophagus of the finest oriental alabaster, only two inches thick, minutely sculptured within and without with several hundred figures, and perfectly translucent when a light was placed within it.

All over the corridors and chambers the walls are adorned with sculptures and paintings in intaglio and relief, representing gods, goddesses, and the hero of the tomb in the most prominent events of his life, priests, religious processions and sacrifices, boats and agricultural scenes, and the most familiar paintings of every day life, in colors as fresh as if they were painted not more than a month ago; and the large saloon, lighted up with the blaze of our torches, seemed more fitting for a banqueting hall, for song and dance than a burial-place of the dead. All travelers concur in pronouncing the sudden transition from the dreary desert without to those magnificent tombs as operating like a scene of enchantment; and we may imagine what might have been the sensations of Belzoni, when wandering with the excitement of a first discoverer through these beautiful chambers and corridors, he found himself in the great saloon leaning over the alabaster sarcophagus. An old Arab who accompanied us remembered Belzoni, and pointed out a chamber where the fortunate explorer entertained a party of European travelers . . . making the tomb of Pharaoh ring with shouts and songs of merriment.[7]

John Lloyd Stephens traveled south at a time when Egypt, while open to travelers, was still an unpredictable country for foreigners. Even getting there took time. The passage from southern France to Alexandria took a month or more under sail until 1837, when the Peninsula and Orient Line (P&O) won government contracts to carry mail by steamship from England to Alexandria. By 1843, the passage from Southampton to Alexandria took only fifteen days. A traveler who went overland to Marseilles could trim four or five days off the journey. In 1844, a mere 275 visitors passed through Egypt on their way to and from India. That number leapt to 3,000 in 1847. Eleven years later, the Suez Canal opened;

thousands of people stopped off in Egypt to see the pyramids and, often, to travel south along the river, especially after the first steamships arrived on the Nile in 1858.

Egypt had obvious biblical associations; it was a place where the European visitor could sample an exotic country in relative comfort, and where there were "biblical scenes" in every village. The devout rode donkeys through bazaars and climbed the pyramids. The Reverend Stephen Olin (1797–1851), a prominent American Methodist and a president of Wesleyan College, drew a moral from Giza in 1840:

> No other ancient place which I have visited makes its instructive homily upon the madness of ambition and the transitoriness of human grandeur, half so touching and impressive. In Rome, and even in Athens, the solemn lesson is perpetually interrupted by the busy pursuits and noisy pleasures of still teeming life; and the monuments of generations long since gone are often blended with, and half concealed by, the habitations or more ambitious structures of the present. At Thebes, everything is left to the desolation to which time and violence have consigned it. The peasants, with their cottages and cornfields, which are seen only here and there upon the ancient plain, are just sufficient to make a good contrast to the fallen temples, yawning tombs, and colossal images that look down in derision upon their puny labours. These monuments are principal objects in the scene, and there is nothing else in the form either of improvement or wealth, or even industry, to distract the attention which they are permitted to engross, or to break in upon the converse into which they insensibly draw us with the men who, at an era beyond the age of authentic history, reared up these memorials of their achievements, literature, and arts.
>
> I think it impossible to sojourn, even for a few days, among such venerable objects, without being inspired with the highest respect for the ancient Egyptians, though the proofs of their debasing superstitions, which so abound here, must inevitably detract a good deal from that feeling. I incline to the opinion that in point of genius they are entitled to the first place among all the ancient nations. True, these structures lack the lightness, the chaste simplicity and faultless proportions, which distinguish Grecian architecture, as exhibited in the Theseion and Parthenon at Athens. It is essential to remember, however, that the Egyptians were the inventors; the Greeks only improved upon their models—an easy task for even inferior minds. This remark is, with some modification, applicable to the statuary as well as the architecture of the two nations. In all that indicates high talent, grandeur of conception, and skill in the applications of science to mechanical operations, the Egyptians were superior, and at least equal in the lower attributes of mere handicraft skill and patient industry.[8]

Artists came, too, some of them to paint "scriptural subjects," using the modern people as inspiration. The architect and designer Owen Jones

5-2 David Roberts's *Abou-Simbel*, a nineteenth-century watercolor, is a fine example of his romantic, yet realistic, style of art.

(1809–1874) used drawings from his Egyptian travels in his designs for the Great Exhibition at London's Crystal Palace in 1854. The greatest and best-known artist to visit Egypt, however, was the Scottish painter David Roberts (1796–1864), who visited in 1838–1839 in an attempt to capture contemporary Egypt as realistically as possible. He succeeded brilliantly with his colorful, romantic paintings not only of the Nile, but also of the Holy Land.

The pyramids were a highlight of any visit to Egypt, but exploring the interiors of the pyramids, with their narrow, lightless, and bat-infested passages, was quite an ordeal. On May 8, 1854, the English Pre-Raphaelite artist William Holman Hunt (1827–1910) wrote of his experiences to his artistic contemporary John Everett Millais:

> I never had any great admiration for the Pyramids such as most people manifest, and this, and perhaps a desire to appear superior to the cockney visitors, had made me leave the duty of particular examination to the last. . . . I wish I could give you any idea of the event. It was a hot day, and when we reached the entrance I was glad to stop a few minutes in the shade before commencing my inner researches; when we started it was along an alley descending at an angle of 35°, without sufficient room to allow us to walk upright. It was a difficult matter to proceed down this slippery pavement and reach out far enough in each stride to come upon a

rudely broken step which perhaps had been made at first for the use of visitors or workmen. I managed, however, here without the assistance of either the Arab before or the one behind. At the end of fifty yards we came upon a halting-place, where they stayed and lighted the candles they had each brought. Behind and upwards we looked on the long cool passage with the hot white sky at the end; for our further passage we had to turn on one side and along a low tunnel requiring one to stoop double: here my guides were divided as before, each holding their candle towards me. I heard through their monotonous chanting shrill and sharp sounds as of creatures frightened; but there was no opportunity for inquiry, the men had chosen a pace and there was no interrupting it, and when we stopped at last it was at such a strange barrier that all my curiosity was drawn towards our own affairs. I had not yet recovered the blindness of the sun, and when I saw our way completely blocked up in front and at the side, it seemed to me that there was no further way; but I was reassured somewhat by seeing one Arab climb the wall. I proceeded to follow his example, but as he seemed to have restricted himself to an inconvenient space, I turned towards the further corner; but here I was arrested by the Arab Abdullah and the illumination of the mouth of a dark well. "Dat go moush, araf-fein; him go down, down, no stop"—a piece of information which induced me to place myself in his offered arm and be quiet, while he wheeled me round as I have seen heavy goods turned about by iron cranes in London; and here I had the hand of Mahommed to grasp to clamber up to a landing leading to another passage, which, as nearly as I can guess, must run upwards at an angle of 35° from the one I had just left here. I held the hand of Abdullah in front and of the other behind, in established order, and in spite of a liberal heat and perspiration suffered by each, we progressed at quick measure as again doled out by the harmonious but most unhappy tune of the true believers. Our pace was suddenly checked by the presence of another deep well, which here went completely across the passage; but, fortunately, a way was left at the side on a kind of step which runs from the bottom to the top, and this we used to pass the terrible opening to the remainder of this and other forgotten ascents and descents, the while I listened to the echoes and the bat screeches, and peered forwards as well as I could with my body bent double, to make out the nature of our way, until at the top of a tiring ascent I was allowed to walk upright for a few paces, and then was told that the place was the central chamber of the Pyramid. My eyes were not prepared for the depth of darkness in that place, and I looked about vainly to discover the walls that I might tell its size; but I was forced to wait further initiation and employ my probation on objects within reach. There was an empty sarcophagus in the middle of the room, which had evidently been broken open for its contents, which had been taken away; nothing was left but an outer case of rude construction, perhaps designedly to deceive any who might find that hidden treasure-house. In a corner of the room was an excavation which had been commenced by some recent investigator, but which had been given up and left as fruitless. At last I could manage to estimate the size of the place, and to my disappointment, since the walls had seemed to contract in becoming visible, it was not more than 30 or 40 feet square, and it had nothing more than the two objects, except the thousands of names written upon the walls of all ages. . . . The structure was still strong for ages to come to bear witness to after people. Some fruit stones have done their work when the kernel is found and their broken pieces are thrown away; while others, as cocoa-nuts and gourd rinds, are saved to commence a new office. Here I left off dreaming about the failure of the original purpose, and I chanted out: "The dead praise not thee, O Lord: neither all they that go down into silence. But we will praise the Lord: from this time forth for evermore. Praise the Lord." And before the sound had settled I got up to go out again, when I was startled by an echo clear as a reply: "The dead praise not thee, O Lord: neither all they that go down into silence. But we will praise the Lord: from this time forth for evermore. Praise the Lord."[9]

Every traveler worth his or her salt ascended to the summit of the Great Pyramid, preferably at sunrise, something that is now forbidden. An American clergyman, David Millard, climbed the 481 feet (146 meters) to the top in 1841:

No man can gaze from the top of the pyramid Cheops, without emotions never to be forgotten. His thoughts roam backward through thousands of years. He gazes with astonishment on the mysterious works of art spread at his feet. He thinks of the countless thousands employed in constructing these vast monuments of human toil. He contemplates the whole as done by men who lived and moved and had a being more than four thousand years ago. Where are they now? Gone! All gone! Their names lost for ever, and even the design of their vast labor enveloped in mystery and uncertainty![10]

There were other visitors who were more taken with the special light at dawn. The French novelist Gustave Flaubert had the following impression:

We wait a good half hour for the sunrise. The sun was rising just opposite; the whole valley of the Nile, bathed in mist, seemed to be a still white sea; and the desert behind us, with its hillocks of sand, another ocean, deep purple, its waves all petrified. But as the sun climbed behind the Arabian chain the mist was torn into great shreds of filmy gauze; the meadows, cut by canals, were like green lawns with winding borders. To sum up: three colors—immense green at my feet in the foreground; the sky pale red—worn vermilion; behind and to the right, a rolling expanse looking scorched and iridescent, with the minarets of Cairo, canges [small Nile boats] passing in the distance, clusters of palms.

Finally the sky shows a streak of orange where the sun is about to rise. Everything between the horizon and us is all white and looks like an ocean; this recedes and lifts. The sun, it seems, is moving fast and climbing above oblong clouds that look like swan's down, of an inexpressible softness; the trees in the groves around the villages (Gizeh, Matariyeh, Bedrashein, etc.) seem to be in the sky itself, for the entire perspective is perpendicular, as I once saw it before, from the harbor of Picade in the Pyrenees; behind us, when we turn around, is the desert—purple waves of sand, a purple ocean.

The light increases. There are two things: the dry desert behind us, and before us an immense, delightful expanse of green, furrowed by endless canals, dotted here and there with tufts of palms; then, in the background, a little to the left, the minarets of Cairo and especially the mosque of Mohammed Ali (imitating Santa Sophia), towering above the others.[11]

Today, the suburbs of Cairo lap at the edge of the pyramids. Where desert used to separate the ancient and once sacred precincts from the city, the middle-class suburb of Giza has expanded to within sight of the pyramids, and narrow streets and flat-roofed, crowded houses jostle for space right up to the protected area. Luxury hotels are proliferating in the area, which is rapidly becoming urbanized.

John Lloyd Stephens, Stephen Olin, and the other early travelers experienced an Egypt startlingly different from that of today. There was no Aswan Dam to regulate the flow of the Nile; Cairo was still a relatively small city; almost all travel was by boat, as it had been since the time of the pharaohs. To visit Egypt was to step back in time, seemingly without effort, into a world of creaking waterwheels and crude sailing boats, of temples still buried in sand, and of villages flourishing among soaring columns. The land cast an irresistible spell on visitors, so much so that Napoleon's regiments spontaneously presented arms when the legendary ruins of the sun god Amun's temple at Karnak came into sight. Then, after the opening of the Suez Canal, the travelers changed in type and number and the enchantment faded somewhat. No longer did the visitor camp out in tombs, eating food cooked with firewood from ancient mummy cases. No longer could artifacts be carried away freely as souvenirs. Egypt became the domain of the middle-class traveler and the package tour, complete with glossy tourist guides and all the comforts of home.

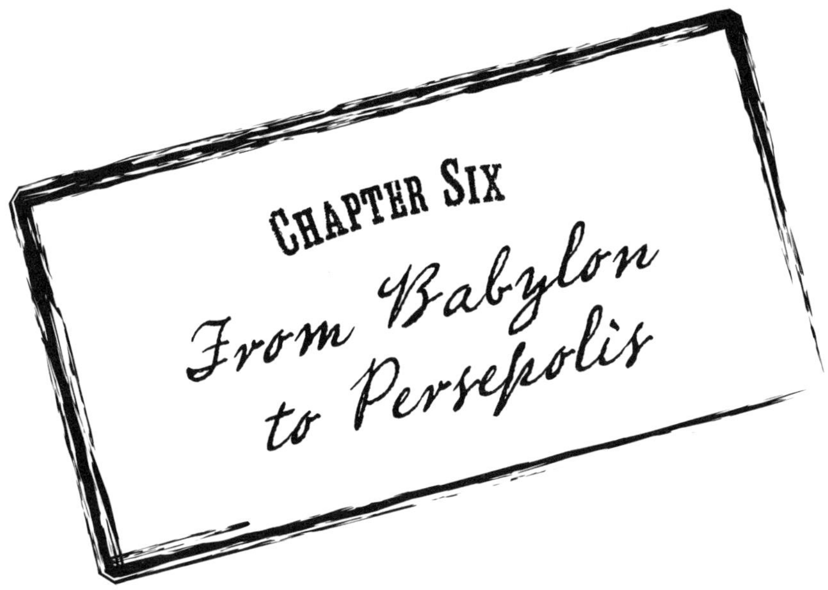

There is no life for miles around. No river glides in grandeur at the base of its mounds, no green dates flourish near its rivers. The shriveled lichen alone, clinging to the weathered surface of the broken brick, seems to glory in its dominion over these barren walls.

WILLIAM KENNETT LOFTUS[1]
on the ancient city of Erech in Mesopotamia, 1857

CHAPTER SIX

From Babylon to Persepolis

Babylon, Nineveh: the ancient cities of the Old Testament lay in a remote Mesopotamian world far off the beaten track for European travelers two centuries ago. In a devout age, Western people knew about the East only through the Scriptures. The biblical cities of Nineveh and Babylon appeared in the Old Testament. At a time when the classics and the Scriptures formed the basis for most education, people considered the Bible the literal historical truth. They remembered how the prophet Zephaniah had thundered against Nineveh: "He will stretch out his hand against the north and destroy Assyria; and he will make Nineveh a desolation, a dry waste like the desert."[2] The writings of the few travelers who crossed the desert to reach the Tigris and Euphrates rivers and Mesopotamia confirmed the prophecies. If these wanderers reached either city, they found nothing more than dusty foundations and crumbling buildings. The eminent Arab geographer al-Mas'udi, who visited Nineveh in 943, found it to be little more than "a complex of ruins." Yet there were small villages among the mounds. "Here," he added presciently, "one finds stone sculptures covered with inscriptions."

The few Europeans who visited what was then an impoverished province of the Ottoman Empire stayed in Baghdad, which had begun modestly as a village before 762, when the caliph al-Mansur turned it into a military camp and, later, into a thriving city that was to become a great center for both commerce and Islamic learning. The wealth and luxury of the Abbasid court resounded through the world. But eighteenth- and nineteenth-century travelers to Baghdad found themselves in a crumbling city living on its past, long-vanished glories. The few Europeans who lived there endured dust storms, sweltering heat, and occasional outbreaks of plague.

Karsten Niebuhr at Persepolis

On January 6, 1766, the Danish traveler Karsten Niebuhr rode into Baghdad on the way home from his long expedition to Persepolis via Egypt. He was the sole survivor of a government expedition to Arabia whose members had never got along with one another. All of them except Niebuhr perished of fever either during or after a long journey through the harsh deserts of Yemen. Niebuhr ended up in India and then traveled overland by mule caravan to Shiraz in modern-day Iran, where he was assured that anyone who gave him trouble would be beheaded immediately. From Shiraz he traveled to Persepolis, which had only received occasional European visitors in previous centuries. But none of them had been as well prepared as Niebuhr, who first saw the valley of ruins at sunset, when the columns were bathed in a rosy glow.

Niebuhr had reached one of the architectural masterpieces of the ancient world. Persepolis lies on a large, bare plain, the Marv Dasht Basin, surrounded by mauve cliffs with sharp contours. It was here, sometime between 518 and 516 B.C., that King Darius decided to build a ceremonial and spiritual center for his empire, since the administrative capital, Susa, lay 300 miles (500 kilometers) to the north. It was named Parsa and was later known to the Greeks as Persepolis (the Iranian name is Takht-e-Jamshid). In an inscription, the king proclaimed that the god "Ahuramazda was of such a mind, together with all the other gods, that this fortress [should] be built. And I built it secure and beautiful and adequate."[3] Later rulers such as Xerxes I (c. 470 B.C.) and Artaxerxes (c. 450 B.C.) enthusiastically embellished the city over the next century. The Persepolis we know today is mainly the work of Xerxes. Persepolis continued to flourish under the later Achaemenian kings, until it was burnt and destroyed by Alexander the Great in 330 B.C.

The Apadana, the structure used by Darius, Xerxes, and later kings for lavish ceremonies, lies atop an artificial terrace 984 feet (300 meters) long and 33 to 66 feet (10 to 20 meters) high. Thirteen of the structure's seventy-two columns still stand on the platform. Two monumental stairways on the north and east sides give access to the summit. Beautiful reliefs showing scenes from the New Year's festival adorn the stairways. The reliefs depict processions of twenty-three subject nations of the Achaemenid Empire, as well as court notables, Medes, and Persians, all followed by guards and with their horses and royal chariots. The delegates in their native costumes bear gifts of gold and silver vessels, weapons, fabrics, jewelry, and exotic animals. Stylized trees separate the different groups in a vast and grandiose display of imperial power. The stairways

6-1 The precision and artistry that enchanted early visitors to southwestern Asia includes this detail of a Persian guard from the relief on the east stairway of the Apadana, Persepolis, Iran.

converge at the summit at an entrance gate guarded by bulls that leads to the Throne Hall near the Apadana. Here the king received representatives of subject nations. Scenes of the monarch in combat with monsters give an impression of royal power. Two huge stone bulls guard the north portico. In building these and other structures at Persepolis, the Achaemenid architects evolved a distinctive monumental style, which used relief sculpture as an adjunct to monumental construction. Although there are marked similarities to Egyptian, Greek, and Assyrian architecture, the Persian architects used more closely fluted, more slender columns than those of Greek temples. The bases are high and often bell-shaped, while the capitals are formed from the foreparts of two bulls set back to back. Persepolis is also a royal necropolis. Darius and his successors carved their monumental tombs into the cliff at Naqsh-i-Rustam, 2.9 miles (4.8 kilometers) northwest of Persepolis.

Totally captivated by this extraordinary place, Niebuhr spent three weeks carefully copying inscriptions, despite suffering from constant attacks of blindness from the white glare off the smooth, inscribed marble walls. He managed to puzzle out forty-two cuneiform, wedge-shaped symbols in the inscriptions. In the process, he identified three separate alphabets, now known to be Babylonian, Elamite, and Old Persian, but did not succeed in deciphering the script. He also realized that the letters spelled out words. Everyone who subsequently worked on cuneiform developed a healthy respect for Niebuhr's careful work, although he himself never returned to the subject.

Nearly dead from fever, Niebuhr paused only briefly in Mesopotamia to examine the dusty mounds of Nebuchadnezzar's Babylon. He was afraid to wander over the site because of a multitude of poisonous snakes. After two months in Baghdad, he joined a caravan to Syria, expecting to depart from Aleppo and to arrive in Copenhagen to popular acclaim. Instead, he was greeted by complete indifference. He was the sole survivor of a long-forgotten government venture sponsored by a now-deceased monarch. Niebuhr retired to his study and wrote an account of his remarkable travels. Even that was largely ignored, so he lived out the rest of his life as clerk to the town council of Meldorf, a small community in western Denmark. By the time he died in 1815, however, his travels had become a model for a new generation of geographers compiling maps of a region that had since assumed considerable strategic importance.

Claudius James Rich at Babylon and Birs Nimrod

At the time of Niebuhr's visit, Baghdad was a decaying caravan center. But the ancient Abbasid capital lay at a strategic position inland from the Persian Gulf and was a potentially important stopping point on an overland route to British India. The East India Company was the first to try to foster trade with Mesopotamia. In 1783, the directors of the company appointed a permanent British agent in Baghdad. Fifteen years later, Napoleon's invasion of Egypt, aimed specifically at controlling the existing routes to India, caused the company to upgrade the agent's position to that of British resident. In 1802, the resident received consular powers. The first man to hold the post was twenty-three-year-old Claudius James Rich (1787–1821), a brilliant, self-taught linguist with a passion for antiquities.

Rich and his eighteen-year-old wife Mary arrived in Baghdad in May 1808, just before the hot season. Rich spoke Arabic and Turkish fluently, and had even spent time in Smyrna attending a school for young Muslim gentlemen. He had previously traveled alone through Syria and Damascus, then across to the Euphrates and Tigris before sailing to Bombay from Basra at the head of the Persian Gulf. In Baghdad, Rich found himself in an ancient city that was so isolated from the Western world that European policy makers knew very little about it. At the time, Baghdad was part of an obscure province of the Turkish Empire, ruled by the sultan in distant Constantinople. Despite his youth, Rich's linguistic abilities soon made him the most influential European in the city. He and his wife lived in considerable style, guarded by thirty Indian soldiers and a troop of sixteen European cavalrymen. The residency, "a large and handsome house in the Turkish style," teemed with servants, and the roof was divided into open-air compartments where everyone would sleep in the hot months. The resident, as Rich was known formally, always called on the pasha of Baghdad in full-dress uniform, accompanied by his guard, drums, and fifes. "Only the most decisive conduct will suffice," Rich wrote. The strategy worked, for Rich exercised remarkable influence over affairs in Baghdad. Nevertheless, the Riches disliked Baghdad. "The view I have of the renowned city is not the most beautiful," wrote Mary Rich. "The streets are extremely narrow and the whole town is built of sun-baked bricks which give it a very dirty appearance. There is nothing at all splendid about Baghdad."[4]

Despite the pressures of diplomacy, Rich devoted considerable time to collecting antiquities, coins, and manuscripts. He also managed to indulge his passion for archaeological travel. In December 1911, he journeyed south to visit ancient Babylon. Diplomatic protocol demanded that he travel in some state, accompanied by his military escort, complete with a field gun and about seventy baggage mules. Rich's insistence on the correct protocol even extended to Mary's traveling arrangements. She was obliged to travel in a covered litter slung between two wooden shafts transported by mules. Her maids fared even worse. They sat in *mohaffas*, cagelike seats slung in pairs across a mule's back. When one maid was heavier than the other, the lighter one had to sit on stones to equalize the load. The resident adhered to this rather uncomfortable protocol until they were clear of Baghdad. Then Mary dismounted and rode her own horse.

The journey to Babylon took two days, across dried-up canals and dusty mounds. The ruins were 2 miles (3.2 kilometers) from the town of Al-Hillah, where the governor greeted them in full state, accompanied by a large crowd and his personal band. Rich found it almost impossible to get a general impression of the dusty mounds. He rode over the length and breadth of the city—a rather hazardous undertaking because the mounds were riddled with holes dug by people looking for bricks. "These ruins consist of mounds of earth, formed by the decomposition of buildings, channeled and furrowed by the weather, and the surfaces of them are strewed with pieces of brick, bitumen, and pottery."[5] There were no temples to admire, no palaces to inspect—just dusty mounds scattered with mud bricks.

Babylon (the Babylonian Bab-ilim, or Babil, "gate of God") was a city long before King Nebuchadnezzar built his fabled Hanging Gardens. It was a subject city of Ur as early as 2100 B.C. and became an independent city-state by 1894 B.C., a city where King Hammurabi promulgated his famous law code that advocated an eye-for-an-eye, tooth-for-a-tooth approach to punishment. Between 1590 and 1155 B.C., the Kassite kings of Babylon brought all of southern Mesopotamia under their sway. Babylon's patron god, Marduk (associated with the planet Mars and known by such other names as Enki and Bel, and also as the biblical Nimrod), became the leading god of the region. Later, the city became part of the Assyrian Empire until 615 B.C., when King Nabopolasser expelled the Assyrians and founded a Neo-Babylonian dynasty. His son Nebuchadnezzar II expanded the Babylonian Empire over most of southwestern Asia. At the same time, he lavished wealth on his imperial capital, which covered more than 2,500 acres (1,000 hectares), with imposing palaces, temples, paved processional ways, and elaborate fortifications including nine major gates. But Nebuchadnezzar's empire was short-lived: Cyrus the Great of Persia captured Babylon in 539 B.C. Thereafter, the city gradually slipped into oblivion.

As Babylon was abandoned, so its mud-brick structures vanished at the hands of quarrymen or melted into dust. Generations of visitors, drawn to the site because of its biblical associations, tried to make sense of the ancient city, which was little more than mounds of dust. Finally, just before World War I, the German archaeologist Robert Koldeway perfected ways of detecting mud brick that was virtually indistinguishable from the surrounding soil by sensitive use of the pickaxe to test soil densities. He recovered imposing structures like the Ishtar Gate, and also processional ways and the foundations of the royal palace.

This expert archaeology was far in the future when Rich spent ten days poring over the huge accumulations of brick and earth that lay on the western bank of the Euphrates. He set his cavalrymen to work as surveyors, giving them tape and line, and hoping to gain a general impression of what had once been a dazzling royal capital known throughout the ancient world. Rich's account of the ruins is at best turgid, but there are highlights:

> The greatest circumference the ancients have ascribed to the city walls, is four hundred and eight stadia; the most moderate, three hundred and sixty. [A stadion was a Greek unit of measurement of about 607 feet (185 meters).] Strabo, who is excellent authority in this particular, as he must have seen the walls in a sufficiently perfect state to form his judgment, allows three hundred and eighty-five; but the smallest computation supposes an area for the city, of which we can now scarcely form an idea. Whatever may have been the size of Babylon, I imagine that its population bore no proportion to it; and that it would convey to a modern the idea of an enclosed district, rather than that of a regular city; the streets, which are said to have led from gate to gate across the area, being no more than roads

through cultivated land, over which buildings were distributed in groups or patches. Quintus Curtius says positively that there was pasture and arable land in the enclosure, sufficient to support the whole of the population during a long siege; and Xenophon reports, that when Cyrus took Babylon (which event happened at night), the inhabitants of the opposite quarter of the town were not aware of it till the third part of the day, ie. three hours after sunrise; which was very possibly owing to the great distance of one cluster of houses from another, since, had they been connected with each other in regular streets, the noise and confusion would, I think, have spread the information of the event with much greater rapidity.

All accounts agree in the height of the walls, which was fifty cubits, having been reduced to these dimensions from the prodigious height of three hundred and fifty feet, by Darius Hystaspes, after the rebellion of the town, in order to render it less defensible. [A cubit was an ancient unit of measurement, equal to the length of the forearm from the tip of the middle finger to the elbow, about 17 to 22 inches (43 to 56 centimeters).] I have not been fortunate enough to discover the least trace of [the walls], in any part of the ruins at Hillah; which is rather an unaccountable circumstance, considering that they survived the final ruin of the town, long after which they served as an enclosure for a park; in which comparatively perfect state, St. Jerome informs us, they remained in his time. Nor can the depredations subsequently committed on them in the building of Hillah, and other similar small places, satisfactorily account for their having totally disappeared.

Similar in solidity and construction to the city walls, was the artificial embankment of the river, with its breast-work, the former of which Diodorus informs us was one hundred stadia in length. The traces of these are entirely obliterated; for though on a cursory view, the mound which now forms the eastern bank of the river, (and which for perspicuity's sake I have called the embankment,) would be likely to deceive observers, yet the alteration in the course of the river at that place, the form of the southern part of the mound, and, above all, the sepulchral urns found built up in it, close to the water's edge, are sufficient proofs that it cannot be the remains of the ancient embankment.

The most extraordinary building within the city was the tower, pyramid, or sepulchre of Belus, the base of which Strabo says was a square of a stadium each side, and it was a stadium in height. It has been generally considered that Herodotus has given an extravagant account of its dimensions: he says that the first platform, or largest and lowest of the eight towers of which it was composed, was . . . "a stadium in height and breadth:" which, supposing the seven other towers to have borne some proportion to it, may be clearly pronounced an absurdity: but . . . also signifies length, space, prolixity. On this principle we take the present fashion of building as some example of the mode heretofore practiced in Babylon, the houses that had more than one story must have consisted of the ground-floor or bassecour, occupied by stables, magazines, and serdaubs or cellars, sunk a little below the ground, for the comfort of the inhabitants during the heats; above this a gallery with the lodging rooms opening into it, and over all the flat terrace for the people to sleep on during the summer.

From what remains of Babylon, and even from the most favourable account handed down to us, there is every reason to believe that the public edifices which adorned it were remarkable more for vastness of dimensions than elegance of design, and solidity of fabric rather than beauty of execution. The tower of Belus appears merely to have been astonishing from its size. It was inferior in some respects to the pyramids [of Giza], and did not surpass either them or probably the great temple of Mexico in external appearance; and the ornaments of which Xerxes despoiled it, convey an idea of barbaric richness, rather than taste: all the sculptures which are found among the ruins, though some of them are executed with the greatest apparent care, speak a barbarous people, indeed with a much greater degree of refinement than the Babylonians seem to have been in possession of; it would be difficult to make any thing of such unpropitious materials as brick and bitumen.[6]

One day, Rich and his party rode out some 6 miles (10 kilometers) to the vast mass of the *ziggurat* (temple mound) at Birs Nimrod (or Nimrud). This was once the temple of the city of Borsippa, an ancient religious center with the Ezida temple dedicated to Marduk. King Hammurabi built the first temple in as early as 1780 B.C. Borsippa flourished greatly under Nebuchadnezzar between 604 and 562 B.C., but was destroyed by the Achaemenid king Xerxes I in the fifth century.

The visit to Birs Nimrod etched itself on Rich's memory. "The morning was at first stormy, but as we approached the object of our journey, the heavy clouds separating, discovered the Birs frowning over the plain, and presenting the appearance of a circular hill, crowned by a tower, with a high ridge extending along the foot of it." The clouds disappointed him, for they prevented him from "acquiring the gradual idea," as he had been able to do with the pyramids of Giza in Egypt some years before. But there were consolations, as Rich tells us at his romantic best. "Just as we were within the proper distance, it burst at once about our sight, in the midst of the rolling masses of dark clouds partially obscured by that kind of haze whose indistinctness is one great cause of sublimity, while a few strong catches of stormy light, thrown upon the desert in the background, served to give some idea of the immense and dreary solitude of the wastes in which this venerable ruin stands."[7]

Hastily, Rich measured and sketched the Birs, which he estimated to be 235 feet (72 meters) high—an enormous, oblong mound of decaying and vitrified brickwork.

Claudius Rich did little to disentangle the confusion of ruins at Babylon, but he provided generations of travelers with a map that gave at least some reliable information about the ruins. His "Memoir on the Ruins of Babylon" appeared in a Viennese journal, *Les mines de l'Orient*, in 1812 and caused a considerable stir, moving Lord Byron to write in his *Don Juan*:

> . . . Claudius Rich, Esquire, some bricks has got
> And written lately two memoirs upon't.

Sir Robert Ker Porter Sees Desolation

In 1818, the Riches entertained the noted artist and adventurer Sir Robert Ker Porter (1777–1842). He was a painter of some acclaim, well known in particular for his battle scenes, including his painting—which was nearly 120 feet (37 meters) long—of the storming of Seringapatam in India in 1799. Porter had traveled to Russia in 1804, where he became painter to the czar. He also wandered extensively in central Asia before heading south to Baghdad in 1818 via Persepolis on his way to sketch at Babylon. The artist found a kindred soul in Rich, who was fascinated by Porter's illustrations of Persepolis and of King Darius's inscription on the Great Rock at Behistun near Kermanshah in Iran. Porter was the first Western artist to sketch Behistun, 1,200 square feet (111 square meters) of inscriptions in Old Persian, Elamite, and Babylonian cuneiform commemorating King Darius's victory over rebel kings in 522 B.C. "What a treasure of information doubtless was there to the happy man who could decipher [the scripts]," he wrote.[8] Porter and Rich discussed the apparently insurmountable problems of copying and deciphering the scripts on the high rock face, which were not copied successfully for another twenty years, until a British cavalry officer, Henry Rawlinson, hired nimble Kurds to clamber across the smooth rock, clinging to tiny cracks in the surface with their hands and feet. Porter enjoyed his stay in Baghdad, combining work on archaeology and inscriptions with the lavish hospitality of the wealthier inhabitants. Dinners featured male dancers performing violent dances "by twisting their bodies into all kinds of odious postures, accompanied by a machine-like dodder of the head, which is duly answered by a wriggle from the back or hips."[9]

The countryside around Babylon was unstable, so Rich insisted that Porter travel with a full escort. Porter was in a high state of anticipation, his mind full of city walls 60 miles (96 kilometers) in circumference, with brass gates and Hanging Gardens described by the ubiquitous Herodotus. In the event, Porter first went to Birs Nimrod, where his escort turned out to be particularly useful:

At the moment of my first seeing it, the tower bore from us south 10 west ["south 10 degrees west," or 190 degrees, in modern parlance]; to which point we made direct forward, hastening our speed as we approached nearer the stupendous pile. But having been about an hour in our course, we were suddenly startled by a cloud of horsemen just discoverable on our left; and who, gradually becoming more distinctly visible, continued to keep on in a parallel line with ourselves. Their unexpected appearance gave an instant check to the ardent career of my own troop, who now, at a more restrained pace, interrupted by short conferences, maintained our advance. By this cautious marching, we had leisure to observe that the movements of our apprehended adversaries did not point immediately to ourselves, but to the very spot whither we were intending to go. As soon as we saw they had arrived at the Birs, which stood like an immense hill overshadowing their squadrons, several of our Arabs were dispatched to descry what they were, and their strength; my commandant assuring me, "there were none of the pasha's warriors, save ourselves, on this side of the Euphrates; therefore I must deem it advisable to proceed circumspectly, that we might not *lose the advantage of distance in a fair start*"; he being certain it would prove that the enemy far outnumbered us.

Our gallop having gradually subsided to a walk, we were slowly proceeding, when in little more than a quarter of an hour, our scouts returned with the comfortable intelligence, that the apparitions of our dread were no other than the kiahya himself, and a numerous escort, who were now quietly disposing themselves on and about the object of my expedition. On this news, several of my valiant troop scampered off like madmen, to join their comrades; but for myself, since so strong an advanced guard gave us now absolute security, I followed with the rest of my party at a more moderate pace; having come upon ground bearing marks to engage my lively interest, even to the foot of the Birs itself. . . .

It is a common idea with the Turks here, that the true object with Europeans, in visiting the banks of the Euphrates, is not to explore antiquities, as we pretend, but to make a laborious pilgrimage to these almost shapeless relics of a race of unbelievers more ancient than ourselves; and to perform certain mysterious religious rites before them; which excite no small curiosity amongst the Faithful, to pry into.[10]

Porter was impressed by the "stupendous work" of the incomplete ziggurat. In a devout age, his only source of information was the Scriptures, and Porter was well versed in the Old Testament. All around him, he saw signs of Divine Wrath. That this was the Tower of Babel seemed beyond question. "It does not seem improbable that what we now see as the fire-blasted summit of the pile, its rent wall and scattered fragments, with their partially vitrified masses, may be a part of that very stage of the primeval tower, which felt the effects of the divine vengeance."[11]

The impression of desolation and wilderness became stronger during a second visit, when the approaching travelers saw several dark figures moving along the summit of the Birs. At first they suspected robbers, but were astounded to see "two or three majestic lions, taking the air upon the heights of the pyramid. Perhaps I never had beheld so sublime a picture to the mind, as well as to the eye."[12] Reminded of the prophets' dire predictions about the destruction of Babylon, Porter quoted Isaiah 31:21: "But wild beasts will lie down there, and its houses will be full of howling creatures." Although well read in the Scriptures, Porter was not a particularly religious man; still, he had no other sources to turn to for history other than the Old Testament, where there were harsh prophecies of divine vengeance. The sheer desolation of Birs Nimrod moved him profoundly. Given his classical and religious upbringing, it was hardly surprising that he invoked the Scriptures.

For Porter, the impression of desolation lingered at Babylon itself, which seemed to be another powerful demonstration of the Lord's handiwork. Like most archaeological travelers of the day, Robert Ker Porter was serious about the past. He measured walls and buildings and sketched sites large and small, spending days at each major location—far more time than a casual tourist. The dusty mounds of Babylon exercised all his antiquarian and artistic skills, and he filled his book about his wanderings with musings on the destruction that had surrounded him. Porter was struck, too, by the antiquity of the city, yet impressed by the freshness of the cuneiform inscriptions on the undersurfaces of Babylon's innumerable bricks:

From her fallen towers have arisen, not only all the present cities in her vicinity, but others, which, like herself, are long ago gone down into the dust. Since the days of Alexander, we find four capitals, at least, built out of her remains: Selearia by the Greeks, Ctaiphon by the Parthians, Al Alaidan by the Persians, Kufa by the Caliphs; with towns, villages, and caravansaries without number. Baghdad too, (had it not, most probably, completed its walls from a nearer neighbour, the ruins of the city, which appears to have occupied the tract of Akarkouff,) might, by some trouble, boast its towers from the great parrot city also. That the fragments of one city should travel so far, to build or repair the breaches of another, on the first view of the subject, appeared unlikely to myself; but on traversing the country between the approximating shores of the two rivers, and observing all the facilities of water-carriage from our side to the other, I could no longer be incredulous of what had been told me; particularly when scarce a day passed without my seeing people digging the mounds of Babylon for bricks, which they carried to the verge of the Euphrates, and thence conveyed in boats to whereever they might be wanted. From the consequent excavations in every possible shape and direction, the regular layers of the original ruins have been so broken, that nothing but confusion is seen to exist between our course and another, when any traveller would attempt seeking a distinct plan amongst those eternally traversing minor heaps, hollows, arid ravines. But certain huge and rugged masses yet stand pre-eminent; which, by their situation, and other local circumstances, seem sufficiently to warrant the conclusions which have been drawn of their original purpose. These vaster mounds are surrounded by subordinate ranges, now bearing the appearance of embankments and which, doubtless, have been the cause of the interior pile's comparatively unimpaired state. The yearly overflowing of the whole country, from the decay of the canals, made to draw off the superflux of the river, having for ages swept unimpeded over the faces of all the ruins which had not the protection of these, I may call them, break-waters, could not fail producing the devastation we see. All such exposed parts of the city must necessarily be broken down into wider and more shapeless ruin, and be gradually washed down into lower and lower hillocks, till, in most places, all traces would be entirely swept away. The piles which I am now going to describe have, therefore, not only been saved by their extraordinary magnitude from the over-topping of the floods, but their foundations greatly preserved, by the majestic length of these banks inclosing them nearly on all sides. . . .[13]

Porter spent days sketching and wandering over the confusing mass of the citadel and city walls. It was hard for him to imagine the great palace in its heyday, but he tried:

The palace itself; it was splendidly decorated with statues of men and animals; with vessels of gold and silver, and indeed luxuries from every quarter of the world, brought thither from the conquests of Egypt, Palestine, and Tyre; but its greatest boast were the magnificent hanging gardens, which acquired even from Grecian writers the appellation of one of the wonders of the world. They are attributed to the gallantry of Nebuchadnezzar, in compliance with a wish of his queen Amytis, to possess elevated groves in the manner she had enjoyed them on the hills around her native Echatana. Babylon was all a flat; and to accomplish so extravagant a desire, an artificial mountain must be constructed: accordingly, we find the plan of this most extraordinary exertion of human labour. The foundation of the mount presented a square of four plethra (400 feet) on each side, while the terraces, one above the other, rose to a height that over-topped the walls of the city; consequently must have stood more than 200 feet high, the altitude of the walls before Darius Hystaspes lowered them. The ascent from terrace to terrace was made by answering flights of steps; while the terraces themselves, it appears, were reared to their various stages, not by solid masses, but on ranges of regular piers; I cannot call them arches, that form never having been found in any Babylonian structure. These piers, forming a kind of vaulting, rose in succession one over the other, to the required height of each terrace; the whole being bound together by a wall 22 feet in thickness.[14]

The brickwork fascinated Porter most of all:

It was nearly impossible to separate [the bricks] and to this circumstance the present masses owed their preservation. . . . The bricks of which they are composed are of a very pale yellow; having so fresh an appearance as to strike me at first, as . . . a more modern erection . . .; but on a minute examination, no doubt remained on my mind of their equal antiquity. After considerable labour, I succeeded in having several pieces of the brick chipped off from an immense fragment which had fallen from an adjacent mass; and on clearing my specimens from the lower course, I plainly traced sufficient of the cuneiform characters, to discover them to be pacts of inscriptions in seven lines. Each brick was placed with its written fare downwards, on a layer of cement so spacing, that it did not exceed the twentieth part of an inch in thickness; appearing, where it united the two bricks, like a fine white line, subdivided by another of a reddish brown, with a granulated sparkling effect. The hardness of this mass was inconceivable and it seemed not less wonderful that so slender a line of cement should hold so tenaciously its respective courses of such massive bricks. I was also much struck with the singular appearance of several of these buttress-like walls, standing, or rather inclining from their centre, as if shaken by some convulsion of nature: part are half tore asunder; and others seem actually pushed beyond the smooth and regular hue of their original front. On examining a projecting ledge thus formed, and looking up under its protruding bricks, I plainly discerned the cuneiform inscriptions on their downward faces . . .; a sufficient proof of the very ancient antiquity of the structure, notwithstanding the fresh, untarnished aspect of the materials.[15]

Rich at Persepolis

At heart, both Porter and Rich were romantics, seduced by the romance of dark clouds, brilliant rays of sunlight, and the full moon. Porter had spent days sketching at Persepolis and waxed lyrical about the beauty of the site. Rich decided to enjoy the site to the full. He knew full well that the impact of Persepolis would be magnified a hundredfold by evocative light, by shadows, and by leisurely contemplation. Far from following the formal protocol of diplomatic life, Rich timed a visit to Persepolis—already thoroughly surveyed by Niebuhr and Porter—to coincide with a full moon. His diary records:

August 14 [1821].—The moon-light nights are now so uncommonly beautiful that I am resolved not to let them slip, but to avail myself of them for my antiquarian excursion. The moon is the only thing that can alleviate the tedium of a night-march. There is besides something in viewing Persepolis and the tomb of Cyrus, "by the pale moonlight," especially as I visit them merely for the sake of the impressions I hope they will make on my mind and fancy and this makes me undertake the expedition, I suppose I ought to he ashamed to say, with more alacrity than I usually do antiquarian excursions. The ruins I propose visiting have been so accurately described, measured, and delineated by our friend Porter, that nothing remains to be done; and I can abandon myself entirely to the luxury of imagination, of which the line, compass, and pencil, and the intolerable labour they bring on, are eminently destructive. There is certainly a great pleasure in discovering, and afterwards showing complete delineations of places which it falls to the lot of very few to see; but at the moment I prefer lying down, and idly contemplating the traces of the march of time, and allowing the fancies to rise and pursue each other, to the preparation of a whole portfolio, and all the glory that might accrue from it. *Tout cela étant*, to-morrow afternoon we propose beginning our trip: first to Morgaub, as that is the farthest point, where I hope to contribute towards settling what seems as yet a very equivocal matter about Cyrus's tomb and Pasagardae. On our return, we inspect Persepolis and Nakshi Rustum, which will probably find us amusement for a couple of days. . . . It may be done at one march; I shall make two easy stages of it.

Persepolis has long attracted my wishes. Other places charm by a knowledge of what they were; but there is something even in the uncertainty of Persepolis that throws a kind of additional interest over it. . . .

August 31.—I returned last night from my expedition. We set off about sunset on the 15th. My permanent travelling party was reduced to Mr. Tod, who was a very pleasant companion. Our first stage was to Zergoon, which we left in the evening of the 16th, and rode along the plain of Persepolis. It was dark when we left the bridge of the Araxes. My expectation was greatly excited. Chardin, when I was a mere child, had inspired me with a great desire to see these ruins, and the desires excited in us in childhood are too vivid ever to be effaced. Their gratification has a relish which motives suggested by reason and judgment are unable afterwards to equal. My late antiquarian researches had, however, also added their interest to my other inducements; and as I rode over the plain by the beautiful star-light, reflections innumerable on the great events that had happened there crowded on my memory. I was in the moment of enjoying what I had long wished for; and what a delightful moment that is. At last the pointed summit began to detach itself from the line of mountains to which we were advancing. Mr. Tod pointed it out: "Under that lie the ruins." At that moment the moon rose with uncommon beauty behind it. Ages seemed at once to present themselves to my fancy.

We were lodged in a half-ruined garden-house, fronting the ruins, and at the distance of about a mile from them. You may he assured that my last looks at night, and first in the morning (I did not go to bed till twelve and rose with the dawn) were directed to that spot. Yet I took a capricious kind of pleasure in not going to them, and forcing myself to be contented with this general survey. This may be foolish, but I determined to put off my minute inspection of them until our return, and enjoy for the present the general impressions caused by this distant view. Lord Byron would have enjoyed the interval better than I could do.[16]

Tragically, Rich died of cholera only a few weeks later, so he never returned to Persepolis. But his brief moment of joy captures the profoundest satisfaction that sometimes awaits the archaeological traveler when, just occasionally, the past comes to light as a deeply emotional experience. Porter had the same experience. "I invariably rode my horse up and down them [the stairs] during my visits to their interesting summit," he wrote in 1821.[17] But despite his awe, Porter, like so many of his contemporaries and successors, carved his name on Persepolis, an act of archaeological vandalism that was almost a rite of passage for travelers of the day.

More and more tourists visited Persepolis in the years that followed, as the inevitable excavations began. The British travel writer Robert Byron (1905–1941) was a connoisseur of ancient civilizations. He wrote of Persepolis,

> Patience! In the old days, you rode up the steps on to the platform. You made a camp there, while the columns and winged beasts kept their solitude beneath the stars, and not a sound or a movement disturbed the empty moonlit plain. You thought of Darius and Alexander. You were alone with the ancient world. You saw Asia as the Greeks saw it, and you felt their magic, and you felt their magic breath stretching out towards China itself. . . . Today you step out of a motor, while a couple of lorries thunder by in a cloud of dust. You find the approaches guarded by walls. You enter by leave of a porter, and are greeted on reaching the platform by a light railway, a neo-German hostel, and a code of academic malice compiled from Chicago. These useful additions clarify the intelligence. You may persuade yourself, in spite of them, into a mood of romance. But the mood they invite is one of a critic at an exhibition. That is the penalty of greater knowledge.[18]

To approach Persepolis in the right frame of mind today you would need to arrive by horse, as Colonel P. M. Sykes did in 1914. He scaled the stairway on his sixteen-hand cavalry steed and was overwhelmed by the view at the top. Alas, these things are no longer possible. Persepolis is readily accessible, but the visitor count is far below that of Petra or the pyramids of Giza in Egypt. The site is well protected and fenced, but the average visitor spends far less time there than his nineteenth-century predecessors did. The average package-tourists pass through Persepolis in a mere two hours. What they enjoy is a controlled archaeological environment, one that can be visited only between set hours. No longer is it possible to experience the delight of standing atop the platform during the full moon; nor is there a chance to camp among the ruins or wander for hours enjoying a place that is magic when alone. Persepolis is still an inspiration for students of ancient art and architecture, even for writers like myself who watch the changing shadows on the staircase reliefs and the

6-2 The relief, which shows the procession of the Persian army, found on the north staircase of the audience hall of Darius I at the Apadana, Persepolis, Iran, is now difficult to appreciate amid growing numbers of tourists.

soft lights of approaching twilight. But it is not, alas, the same as it was in Rich's day, when he had the place to himself and all the time in the world to enjoy it. Once you have a visa, you can freely visit the site—but the visit is more like a visit to a museum than to an evocative place. Rich and Porter would not enjoy themselves.

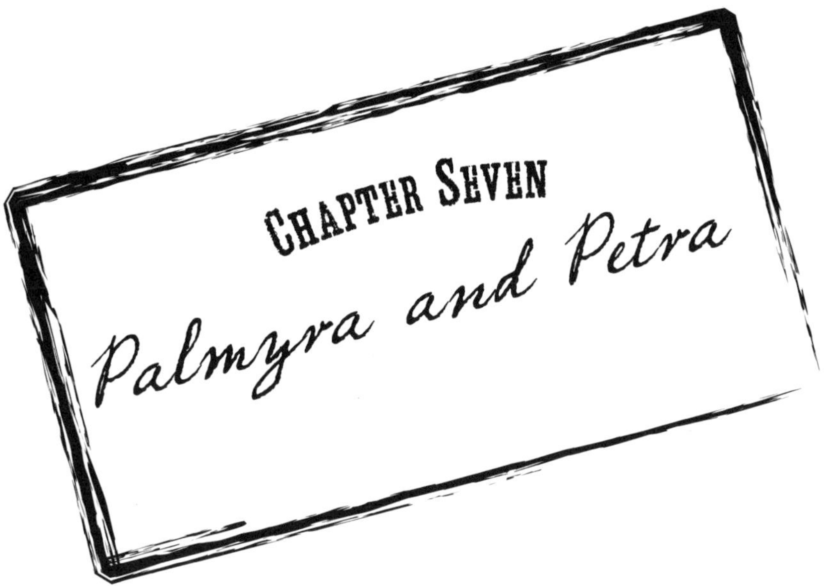

> O Ruins! to your school I will return! I will seek again the calm of your solitudes; and there, far from the afflicting spectacle of the passions, I will cherish in remembrance the love of man, I will employ myself on the means of effecting good for him, and build my own happiness on the promotion of his.
>
> C. F. VOLNEY[1]
> *The Ruins* (1796), Invocation

CHAPTER SEVEN

Palmyra and Petra

Syria is a palimpsest of antiquity, a country scattered with evocative ruins from a tumultuous past. "This kingdom hath suffered many alterations," wrote the Scottish traveler William Lithgow, who wandered through the country in 1612. The landscape teems with Crusader castles, Roman ruins, traces of Byzantium. Early travelers found a strange incongruity, with magnificent temples rising among "hovels," and with what the nineteenth-century English artist William H. Bartlett called "the shapeless structures of the peasantry." He added, "It is a strange irony to find baths and theatres in such a country, or triumphal avenues down which only a flock of ragged goats are driven out and back at dawn and sunset."[2]

Bartlett visited Bostra, 9 miles (14 kilometers) south of Damascus, which was once a great desert caravan city and the capital of Roman Arabia before Palmyra came into prominence. After the decline of the Roman Empire, Bostra was the first Byzantine city to fall to Islam, and it became an important stop on the pilgrimage route to Mecca. Today, Bostra is most famous for its Roman amphitheater with its perfect acoustics and seating for 15,000 people. Bartlett observed the city from miles away:

Bostra stood up, black and imposing, before us for miles before we arrived, a mass of columns and triumphal arches with the castle dominating the whole. I went up the square tower of the minaret and looked out over the town—columns and black square towers over every ruined church and mosque, and the big castle, and the countless masses of fallen stone. . . . Such a spectacle of past magnificence and present squalor it would be difficult to conceive. There were inscriptions everywhere, Latin, Greek, Cufic and Arabic, built into the walls of the Fellahin houses, topsy turvy, together with the perforated slabs that were once windows, and bits of columns and capitals of pillars. . . . At last he [the Mamur, Bartlett's self-appointed guide] took me to the top of the castle and introduced me to the head of the soldiers, who produced chairs and coffee on his roof-top, and subsequently glasses of arack [commonly "arrack," a strong alcoholic drink made of fermented palm sap, rive, or molasses] and water in his room below.

Such are the amenities: coffee on roof-tops, views of the great jumble of medieval ruin, arack and water with cheerful handsome Mamurs, the general sense of magnificence. Behind these the ghosts of Roman legions stalk Trajan's streets between ghostly columns; a Roman triumphal arch still stands, ruins of temples, colonnades, baths, lie about.

First Visitors to Palmyra

Palmyra, in an oasis northeast of Damascus, is one of the most glorious archaeological sites in the world. An ancient commercial metropolis, the city prospered greatly under Roman rule after A.D. 14. Situated at the crossroads of several civilizations, it became a wealthy caravan city after the decline of Petra in 105. Its art and architecture married Greek and Roman techniques with local and Persian influences. For example, the temple to the god Bel, ruler of the heavens, had a large outer wall, an inner sanctuary, and a sacrificial altar like those at many Mesopotamian and Semitic shrines. The pedimented walls and off-center doorway of the inner sanctuary, or cella, also reflect Eastern design. On the other hand,

7-1 For hundreds of years travelers and explorers have ventured to Syria to visit the ancient ruins in Palmyra, shown here in the early morning light.

the temple's fluted Corinthian columns, boldly painted sculpture, and general proportions come from the Greek and Roman tradition. Many scholars believe that the Hellenistic architect Hermogenes influenced many of the architectural details. The temple was intended as a central meeting place for all Palmyra's many ethnic groups.

When Rome and Persia came into conflict during the third century A.D., Palmyra's ruler, Auzaina, managed to hold off the Persian armies, but he was assassinated under mysterious circumstances. His second wife, Queen Zenobia, a woman of strong character, great administrative ability, and strong cultural interests, took over the throne, defied Rome, and carved out a huge domain that extended by 270 to as far as Egypt. The Romans eventually defeated her and took her as a captive to Rome, where she committed suicide. Palmyra never recovered, and it went into further decline after the Islamic expansion. The Greco-Roman ruins have provoked admiration since the time of early Islamic travelers. The ruins first came to the attention of Western antiquarians as a result of an account in 1760 in the *Philosophical Transactions of the Royal Society* that was written by Aleppo merchants of local earthquakes. Palmyra seemed like a mirage in the heart of remote desert because it was so difficult to access, requiring camels, tents, and all the impedimenta of desert travel. A journey to Palmyra was an expensive undertaking, but an experience worth savoring. The French scholar Constantin-François de Chassebœuf, Comte de Volney (1757–1820), was profoundly moved by Palmyra, where he communed with the ghost of Zenobia.

Arrived at the city of Hems, on the border of the Orontes, and being in the neighborhood of Palmyra of the desert, I resolved to visit its celebrated ruins. After three days journeying through arid deserts, having traversed the Valley of Caves and Sepulchres, on issuing into the plain, I was suddenly struck with a scene of the most stupendous ruins—a countless multitude of superb columns, stretching in avenues beyond the reach of sight. Among them were magnificent edifices, some entire, others in ruins; the earth every where strewed with fragments of cornices, capitals, shafts, entablatures, pilasters, all of white marble, and of the most exquisite workmanship. After a walk of three-quarters of an hour along these ruins, I entered the enclosure of a vast edifice, formerly a temple dedicated to the Sun; and accepting the hospitality of some poor Arabian peasants, who had built their hovels on the area of the temple, I determined to devote some days to contemplate at leisure the beauty of these stupendous ruins.

Daily I visited the monuments which covered the plain; and one evening, absorbed in reflection, I had advanced to the Valley of Sepulchres. I ascended the heights which surround it from whence the eye commands the whole group of ruins and the immensity of the desert. The sun had sunk below the horizon: a red border of light still marked his track behind the distant mountains of Syria; the full-orbed moon was rising in the east, on a blue ground, over the plains of the Euphrates; the sky was clear, the air calm and serene; the dying lamp of day still softened the horrors of approaching darkness; the refreshing night breezes attempered the sultry emanations from the heated earth; the herdsmen had given their camels to repose, the eye perceived no motion on the dusky and uniform plain; profound silence rested on the desert; the howlings only of the jackal, and the solemn notes of the bird of night, were heard at distant intervals. Darkness now increased, and through the dusk could only be discerned the pale phantasms of columns and walls. The solitude of the place, the tranquillity of the hour, the majesty of the scene, impressed on my mind a religious pensiveness. The aspect of a great city deserted, the memory of times past, compared with its present state, all elevated my mind to high contemplations. I sat on the shaft of a column, my elbow reposing on my knee, and head reclining on my hand, my eyes fixed, sometimes on the desert, sometimes on the ruins, and fell into a profound reverie.

Here, said I, once flourished an opulent city; here was the seat of a powerful empire. Yes! these places now so wild and desolate, were once animated by a living multitude; a busy crowd thronged in these streets, now so solitary. Within these walls, where now reigns the silence of death, the noise of the arts, and the shouts of joy and festivity incessantly resounded; these piles of marble were regular palaces; these fallen columns adorned the majesty of temples; these ruined galleries surrounded public places. Here assembled a numerous people for the sacred duties of their religion, and the anxious cares of their subsistence; here industry, parent of enjoyments, collected the riches of all climes, and the purple of Tyre was exchanged for the precious thread of Serica; the soft tissues of Cassimere for the sumptuous tapestry of Lydia; the amber of the Baltic for the pearls and perfumes of Arabia; the gold of Ophir for the tin of Thule.

And now behold what remains of this powerful city: a miserable skeleton! What of its vast domination: a doubtful and obscure remembrance! To the noisy concourse which thronged under these porticoes, succeeds the solitude of death. The silence of the grave is substituted for the busy hum of public places; the affluence of a commercial city is changed into wretched poverty; the palaces of kings have become a den of wild beasts; flocks repose in the area of temples, and savage reptiles inhabit the sanctuary of the gods. Ah! how has so much glory been eclipsed? how have so many labors been annihilated? Do thus perish then the works of men—thus vanish empires and nations?

And the history of former times revived in my mind; I remembered those ancient ages when many illustrious nations inhabited these countries; I figured to myself the Assyrian on the banks of the Tygris, the Chaldean on the banks of the Euphrates, the Persian reigning from the Indus to the Mediterranean. I enumerated the kingdoms of Damascus and Idumea, of Jerusalem and Samaria, the warlike states of the Philistines, and the commercial republics of Phoenicia. This Syria, said I, now so depopulated, then contained a hundred flourishing cities, and abounded with towns, villages, and hamlets. In all parts were seen cultivated fields, frequented roads, and crowded habitations. Ah! whither have flown those ages of life and abundance?—whither vanished those brilliant creations of human industry? Where are those ramparts of Nineveh, those walls of Babylon, those palaces of Persepolis, those temples of Balbec and of Jerusalem? Where are those fleets of Tyre, those dock-yards of Arad, those work-shops of Sidon, and that multitude of sailors, of pilots, of merchants, and of soldiers? Where those husbandmen, harvests, flocks, and all the creation of living beings in which the face of the earth rejoiced? Alas! I have passed over this desolate land! I have visited the palaces, once the scene of so much splendor, and I beheld nothing but solitude and desolation. I sought the ancient inhabitants and their works, and found nothing but a trace, like the foot-prints of a traveller over the sand. The temples are fallen, the palaces overthrown, the ports filled up, the cities destroyed; and the earth, stripped of inhabitants, has become a place of sepulchres. Great God! Whence proceed such fatal revolutions? What causes have so changed the fortunes of these countries? Wherefore are so many cities destroyed? Why has not this ancient population been reproduced and perpetuated?[3]

Other less romantically inclined visitors arrived to map and sketch, but not the eccentric Lady Hester Stanhope (1776–1839), who rode boldly into Palmyra on a white Arab stallion in 1813 accompanied by Dr. Charles Meryon, her private physician; her lover, a twenty-year-old Englishman, Michael Bruce; and a large retinue. Stanhope, the daughter of the wealthy but profligate Earl of Stanhope, was orphaned at the age of twenty-seven. Socially well connected, she was so successful at cultivating people that the government granted her a generous pension for life. Grieved by the rapid loss of five men in succession, she left England in 1810 at the age of thirty-three, never to return.

Lady Hester sailed for the Mediterranean, was shipwrecked off Rhodes, visited Cairo, and then made a grand tour of the Holy Land in safety by bribing the major bandit in the region. Dressed in largely male clothing, smoking a bubble pipe, and swearing at her mule drivers in three languages, she was a fearless woman who wore no veil when she rode a horse into Damascus, confronted powerful leaders in their palaces, and wangled safe conducts and invitations by brazen effrontery.

When she wanted to visit Palmyra, she obtained an invitation from the Bedouin emir of the 'Anazah tribe. He was captivated by her and arranged an entertaining visit. As drums throbbed, she led a procession of Bedouin notables, followed by lesser tribesmen, down one of the few well-preserved colonnaded Roman avenues that led to the great temple standing in the center of the city. Beside each column was stationed a young maiden, and as the procession passed, each fell in beside the mounted Lady Hester as escort, all the way to the temple. "I have been crowned Queen of the Desert, under the triumphal arch at Palmyra," she later proclaimed.

After resting for a day, she rode around the ruins, exhausting her elderly guide before storytelling, dancing, and coffee drinking in the midst of the ruins after nightfall. In the end, she had to leave hastily, pursued by other hostile tribesmen. Stanhope subsequently visited Baalbek (see below), where she camped in the ruins of an old mosque and complained of the cold. She was not enthused by the ancient city, departed without leaving any impressions of the site, and eventually settled among the Druze people of Syria, who regarded her as a prophetess, a role she assumed with quiet pleasure.

Nineteenth-century Palmyra was definitely off the beaten track, as we learn from the itinerant historian Philip Van Ness Myers, who spent a few days there while on an extended trip through the region in the 1870s:

> Just at nightfall we halted, made a cup of coffee over a fire of camel's thorn [a shrub commonly used as firewood], and then, as it was raining, and our soldiers were unprovided with tents, we remounted, and rode all night through a severe storm, which at times swept the desert with snow and hail. In the gray light of the morning we discovered the tower-tombs of Palmyra, standing like spectres in the pass that led through the low range of verdureless hills which lay across our trail. We reached the summit of the pass, and the wonderful ruins were all before us, lying on the edge of the plain, which, from the foot of the range we were upon, rolled out in unbroken desolation to the eastern horizon. Baalbec dwindled into insignificance. One pile alone, the ruined Temple of the Sun, which rose up grandly from the most distant part of the city, but which the eye did not reach till it had wandered over a long mile of fallen mausoleums and temples, swept down through grand avenues flanked with columns, amid triumphal arches, clustered pillars, and monumental shafts—that grand pile alone, that at last arrested the eye at the end of the pillared vista of the great colonnade, rivaled in beauty and impressiveness all the combined ruins of the famous Syrian City of the Sun [Baalbek].
>
> Descending from the pass, we wound through the ruins to the gate of the temple court. The enclosure was crowded with the miserable mud hovels of Arabs and Turkish soldiers. We were escorted through the irregular streets to the residence of the officer of the post. It was a little mud hut, twelve by eighteen feet, stuck against the very walls of the shrine, with two of the lofty, beautifully fluted pillars of the temple, which were built into the walls of the hovel, projecting thirty feet or more above the roof. Here we were kindly but curiously entertained during the several days spent in exploring the ruins.[4]

Baalbek

Baalbek was a Bronze Age city, flourishing as early as 2900 B.C. The Greeks and Romans called it Heliopolis, "City of the Sun," a name that commemorated the important religious associations of the city with

Egyptian sun worship when it was ruled by the Ptolemies. The great age of Roman building at Baalbek began in A.D. 15, sometime after Julius Caesar stationed a legion there and started construction of a religious precinct. For the next three centuries, successive emperors spent lavishly on the temple and its associated buildings until Christianity became the empire's official religion in 313. The emperor Augustus began construction of the temple of Jupiter in the late first century B.C. It was completed soon after A.D. 60. One hundred and four massive granite columns imported from Aswan in Egypt lined the immense sanctuary of Jupiter Heliopolitanus, and held a temple surrounded by fifty additional columns, each almost 62 feet (19 meters) high.

Baalbek had a long and tumultuous history, achieving prosperity under Muslim rule before becoming a nominally Ottoman town. But it was a dangerous place for travelers until the 1840s, when Ottoman rule was firmly established. By the 1860s, Baalbek had many tourists as it became a popular resort on the Aleppo-Damascus route. An English antiquarian traveler, Richard Pococke, passed through Baalbek as early as 1740. Others camped in the shadow of the mighty temple of Jupiter itself, for Baalbek was still a jumble of confusing ruins. Another visitor, the English scholar James Wood, wryly remarked in 1853 that the local people liked to talk about the long "hours of dalliance" enjoyed by King Solomon in Baalbek, "a subject on which the warm imagination of the Arabs is apt to be too particular."

Inaccessible Petra

Petra, from the Greek word meaning "rock," immediately conjures up visions of Indiana Jones galloping through the *Siq*, the narrow defile that twists and turns through high sandstone cliffs. The film *The Last Crusade* has Jones in quest of the Holy Grail, with Hollywood special effects to match. Petra was a suitably evocative setting for a stirring adventure story. It is also a place that satisfies the most romantic of archaeological travelers. The city was founded in about the sixth century B.C. by nomadic Nabateans. By the late first century B.C., Petra had become prominent as the principal city of Nabatea, a center of the camel-borne spice trade from Arabia and Aqaba to the Syrian Desert and beyond. Petra was famous not only for its importance to trade, but also for its elaborate hydraulic systems developed to capture and control winter rains and flash floods. For centuries, Petra remained independent, until the Roman general Pompey conquered it in 64–63 B.C.; still, it did not come under full Roman rule until A.D. 103, when the emperor Trajan made it the capital of a province named Arabia Petraea. The city continued to prosper, despite an earthquake in A.D. 363, and became the seat of a Byzantine bishopric in the sixth century. But changes in trading patterns and another catastrophic earthquake in A.D. 551 led to Petra's decline and eventual ruin. It withered to little more than a village in Islamic times.

For all its ancient prosperity, Petra, with its spectacular rock-cut temples and tombs, was virtually unknown to the Western world until 1812, when the Swiss traveler Johann Ludwig Burckhardt, journeying from Damascus to Cairo, heard tales from desert Bedouins of an ancient city in the remote Sharra Mountains in what is now Jordan. No European had seen the ruins. Six years earlier, a German traveler had been murdered when he tried to enter them. Burckhart posed as a mendicant beggar. He persuaded the Bedouin inhabitants of a small nearby settlement (now Wadi Mousa) to guide him to a local mountain called Jebel Haroun—named after Aaron, the brother of Moses—just outside Petra. He told them that he wished to sacrifice a goat at Aaron's mountaintop shrine. The only reasonably safe path to the shrine led through the *Siq* into the heart of Petra. Burckhardt came unexpectedly on the Khazneh, the spectacular rock-cut temple that fronts the narrow defile. By this time, Burckhardt's guides

7-2 The largest tomb façade at Petra is known as the Monastery. Fifty meters high and forty-five meters wide, it might have acquired its name because of the crosses inscribed on the interior walls. The tomb has two stories surmounted by an imposing urn.

were becoming suspicious of his intentions, so he pretended to make his sacrifice and left hastily. Burckhardt considered his visit to Petra his most dangerous desert experience. The local people coveted everything he possessed, despite his traveling with nothing that he thought would attract them. They even stripped off some of the rags covering his blistered ankles.

Petra was inaccessible, in country inhabited by volatile Bedouin groups who looked on all strangers with a jaundiced eye. Nevertheless, other visitors followed Burckhardt, most of them dressed as Bedouin, wearing a woolen coat (a *mashlak*), a long canvas shirt secured by a leather or woolen belt, and a kaffiyeh secured with a camel-hair cord. Such visitors praised the "awful sublimity of the approach" and the rock formations that presented "nature in her most savage and romantic form." Lengthy stays were impracticable as the Bedouin did not make outsiders welcome and were said to be bloodthirsty murderers. But the ruins had a powerful allure. The American biblical scholar Edward Robinson was moved to write in 1838 of a strange contrast, "where a taste for the frivolities of the day was at the same time gratified by the magnificence of the tombs; amusement in a cemetery; a theater in the midst of the sepulchers."

In 1840, the Englishman Austen Henry Layard, soon to become world famous for his excavations into Assyrian cities along the Tigris, rode out of Jerusalem for Petra. He traveled alone, accompanied only by a boy, departing with the dire warnings of everyone in his ears. Layard was accustomed to roughing it—he had recently ridden across Syria and Turkey, sleeping in his cloak in the open desert—but nothing prepared him for the Bedouin, who threatened to kill him, robbed him of all his possessions, and then held him hostage. He wandered with them for weeks while they debated his fate before they released him unscathed. Still, the experience gave him an understanding of the character of the tribe, an understanding that was to serve him well in coming years. He took a poor view of Petra's architecture, however, which he considered "debased," but admitted that the site was unique.

The first detailed descriptions of Petra come from the pen of Léon de Laborde (1807–1869), the twenty-year-old son of a French privy councilor and politician. The father, Alexandre de Laborde, and his son took a leisurely trip through the eastern Mediterranean in 1824, but "circumstances prevented" them from visiting Petra. While his father returned home, Léon stayed in Cairo, where he met Linant de Bellefonds, a naval officer turned desert traveler of considerable experience. The two of them set out with fifteen camels and eighteen people in February 1828, dressed like Bedouin so as not to attract attention. Traveling via Aqaba, they were able to reach Petra safely, where they settled down to paint and sketch at their leisure. They managed to stay for six days unmolested, unashamedly distributing lavish gifts to the local people (and thereby making life harder for later travelers). But soon their guides hustled them away because the plague was raging in nearby villages.

Laborde was enraptured by Petra, which he considered remarkable and romantic. Like many other early visitors, he quoted from the Scriptures, repeating the curses on Edom, a shadowy Old Testament kingdom south of the Dead Sea. According to 2 Kings, Petra (Selah) was one of Edom's strongholds. The Edomites took part in the plundering of Jerusalem by the Babylonian king Nebuchadnezzar and in the slaughtering of Jews. They were roundly denounced by the prophets as a result. Laborde recalled the words of Jeremiah:

> O thou that dwellest in the clefts of the rock, that holdest the height of the hill, though thou shouldst make thy nest as high as the eagle, I will bring thee down from thence, saith the Lord. Also Edom shall be a desolation: everyone that goes by it shall be astonished, and shall hiss at all the plagues thereof.[5]

Until the celebrated artist David Roberts published his paintings of Petra in 1842–1849, the plates and sketches in Laborde's *Voyage de l'Arabie Pétrée* (1830) were the only depictions of the site. They attracted a handful of intrepid travelers to the city, which was still in remote, dangerous country. Laborde went on to become a successful art historian, diplomat, and politician. Linant studied hydrography and became the chief engineer of Egypt.

As with the antiquarians in Europe, Petra's biblical associations were irresistible with everyone in such a devout age. When William Bartlett and a gang of well-armed tribesmen reached Petra in the 1840s, he praised "the rock-hewn capital of Edom, which, by its singular wildness, even yet seems any other place, to thrill the imagination and waken the love of adventure."

Perhaps the best-known traveler to visit Petra in the early days was the New York lawyer and writer John Lloyd Stephens (1805–1852), later to achieve archaeological and literary immortality for his descriptions of ancient Maya ruins (see Chapter 9). Tired of the law, he set off on a journey to Europe that eventually took him to Poland, Turkey, and Russia. Without turning home, he then traveled to Alexandria and up the Nile, where he decided to travel east. On March 14, 1836, he became Abdel Hasis, a respectable Cairo merchant dressed in flowing, colorful robes and armed with a brace of Turkish pistols. After an arduous and often thirsty journey, Stephens entered the Wadi Mousa (the valley nearest Petra, now the name of the local town) and emerged at the temple façade of the Khazneh, carved from the "rosiest red of all rocks of Petra." The normally eloquent Stephens was, for once, at a loss for words to describe the magnificent, often subtle hues of the rock faces. In his best-selling *Incidents of Travel in Egypt, Arabia Petraea, and the Holy Land*, published in 1837, he nonetheless gives us a memorable impression:

> And this was the city at whose door I now stood. In a few words, this ancient and extraordinary city is situated within a natural amphitheatre of two or three miles in circumference, encompassed on all sides by rugged mountains five or six hundred feet in height. The whole of this area is now a waste of ruins, dwelling-houses, palaces, temples, and triumphal arches, all prostrate together in undistinguishable confusion. The sides of the mountains are cut smooth, in a perpendicular direction, and filled with long and continued ranges of dwelling-houses, temples, and tombs, excavated with vast labor out of the solid rock; and while their summits present Nature in her wildest and most savage form, their bases are adorned with all the beauty of architecture and art, with columns, and porticoes, and pediments, and ranges of corridors, enduring as the mountains out of which they are hewn, and fresh as if the work of a generation scarcely yet gone by.
>
> Nothing can be finer than the immense rocky rampart which encloses the city. Strong, firm, and immovable as Nature itself, it seems to deride the walls of cities and the puny fortifications of skillful engineers. The only access is by clambering over this wall of stone, practicable only in one place, or by an entrance the most extraordinary that Nature, in her wildest freaks, has ever framed. The loftiest portals ever raised by the hands of man, the proudest monuments of architectural skill and daring, sink into insignificance by the comparison. It is, perhaps, the most wonderful object in the world, except the ruins of the city to which it forms the entrance.
>
> Unfortunately, I did not enter by this door, but by clambering over the mountains at the other end; and when I stood upon the summit of the mountain, though I looked down upon the vast area filled with ruined buildings and heaps of rubbish, and saw the mountainsides cut away so as to form a level surface, and presenting long ranges of doors in successive tiers or stories, the dwelling and burial places of a people long since passed away; and though immediately before me was the excavated front of a large and beautiful temple, I was disappointed. . . . Several times the sheik had told me, in the most positive manner, that there was no other entrance; and I was moved to indignation at the marvellous and exaggerated, not to say false representations, as I thought, of the only persons who had given any account of this wonderful entrance. . . .
>
> I was disappointed, too, in another matter. Burckhardt had been accosted, immediately upon his entry, by a large party of Bedouins, and been suffered to remain but a very short time. Messrs. Legh, Banks, Irby, and Mangles had been opposed by hundreds of Bedouins, who swore "that they should never enter their

territory nor drink of their waters," and "that they would shoot them like dogs if they attempted it." And I expected some immediate opposition from at least the thirty or forty, fewer than whom, the sheik had told me, were never to be found in Wadi Musa. I expected a scene of some kind; but at the entrance of the city there was not a creature to dispute our passage; its portals were wide open, and we passed along the stream down into the area, and still no man came to oppose us. We moved to the extreme end of the area; and, when in the act of dismounting at the foot of the rock on which stood the temple that had constantly faced us, we saw one solitary Arab, straggling along without any apparent object, a mere wanderer among the ruins; and it is a not uninteresting fact, that this poor Bedouin was the only living being we saw in the desolate city of Petra. After gazing at us for a few moments from a distance, he came towards us, and in a few moments was sitting down to pipes and coffee with my companions. I again asked the sheik for the other entrance, and he again told me there was none; but I could not believe him, and set out to look for it myself; and although in my search I had already seen enough abundantly to repay me for all my difficulties in getting there, I could not be content without finding this desired avenue.

In front of the great temple, the pride and beauty of Petra, of which more hereafter, I saw a narrow opening in the rocks, exactly corresponding with my conception of the object for which I was seeking. A full stream of water was gushing through it, and filling up the whole mouth of the passage. Mounted on the shoulders of one of my Bedouins, I got him to carry me through the swollen stream at the mouth of the opening, and set me down on a dry place a little above, whence I began to pick my way, occasionally taking to the shoulders of my follower, and continued to advance more than a mile. I was beyond all peradventure in the great entrance I was seeking. There could not be two such, and I should have gone on to the extreme end of the ravine, but my Bedouin suddenly refused me the further use of his shoulders. He had been some time objecting and begging me to return, and now positively refused to go any farther; and, in fact, turned about himself. I was anxious to proceed, but I did not like wading up to my knees in the water, nor did I feel very resolute to go where I might expose myself to danger, as he seemed to intimate. While I was hesitating, another of my men came running up the ravine, and shortly after him Paul and the sheik, breathless with haste, and crying in low gutturals, "El Arab! el Arab!"—"The Arabs! the Arabs!" This was enough for me. I had heard so much of El Arab that I had become nervous. It was like the cry of Delilah in the ears of sleeping Samson, "The Philistines be upon thee." At the other end of the ravine was an encampment of the El Alouins; and the sheik, having due regard to my communication about money matters, had shunned this entrance to avoid bringing upon me this horde of tribute-gatherers for a participation in the spoils. Without any disposition to explore farther, I turned towards the city; and it was now that I began to feel the powerful and indelible impression that must be produced on entering, through this mountainous passage, the excavated city of Petra.

For about two miles it lies between high and precipitous ranges of rocks, from five hundred to a thousand feet in height, standing as if torn asunder by some great convulsion, and barely wide enough for two horsemen to pass abreast. A swelling stream rushes between them; the summits are wild and broken; in some places overhanging the opposite sides, casting the darkness of night upon the narrow defile; then receding and forming an opening above, through which a strong ray of light is thrown down, and illuminates with the blaze of day the frightful chasm below. Wild fig-trees, oleanders, and ivy were growing out of the rocky sides of the cliffs hundreds of feet above our heads; the eagle was screaming above us; all along were the open doors of tombs, forming the great Necropolis of the city; and at the extreme end was a large open space, with a powerful body of light thrown down upon it, and exhibiting in one full view the facade of a beautiful temple, hewn out of the rock, with rows of Corinthian columns and ornaments, standing out fresh and clear as if but yesterday from the hands of the sculptor.[3] Though coming directly from the banks of the Nile, where the preservation of the temples excites the admiration and astonishment of every traveler, we were roused and excited by the extraordinary beauty and excellent condition of the great temple at Petra. Even in coming upon it, as we did, at disadvantage, I remember that Paul, who was a passionate admirer of the arts, when he first obtained a glimpse of it, involuntarily cried out, and moving on to the front with a vivacity I never saw him exhibit before or afterward, clapped his hands, and shouted in ecstasy. To the last day of our being together he was in the habit of referring to his extraordinary fit of enthusiasm when he first came upon that temple; and I can well imagine that, entering by this narrow defile, with the feelings roused by its extraordinary and romantic wildness and beauty, the first view of that superb façade must produce an effect which could never pass away. Even now, that I have returned to the pursuits and thought-engrossing incidents of a life in the busiest city in the world, often in situations as widely different as light from darkness, I see before me the façade of that temple; neither the Colosseum at Rome, grand and interesting as it is, nor the ruins of the Acropolis at Athens, nor the Pyramids, nor the mighty temples of the Nile, are so often present to my memory.

The whole temple, its columns, ornaments, porticoes, and porches, are cut out from and form part of the solid rock; and this rock, at the foot of which the temple stands like a mere print, towers several hundred feet above, its face cut smooth to the very summit, and the top remaining wild and misshapen as Nature made it. The whole area before the temple is perhaps an acre in extent, enclosed on all sides except at the narrow entrance, and an opening to the left of the temple, which leads into the area of the city by a pass through perpendicular rocks five or six hundred feet in height.

It is not my design to enter into the details of the many monuments in this extraordinary city; but, to give a general idea of the character of all the excavations, I cannot do better than go within the temple. Ascending several broad steps, we entered under a colonnade of four Corinthian columns, about thirty-five feet high, into a large chamber of some fifty feet square and twenty-five feet high.

> The outside of the temple is richly ornamented, but the interior is perfectly plain, there being no ornament of any kind upon the walls or ceiling; on each of the three sides is a small chamber for the reception of the dead; and on the back wall of the innermost chamber I saw the names of Messrs. Legh, Banks, Irby, and Mangles, the four English travelers who with so much difficulty had effected their entrance to the city; of Messieurs Laborde and Linant, and the two Englishmen and Italian of whom I have before spoken; and two or three others, which, from the character of the writing, I supposed to be the names of attendants upon some of these gentlemen. These were the only names recorded in the temple; and, besides Burckhardt, no other traveler had ever reached it. I was the first American who had ever been there. Many of my countrymen, probably, as was the case with me, have never known the existence of such a city; and, independently of all personal considerations, I confess that I felt what, I trust, was not an inexcusable pride, in writing upon the innermost wall of that temple the name of an American citizen; and under it, and flourishing on its own account in temples, and tombs, and all the most conspicuous places in Petra, is the illustrious name of Paolo Nuozzo, dragoman.
>
> The whole theatre is at this day in such a state of preservation, that if the tenants of the tombs around could once more rise into life, they might take their old places on its seats, and listen to the declamation of their favorite player. To me the stillness of a ruined city is nowhere so impressive as when sitting on the steps of its theatre; once thronged with the gay and pleasure-seeking, but now given up to solitude and desolation. Day after day these seats had been filled, and the now silent rocks had echoed to the applauding shout of thousands; and little could an ancient Edomite imagine that a solitary stranger, from a then unknown world, would one day be wandering among the ruins of his proud and wonderful city, meditating upon the fate of a race that has for ages passed away. Where are ye, inhabitants of this desolate city? ye who once sat on the seats of this theatre, the young, the high-born, the beautiful, and brave; who once rejoiced in your riches and power, and lived as if there was no grave? Where are ye now? Even the very tombs, whose open doors are stretching away in long ranges before the eyes of the wondering traveler, cannot reveal the mystery of your doom. . . .[6]

Stephens was a wonderful travel writer. He duly paid court to the prophets and their predictions, but wrote with a lively sense of humor and a pleasing element of mischievousness. A devout reviewer of *Arabia Petraea* in the *Christian Examiner* recommended the book to his colleagues but complained of the writer's "levities," which "give a queer air of irreverence . . . about sacred things." For the rest of his life, Stephens thought of Petra as a beautiful city that bore witness to prophetic denunciations: "its very existence being known only to the wandering Arab, the difficulty of reaching it, and the hurried and dangerous manner in which I had reached it, gave a thrilling and almost fearful interest to the time and place, of which I feel it utterly impossible to convey any idea."[7]

Not known to exaggerate his exploits, Stephens described the reality of the threats to his life:

> Every moment the sheik was becoming more and more impatient; and, spurring my horse, I followed him on a gallop among the ruins. We ascended the valley, and rising to the summit of the rocky rampart, it was almost dark when we found ourselves opposite a range of tombs in the suburbs of the city. Here we dismounted; and selecting from among them one which, from its finish and dimensions, must have been the last abode of some wealthy Edomite, we prepared to pass the night within its walls. I was completely worn out when I threw myself on the rocky floor of the tomb. I had just completed one of the most interesting days in my life; for the singular character of the city, and the uncommon beauty of its ruins, its great antiquity, the prophetic denunciations of whose truth it was the witness, its loss for more than a thousand years to the civilized world, its very existence being known only to the wandering Arab, the difficulty of reaching it, and the hurried and dangerous manner in which I had reached it, gave a thrilling and almost fearful interest to the time and place, of which I feel it utterly impossible to convey any idea.
>
> In the morning Paul and I had determined, when our companions should be asleep, to ascend Mount Hor by moonlight; but now we thought only of rest; and seldom has the pampered tenant of a palace laid down with greater satisfaction upon his canopied bed than I did upon the stony floor of this tomb in Petra. In the front part of it was a large chamber, about twenty-five feet square and ten feet high; and behind this was another of smaller dimensions, furnished with receptacles for the dead, not arranged after the manner of shelves extending along the wall, as in the catacombs I had seen in Italy and Egypt, but cut lengthwise in the rock, like ovens, so as to admit the insertion of the body with the feet foremost.
>
> We built a fire in the outer chamber, thus lighting up the innermost recesses of the tombs; and, after our evening meal, while sipping coffee and smoking pipes, the sheik congratulated me upon my extreme good fortune in having seen Petra without any annoyance from the Bedouins; adding, as usual, that it was a happy day for me when I saw his face at Cairo. He told me that he had never been to Wadi Musa without seeing at least thirty or forty Arabs, and sometimes three or four hundred; that when Abdel Hag (Mr. Linant) and Mr. Laborde visited Petra the first time, they were driven out by the Bedouins after remaining only five hours, and were chased down into the valley, Mr. Linant changing his dromedary every three hours on the way back to Aqaba; that there he remained, pretending to be sick, for twenty-four days, every day feasting half the tribe; and during that time sending to Cairo for money, dresses, swords, guns, pistols, ammunition, &c., which he distributed among them so lavishly that the whole tribe escorted him in triumph to Petra. This is so different from Mr. Laborde's account of his visit, that it cannot be true. I asked him about the visit of Messrs. Legh and Banks, and

Captains Irby and Mangles; and drawing close to me, so as not to be overheard by the rest, he told me that he remembered their visit well; that they came from Karak with three sheiks and three or four hundred men, and that the Bedouins of Wadi Musa turned out against them more than two thousand strong.[8]

We marvel at the toughness of the early archaeological traveler, who encountered logistical and day-to-day challenges that seem almost unimaginable today. The logistics of the early travelers' journeys across deserts, through brigand-infested valleys, required meticulous planning, an ability to bargain tenaciously, and a gift for improvisation and being able to melt into the background if necessary. Bold conduct and an ability to bluff were essential, as was constant watchfulness. Not for these travelers the predictable comforts of the grand tour, where inns awaited the traveler and merchants in Rome and Naples catered to every need. Today, you visit Palmyra and Petra in an air-conditioned coach with a trained guide who speaks your language fluently. The ruins are well cared for, and you see the often orderly rows of columns, boulders, and inscriptions. Your only concern is where the next rest stop will be. I have an uneasy feeling that something is missing from our experience—perhaps real adventure. But many of the adventures of our predecessors are ones that we would not wish on our worst enemy.

> Make a public example of any one in your company you catch defacing a monument, either by scribbling his name or by taking fragments of it away. Posterity will bless you.
>
> CANON HARDWICKE D. RAWNSLEY, 1892[1]

CHAPTER EIGHT

Tourists Along the Nile

Until 1830, the traveler to India faced a long, and often stormy, passage around the Cape of Good Hope. The advent of the steamship changed everything. Now you could take a steamer from England or Marseilles to Alexandria, then spend a few days or weeks in Cairo waiting for news that the ship for India was approaching Suez. You then took a camel, horse, or wagon across the desert to meet the vessel at what was then a small village. Hotels opened in Suez and Cairo to accommodate transit passengers. The British Hotel in Cairo, soon to be renamed Shepheard's Hotel after its manager, welcomed its first guests in 1841. This magnificent Victorian institution became world famous, especially after the opening of the Suez Canal in 1869, when it became *the* hotel of choice for the British Raj on its way to and from India. The hotel also catered to a new breed, the archaeological tourist.

Bubonic plague epidemics periodically claimed thousands of lives in Egypt until 1844, when it suddenly and mysteriously disappeared. Cholera arrived from India to take its place, but despite this scourge, Egypt became a recommended destination for travelers wishing to escape damp European winters. By this time, a journey up the Nile to the First Cataract was routine, although one had to endure long quarantines on account of the plague. Nile travel became so popular that the London publisher John Murray commissioned the Egyptologist John Gardner Wilkinson to write a guide, one of a series aimed at a new audience of middle-class tourists. Wilkinson traveled in style, his baggage requiring a small army of porters. The contents of his baggage included an iron bedstead, a sword and other oddities, and "much more," including a chicken coop, ample biscuits (cookies), and potted meats. He lamented the high cost of living in Egypt and the changes brought by a rising tide of visitors. "The travelers who go up the Nile will I fear soon be like Rhine tourists. & Cheapside will pour out its Legions upon Egypt."[2] His *Handbook for*

Travellers in Egypt first appeared in 1847, went through multiple editions until 1873, and was still in common use half a century after its first appearance. Crammed with archaeological, artistic, and architectural information, the *Handbook* also contained much practical advice, including a recommendation that one sink one's *dahabiyya* to rid it of "rats and other noxious inhabitants" before setting sail.

Thomas Cook and Mark Twain

Just as Wilkinson was traveling up the Nile, another Englishman, a devout Baptist and cabinetmaker, Thomas Cook, founded a company in Leicester, in central England, to run rail excursions to temperance meetings. His venture was a success. Soon Cook expanded his business to general excursions, transporting more than 165,000 people to the 1851 Great Exhibition in London and mounting tours to France, Switzerland, and Italy at affordable prices for the up-and-coming middle class. He moved his business to London in 1865 with a view to running package tours to Egypt, which began in 1869. He organized all-inclusive excursions using steamers on the Nile, which were far more reliable than sail-powered *dahabiyyas*, the ubiquitous river-sailing craft. Cook's son opened an office in Shepheard's Hotel two years later, and the business expanded rapidly—to the consternation of many independent, affluent travelers, who considered Cook's tourists to be "common." Tourism soon became big business. By the time the poet and travel writer Douglas Sladen, author of *Oriental Cairo* (1911), traveled up the Nile on a Cook steamer, the routine was well established.

> I have never enjoyed anything more than my voyages up the Nile in Cook's Tourist steamers. They are luxurious without being too elaborate; their food compares with that of any hotel in Egypt; their servants are the best I have ever come across. Most of them have excellent dragomans, and their programme is skilfully adapted to satisfy both the wise and the foolish. The steamers between Cairo and Assuan accommodate about eighty people. Their cabins are large, with beds so high above the floor that an American saratoga will go underneath them; their washing arrangements and baths are particularly good, a great consideration in a hot climate like Egypt. The only fault I have to find with the cabins is that the electric light goes out at eleven, for on the Nile, more than anywhere else, you want to do a good deal of reading at night. All the best books on Egypt are in the ship library. If you read three or four hours every night you would not exhaust all that good writers have written upon the places you see on the voyage, and you can only read at night, because by day you are passing something of interest every few minutes, whether it be a city, or a Nile village, or an exquisite palm grove, or picturesque incidents of native life, or the birds which turn the large shoals into a

kind of zoological gardens, and seem to know quite well that no firing is permitted from Cook's steamers.

Every steamer has a cosy little reading-room fitted with writing-tables, and supplied with the latest newspapers, as well as with a library of books on Egypt. The papers, like the letters, are brought on board every day, and there is a pillar-box on board, cleared every night, for those who wish to post letters. You simply arrange to have your letters sent to Cook's Cairo office; their post clerk knows where their steamers will be each day and forwards the letters by train. The second dragoman is postman. You find your letters beside your plate at breakfast, just as you would at home.

Breakfast is a country-house meal. It starts with porridge and its patent substitutes, and proceeds with bacon and eggs and fish and other hot dishes, and ham and tongue and chicken, and other cold fare, to jam and marmalade. And the bread and the butter are excellent. It needs to be a hearty meal, for one cannot help getting up early when there is an Egyptian sunrise mingling earth and heaven, and the waking life of the villages to watch. I used to have a cup of tea brought to me at sunrise, and then lie in my bunk, looking out of the big window at the early morning Nile effects, until it was time for my bath, unless we were passing through something so exciting that I felt constrained to put on a big overcoat over my pyjamas and go and sit in the sun gallery, glazed all round, which occupies the fore part of the promenade deck. But this saddened the whiterobed Arab servants, who hated a passenger's seeing the deck before they had swept off every particle of dust with their ostrich-feather brooms, and made the brass shine like gold. The ostrich-feather broom plays a great part in the economy of Cook's Nile boats. The decks are dusted with it, and your boots and legs are dusted with it whenever you go on shore 'to shake the dust from off your feet.'

My first bath was rather a shock to me, for the bath and the bath-room are so very white and the Nile water in the bath looks like a cup of chocolate. But it does not make you muddy; it has the same cleansing properties as other waters . . .

There is in the centre of the promenade deck of Cook's Tourist steamers a broad lounge, which goes right across it, awninged above from the sun by day, and awninged all round at night till it looks like a marquee put up for a ball. As it is full of easy chairs and tea-tables and windscreens, the idle and the unintelligent lounge about it all day long when they are not making excursions (which they like for the donkey rides), reading novels, or dozing, or playing bridge. Their day begins with afternoon tea, at which you have half Huntley and Palmer's productions instead of bread and butter. Special friends make up tea-parties, and the beautiful Arab servants, in white robes, and bright red tarbooshes, sashes and slippers, glide about, filling up the tea-cups as fast as they are emptied and bringing fresh varieties of Huntley and Palmer to compel people to over-eat themselves. This goes playfully on till somebody discovers that sunset is beginning. Then even the least intelligent people on the ship hurry to the side, not for the usual reason, and bring up ejaculations for a solid hour while the Egyptian sky proceeds with its marvellous transformation-scenes . . .

In the height of the season, when the tourist steamers are full, on the days when there are no excursions, the particular young man sometimes breaks out into silk suits and wonderful socks, or, at any rate, rare and irreproachable flannels, just as the girl who has come to conquer Cairo society rings the gamut of summer extravagances. They have the moral courage for at least two different costumes between breakfast and dinner; and though a mere man is limited to his theatre jacket for dinner, the irresponsible girl can dress as elaborately as she pleases for the evening, and the climate tempts her . . .

By dinner-time most people are tired—tired of doing nothing if there has been no excursion; tired of long rides over the hot Desert, and hard sight-seeing, if there has been an excursion. They sit down with great content to a good dinner, and when it is over move out to the marquee which has been improvised out of the lounge for their coffee and cigarettes and a little light chatter; and, if they are wise, read their guide-books. On our steamer nobody played bridge except the two clergymen and their wives. Most people had no time for the Devil's picture-books; they were reading their guide-books; you are lost in Egypt if you do not read up. I used to disappear directly after dinner and read in my bunk, where the light was good and the quiet perfect . . .

We were lucky enough, for we had chosen our ship haphazard, to have Mohammed, the *doyen* of Cook's, for our chief dragoman. He is a dragoman of the old school, who knows his subject well, but is even more endeared to the tourist by the picturesqueness of himself and the thirty changes of raiment which he takes on board the ship with him, and his fine manners of the old-fashioned East. He maintains the ideals and the atmosphere of the dragoman of the good old days when nobody but Croesus (for the most part a coronetted Croesus) went to Egypt. He has a fund of good stories, which he tells with unconsciously theatrical attitudes and gestures, for the tourist; a great deal of authority for the native of the donkey-boy, guide, and curio-selling professions; wonderful tact and patience with the exacting and inquisitive or stupid people whom he has to show over ruins in which they are interested in inadequate and widely different ways; and unfailing wit and cheerfulness. Added to which, he is wholly free from the presumption which so often disfigures the attitude of dragomans to ladies.

Every night at dinner-time he used to come in and clap his hands for attention, and announce the programme for the following day, in a witty little speech, which described the nature of the monuments to be visited, and the means to be employed in getting to them—donkeys, boats, or walking—with a little useful advice as to conditions atmospheric or otherwise, and the unfailing reminder that 'monument-tickets would be very much wanted.'[3]

By 1870, about three hundred American tourists registered at the consulate in Cairo in a year. Mark Twain had recently published *Innocents Abroad*, a widely read account of his travels in Europe and the Middle East. But in Egypt he had time to visit only the pyramids and the Sphinx

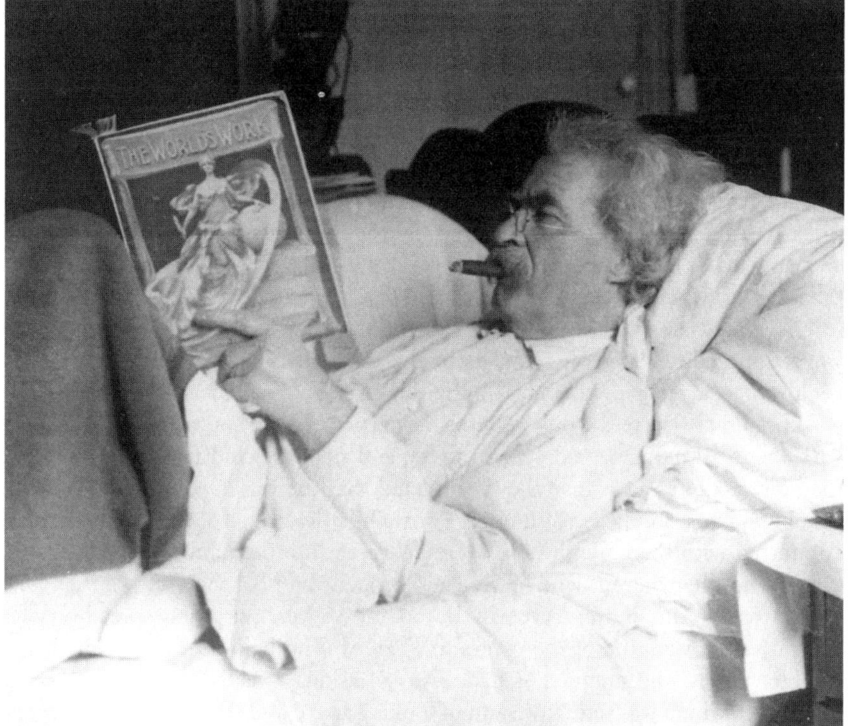

8-1 The witty, cynical, and occasional travel writer Mark Twain (Samuel Langhorne Clemens) rests in bed with a book after various trips abroad.

before turning for home. Twain admired the lushness of Egypt, "the boundless sweep of the level plain, green with luxuriant grain, that gladdens the eye as far as it can pierce through the soft, rich atmosphere." He described Shepheard's Hotel, by then a famed hostelry, as "the worst on earth except the one I stopped at once in a small town in the United States." Twain committed no vandalism, such as carving his name on a temple column. He was content to accuse the Egyptians of feeding mummies to their railway engines. His description of a visit to the pyramids reflects a typical, if somewhat cynical, experience of the day:

> At the distance of a few miles the pyramids rising above the palms looked very clean-cut, very grand and imposing, and very soft and filmy as well. They swam in a rich haze that took from them all suggestions of unfeeling stone and made them seem only the airy nothings of a dream—structures which might blossom into tiers of vague arches or ornate colonnades maybe, and change and change again into all graceful forms of architecture, while we looked, and then melt deliciously away and blend with the tremulous atmosphere.

At the end of the levee we left the mules and went in a sailboat across an arm of the Nile or an overflow, and landed where the sands of the great Sahara left their embankment, as straight as a wall, along the verge of the alluvial plain of the river. A laborious walk in the flaming sun brought us to the foot of the great pyramid of Cheops. It was a fairy vision no longer. It was a corrugated, unsightly mountain of stone. Each of its monstrous sides was a wide stairway which rose upward, step above step, narrowing as it went, till it tapered to a point far aloft in the air. Insect men and women—pilgrims from the *Quaker City*—were creeping about its dizzy perches, and one little black swarm were waving postage stamps from the airy summit—handkerchiefs will be understood.

Of course we were besieged by a rabble of muscular Egyptians and Arabs who wanted the contract of dragging us to the top—all tourists are. Of course you could not hear your own voice for the din that was around you. Of course the sheikhs said *they* were the only responsible parties, that all contracts must be made with them, all moneys paid over to them, and none exacted from us by any but themselves alone. Of course they contracted that the varlets who dragged us up should not mention baksheesh once. For such is the usual routine. Of course we contracted with them, paid them, were delivered into the hands of the draggers, dragged up the pyramids, and harried and bedeviled for baksheesh from the foundation clear to the summit. We paid it, too, for we were purposely spread very far apart over the vast side of the pyramid. There was no help near if we called, and the Herculeses who dragged us had a way of asking sweetly and flatteringly for baksheesh, which was seductive, and of looking fierce and threatening to throw us down the precipice, which was persuasive and convincing.

Each step being full as high as a dinner table; there being very, very many of the steps; an Arab having hold of each of our arms and springing upward from step to step and snatching us with them, forcing us to lift our feet as high as our breasts every time, and do it rapidly and keep it up till we were ready to faint—who shall say it is not lively, exhilarating, lacerating, muscle-straining, bone-wrenching and perfectly excruciating and exhausting pastime climbing the pyramids? I beseeched the varlets not to twist *all* my joints asunder; I iterated, reiterated, even *swore* to them that I did not wish to beat anybody to the top; did all I could to convince them that if I got there the last of all, I would feel blessed above men and grateful to them forever; I begged them, prayed them, pleaded with them to let me stop and rest a moment—only one little moment—and they only answered with some more frightful springs, and an unenlisted volunteer behind opened a bombardment of determined boosts with his head which threatened to batter my whole political economy to wreck and ruin.

Twice, for one minute, they let me rest while they extorted baksheesh, and then continued their maniac flight up the pyramid. They wished to beat the other parties. It was nothing to them that I, a stranger, must be sacrificed upon the altar of their unholy ambition. But in the midst of sorrow, joy blooms. Even in this dark hour I had a sweet consolation. For I knew that except these Muhammadans repented, they would go straight to perdition someday. And *they* never repent—

they never forsake their paganism. This thought calmed me, cheered me, and I sank down, limp and exhausted, upon the summit, but happy, *so* happy and serene within.

On the one hand, a mighty sea of yellow sand stretched away toward the ends of the earth, solemn, silent, shorn of vegetation, its solitude uncheered by any forms of creature life; on the other, the Eden of Egypt was spread below us—a broad green floor, cloven by the sinuous river, dotted with villages, its vast distances measured and marked by the diminishing stature of receding clusters of palms. It lay asleep in an enchanted atmosphere. There was no sound, no motion. Above the date plumes in the middle distance swelled a domed and pinnacled mass, glimmering through a tinted, exquisite mist; away toward the horizon a dozen shapely pyramids watched over ruined Memphis; and at our feet the bland impassible sphinx looked out upon the picture from her throne in the sands as placidly and pensively as she had looked upon its like full fifty lagging centuries ago.

We suffered torture no pen can describe from the hungry appeals for baksheesh that gleamed from Arab eyes and poured incessantly from Arab lips. Why try to call up the traditions of vanished Egyptian grandeur; why try to fancy Egypt following dead Rameses to his tomb in the pyramid or the long multitude of Israel departing over the desert yonder? Why try to think at all? The thing was impossible. One must bring his meditations cut and dried, or else cut and dry them afterward.

The traditional Arab proposed, in the traditional way, to run down Cheops, cross the eighth of a mile of sand intervening between it and the tall pyramid of Cephron, ascend to Cephron's summit and return to us on the top of Cheops—all in nine minutes by the watch, and the whole service to be rendered for a single dollar. In the first flush of irritation I said let the Arab and his exploits go to the mischief. But stay. The upper third of Cephron was coated with dressed marble smooth as glass. A blessed thought entered my brain. He must infallibly break his neck. Close the contract with dispatch, I said, and let him go. He started. We watched. He went bounding down the vast broadside, spring after spring, like an ibex. He grew small and smaller till he became a bobbing pygmy, away down toward the bottom—then disappeared. We turned and peered over the other side—forty seconds—eighty seconds—a hundred—happiness, he is dead already!—two minutes—and a quarter. "There he goes!" Too true—it was too true. He was very small now. Gradually, but surely, he overcame the level ground. He began to spring and climb again. Up, up, up—at last he reached the smooth coating—now for it. But he clung to it with toes and fingers, like a fly. He crawled this way and that—away to the right, slanting upward—away to the left, still slanting upward—and stood at last, a black peg on the summit, and waved his pygmy scarf! Then he crept downward to the raw steps again, then picked up his agile heels and flew. We lost him presently. But presently again we saw him under us, mounting with undiminished energy. Shortly he bounded into our midst with a gallant war whoop. Time: eight minutes, forty-one seconds. He had won. His bones were intact. It was a failure. I reflected. I said to myself, "He is tired and must grow dizzy. I will risk another dollar on him."

He started again. Made the trip again. Slipped on the smooth coating—I almost had him. But an infamous crevice saved him. He was with us once more—perfectly sound. Time: eight minutes, forty-six seconds.

I said to Dan. "Lend me a dollar—I can beat this game yet."

Worse and worse. He won again. Time: eight minutes, forty-eight seconds. I was out of all patience now. I was desperate. Money was no longer of any consequence. I said, "Sirrah, I will give you a hundred dollars to jump off this pyramid head first. If you do not like the terms, name your bet. I scorn to stand on expenses now. I will stay right here and risk money on you as long as Dan has got a cent."

I was in a fair way to win now, for it was a dazzling opportunity for an Arab. He pondered a moment, and would have done it, I think, but his mother arrived then and interfered. Her tears moved me—I never can look upon the tears of woman with indifference—and I said I would give her a hundred to jump off, too.

But it was a failure. The Arabs are too high-priced in Egypt. They put on airs unbecoming to such savages.

We descended, hot and out of humor. The dragoman lit candles, and we all entered a hole near the base of the pyramid, attended by a crazy rabble of Arabs who thrust their services upon us uninvited. They dragged us up a long inclined chute and dripped candle grease all over us. This chute was not more than twice as wide and high as a Saratoga trunk, and was walled, roofed, and floored with solid blocks of Egyptian granite as wide as a wardrobe, twice as thick, and three times as long. We kept on climbing, through the oppressive gloom, till I thought we ought to be nearing the top of the pyramid again, and then came to the "Queen's Chamber" and shortly to the chamber of the King. These large apartments were tombs. The walls were built of monstrous masses of smoothed granite, neatly joined together. Some of them were nearly as large square as an ordinary parlor. A great stone sarcophagus like a bathtub stood in the center of the King's Chamber. Around it were gathered a picturesque group of Arab savages and soiled and tattered pilgrims, who held their candles aloft in the gloom while they chattered, and the winking blurs of light shed a dim glory down upon one of the irrepressible memento-seekers who was pecking at the venerable sarcophagus with his sacrilegious hammer.

We struggled out to the open air and the bright sunshine, and for the space of thirty minutes received ragged Arabs by couples, dozens, and platoons, and paid them baksheesh for services they swore and proved by each other that they had rendered, but which we had not been aware of before—and as each party was paid, they dropped into the rear of the procession and in due time arrived again with a newly invented delinquent list for liquidation. We lunched in the shade of the pyramid, and in the midst of this encroaching and unwelcome company, and then Dan and Jack and I started away for a walk. A howling swarm of beggars followed us—surrounded us—almost headed us off. A sheikh, in flowing white burnoose and gaudy headgear, was with them. He wanted more baksheesh. But we had adopted a new code—it was millions for defense, but not a cent for baksheesh. I asked him if he could persuade the others to depart if we paid him. He said yes—for ten francs. We accepted the contract, and said:

"Now persuade your vassals to fall back."

He swung his long staff round his head and three Arabs bit the dust. He capered among the mob like a very maniac. His blows fell like hail, and wherever one fell a subject went down. We had to hurry to the rescue and tell him it was only necessary to damage them a little—he need not kill them. In two minutes we were alone with the sheikh, and remained so.[4]

"A boating trip interspersed with ruins"

Most affluent visitors came to be entertained and informed, taking what one French writer called a "donkey-ride and a boating trip interspersed with ruins." Such tourists almost invariably traveled in a slow-moving *dahabiyya*. These ageless Nile craft were sailing vessels rigged with a single mast and sail on an enormous yardarm. The most luxurious were quite spacious, even equipped with grand pianos. Boats sailed upriver with the prevailing winds of the Mediterranean behind them. When the wind dropped, the crew laboriously towed the boat to its destination. The current carried vacationers back downstream to Cairo.

8-2 Two of the most common forms of conveyance for early tourists in Egypt are shown here at rest: a boat and a donkey.

Discerning travelers with plenty of time to spare found *dahabiyya* travel both civilized and soothing. They would socialize with other travelers, pausing for days or even weeks at Luxor, Aswan, and elsewhere to sketch and explore at their leisure. The trip could occupy two months or more, especially if you elected to go as far south as Abu Simbel and the Second Cataract. Many visitors came for their health, rented houses, and stayed for months. One such émigré was the aristocratic Englishwoman Lady Lucie Duff-Gordon, who suffered from tuberculosis and took up residence in a ramshackle residence known as the French House, perched on the roof of the Luxor temple and then largely buried in sand. From 1863 to 1869, she surveyed local society with a powerful compassion, writing letters home about the oppressive policies of the authorities, about sandstorms, and about the endless cycle of planting and harvest. She met an old foreman who had worked for the notorious Italian tomb robber and adventurer Giovanni Belzoni when he had found the tomb of the pharaoh Seti I in the Valley of the Kings half a century earlier. She visited this tomb with its vivid paintings, which had now become a popular tourist attraction. She sent her husband a gift of a pharaonic lion, which she admitted that she stole from a temple, where it had served as a footstool for tourists to mount their donkeys. Lady Lucie Duff-Gordon died of her tuberculosis atop the temple, far from her family but surrounded by her Egyptian friends, who are remembered in her letters.

A Thousand Miles up the Nile

In November 1873, an inquisitive, suntanned traveler, Amelia B. Edwards, checked into Shepheard's Hotel. Edwards was one of that distinctive Victorian breed of prolific romantic novelist whose literary output more than compensated for the lack of radio and television. During her sixty-one years, an immense number of articles, lectures, books, reviews, and pamphlets streamed from her facile pen. The daughter of an army officer who served under the Duke of Wellington in the Peninsular War, Edwards showed even in childhood a remarkable talent for writing and drawing, and she possessed a potentially professional-caliber voice. Her first poem was published when she was seven years old.

Ultimately Amelia Edwards became a journalist, contributing articles on all manner of subjects to popular periodicals such as *Chamber's Journal* and the *Saturday Review*. She also wrote eight forgettable romance novels between 1855 and 1880, and she edited books on history and art aimed at general audiences, most of which sold well and allowed her to live the life of a leisured literary traveler, a life that was the right of a successful late-Victorian author.

In 1872, Edwards explored the Dolomite Mountains in northern Italy, at the time an out-of-the-way destination even for well-traveled men. Her first best-selling book, issued originally as *A Midsummer Ramble in the Dolomites* and later as *Untrodden Peaks*, resulted from this trip. During the summer of 1873, she and her travel companion, Lucy Renshawe, planned a walking tour in France. For days, the rain would not stop, so they decided on impulse to travel to Cairo instead, the start of what would become an extended tour through Syria and Egypt in 1873 and 1874. The trip changed Edwards's life and led to her best-known book, *A Thousand Miles up the Nile*, published three years later.

A Thousand Miles was a deservedly popular travel book that went through several editions and displays Edwards's lush writing style at its best. She describes a typical, fairly luxurious trip to the Second Cataract in two *dahabiyyas*. The party consisted of five English gentlefolk traveling in company with two English ladies in another craft. They all seem to have been typical Nile-goers: young and old, well-dressed and ill-dressed, learned and unlearned, eager for any new experience, and, like so many Victorians, secure in their own society and conscious of the superiority of its values, religion, and morals over those of "foreigners" and certainly over those of the Egyptians, whose ancient history they nonetheless found so compelling.

Amelia Edwards made full use of her river journey. She wrote a book that delightfully evokes both the unchanging peasant life along the banks of the river, which seemed virtually unchanged from ancient Egyptian times, and from the tourist life of a century and a half ago. *A Thousand Miles* is knowledgeable and yet bears its knowledge lightly. At the time of her journey, Edwards was lamentably ignorant of archaeology, so her impressions of and reactions to temple and tomb were emotional rather than scientific. This led to some notably lush prose in a Victorian genre that relished evocative description. Of a Nile sunset, she wrote: "Every cast shadow in the recesses of the cliffs turns to pure violet; and the face of the rock glows with a ruddier gold; and the palms on the western bank stand up in solid bronze against a crimson horizon. Then the sun dips, and instantly the whole range of cliffs turns into a deadly, greenish grey, while the sky above and behind them is suddenly suffused with pink."[5] Everywhere the party went, they moved around in a capsule of luxury, fine service, and soft-footed attendants. They would eat luncheon in temple or tomb, with the locals kept at a respectful distance. The servants would spread rugs and serve lemonade or wine along with a cold collation.

We had luncheon that morning, I remember, with the M.B.'s in the second hall of the Ramesseum. It was but one occasion among many; for the Writer was constantly at work on that side of the river, and we had luncheon in one or other of the western Temples every day. Yet that particular meeting stands out in my memory apart from the rest. I see the joyous party gathered together in the shade of the great columns—the Persian rugs spread on the uneven ground—the dragoman in his picturesque dress going to and fro—the brown and tattered Arabs, squatting a little way off, silent and hungry-eyed, each with his string of forged scarabs, his imitation gods, or his bits of mummy-case and painted cartonnage for sale—the glowing peeps of landscape framed in here and there through vistas of columns—the emblazoned architraves laid along from capital to capital overhead, each block sculptured with enormous cartouches yet brilliant with vermilion and ultramarine—the patient donkeys munching all together at a little heap of vetches in one corner—the intense depths of cloudless blue above. Of all Theban ruins, the Ramesseum is the most cheerful. Drenched in sunshine, the warm limestone of which it is built seems to have mellowed and turned golden with time. No walls enclose it. No towering pylons overshadow it. It stands high, and the air circulates freely among those simple and beautiful columns. There are not many Egyptian ruins in which one can talk and be merry; but in the Ramesseum one may thoroughly enjoy the passing hour.[6]

Amelia Edwards's *dahabiyya* stopped at Luxor for a leisurely stay that included a memorable passage through the temple of Amun at Karnak. This temple was a masterpiece of Egyptian architecture, adorned with lavish offerings and ornaments by generations of New Kingdom pharaohs during several centuries of flamboyant imperial power after 1530 B.C. The greatest of Egypt's pharaohs—Amenophis II, Seti I, and Rameses II—trod these same precincts, where they honored the sun god Amun in all his radiant glory.

The trip that inspired *A Thousand Miles up the Nile* changed Edwards's life. She was so entranced with Egypt and so horrified by the wholesale destruction and looting of its past that she devoted the rest of her life to saving the ancient Egyptians for posterity. Her book rapidly became a best-seller, for she clothed ancient Egypt in a romantic aura, writing in a style that appealed to a Victorian audience accustomed to luxuriant narratives. Her book made Egypt and its monuments come alive, and it entertained thousands of readers who purchased it at railway bookstores throughout Britain. Her description of the temple of the sun god Amun at Karnak is Edwards at her evocative best:

I seem to remember the rest as if it had all happened in a dream. Leaving the Temple, we turned towards the river, skirted the mud-walls of the native village, and approached the Great Temple by way of its main entrance. Here we entered upon what had once been another great avenue of sphinxes, ram-headed, couchant on plinths deep cut with hieroglyphic legends, and leading up from some grand landing-place beside the Nile.

And now the towers that we had first seen as we sailed by in the morning rose straight before us, magnificent in ruin, glittering to the sun, and relieved in creamy light against blue depths of sky. One was nearly perfect; the other, shattered as if by the shock of an earthquake, was still so lofty that an Arab clambering from block to block midway of its vast height looked no bigger than a squirrel.

On the threshold of this tremendous portal we again dismounted. Shapeless crude-brick mounds, marking the limits of the ancient wall of circuit, reached far away on either side. An immense perspective of pillars and pylons leading up to a very distant obelisk opened out before us. We went in, the great walls towering up like cliffs above our heads, and entered the First Court. Here, in the midst of a large quadrangle open to the sky, stands a solitary column, the last of a central avenue of twelve, some of which, disjointed by the shock, lie just as they fell, like skeletons of vertebrate monsters left stranded by the Flood.

Crossing this Court in the glowing sunlight, we came to a mighty doorway between two more propylons—the doorway splendid with coloured bas-reliefs; the propylons mere cataracts of fallen blocks piled up to right and left in grand confusion. The cornice of the doorway is gone. Only a jutting fragment of the lintel stone remains. That stone, when perfect, measured forty feet and ten inches across. The doorway must have been full a hundred feet in height

We went on. Leaving to the right a mutilated colossus engraven on arm and breast with the cartouche of Rameses II., we crossed the shade upon the threshold, and passed into the famous Hypostyle Hall of Seti the First.

It is a place that has been much written about and often painted; but of which no writing and no art can convey more than a dwarfed and pallid impression. To describe it, in the sense of building up a recognisable image by means of words, is impossible. The scale is too vast; the effect too tremendous; the sense of one's own dumbness, and littleness, and incapacity, too complete and crushing. It is a place that strikes you into silence; that empties you, as it were, not only of words but of ideas. Nor is this a first effect only. Later in the year, when we came back down the river and moored close by, and spent long days among the ruins, I found I never had a word to say in the Great Hall. Others might measure the girth of those tremendous columns; others might climb hither and thither, and find out points of view, and test the accuracy of Wilkinson and Zincke; but I could only look, and be silent.

Yet to look is something, if one can but succeed in remembering; and the Great Hall of Karnak is photographed in some dark corner of my brain for as long as I have memory. I shut my eyes, and see it as if I were there—not all at once, as in a picture; but bit by bit, as the eye takes note of large objects and travels over an extended field of vision. I stand once more among those mighty columns, which radiate into avenues from whatever point one takes them. I see them swathed in coiled shadows and broad bands of light. I see them sculptured and painted with shapes of Gods and Kings, with blazonings of royal names, with sacrificial altars, and forms of sacred beasts, and emblems of wisdom and truth. The shafts of these columns are enormous. I stand at the foot of one—or of what seems to be the foot; for the original pavement lies buried seven feet below. Six men standing with extended arms, finger-tip to finger-tip, could barely span it round. It casts a shadow twelve feet in breadth—such a shadow as might be cast by a tower. The capital that juts out so high above my head looks as if it might have been placed there to support the heavens. It is carved in the semblance of a full-blown lotus, and glows with undying colours—colours that are still fresh, though laid on by hands that have been dust these three thousand years and more. It would take not six men, but a dozen to measure round the curved lip of that stupendous lily.

Such are the twelve central columns. The rest (one hundred and twenty-two in number) are gigantic too; but smaller. Of the roof they once supported, only the beams remain. Those beams are stones—huge monoliths carved and painted, that bridge the space from pillar to pillar, and pattern the trodden soil with bands of shadow.

Looking up and down the central avenue, we see at the one end a flame-like obelisk; at the other, a solitary palm against a background of glowing mountain. To right, to left, showing transversely through long files of columns, we catch glimpses of colossal bas-reliefs lining the roofless walls in every direction. The King, as usual, figures in every group, and performs the customary acts of worship. The Gods receive and approve him. Half in light, half in shadow, these slender, fantastic forms stand out sharp, and clear, and colourless; each figure some eighteen or twenty feet in height. They could scarcely have looked more weird when the great roof was in its place and perpetual twilight reigned. But it is difficult to imagine the roof on, and the sky shut out. It all looks right as it is; and one feels, somehow, that such columns should have nothing between them and the infinite blue depths of heaven.

The great central avenue was, however, sufficiently lighted by means of a double row of clerestory windows, some of which are yet standing. Certain writers have suggested that they may have been glazed; but this seems improbable, for two reasons. Firstly, because one or two of these huge window-frames yet contain the solid stone gratings which in the present instance seem to have done duty for a translucent material: and, secondly, because we have no evidence to show that the early Egyptians, though familiar since the days of Cheops with the use of the blow-pipe, ever made glass in sheets, or introduced it in this way into their buildings.

How often has it been written, and how often must it be repeated, that the Great Hall at Karnak is the noblest architectural work ever designed and executed by human hands? One writer tells us that it covers four times the area occupied by the Cathedral of Nôtre Dame in Paris. Another measures it against St. Peter's. All admit their inability to describe it; yet all attempt the description. To convey a concrete image of the place to one who has not seen it, is however, as I have already said, impossible. If it could be likened to this place or that, the task would not be so difficult; but there is, in truth, no building in the wide world to compare with it. The Pyramids are more stupendous. The Colosseum covers more ground. The Parthenon is more beautiful. Yet in nobility of conception, in vastness of detail, in majestic beauty of the highest order, the Hall of Pillars exceeds them every one. This doorway, these columns, are the wonder of the world. How was that lintel-stone raised? How were those capitals lifted? Entering among those mighty pillars, says a recent observer, "you feel that you have shrunk to the dimensions and feebleness of a fly." But I think you feel more than that. You are stupified by the thought of the mighty men who made them. You say to yourself:—"There were indeed giants in those days."

It may be that the traveller who finds himself for the first time in the midst of a grove of *Wellingtonia gigantea* feels something of the same overwhelming sense of awe and wonder, but the great trees, though they have taken three thousand years to grow, lack the pathos and the mystery that comes of human labour. They do not strike their roots through six thousand years of history. They have not been watered with the blood and tears of millions. Their leaves know no sounds less musical than the singing of birds, or the moaning of the night-wind as it sweeps over the highlands of Calaveros. But every breath that wanders down the painted aisles of Karnak seems to echo back the sighs of those who perished in the quarry, at the oar, and under the chariot-wheels of the conqueror.

Amelia Edwards and her contemporaries traveled with all the assurance and certainty of visitors who considered their civilization superior to all others. By the late nineteenth century, Egypt was a safe place for even the most unsophisticated traveler. One traveled in a capsule of steamships and luxury hotels, with the bustle and unchanging routine of Egyptian life at arm's distance. The American adventurer and travel writer John Lloyd Stephens made a trip up the Nile in 1826, before his journey to Petra described in Chapter 7. His impressions are typical of many nineteenth-century visitors:

I have heard all manners of opinion expressed in regard to a voyage on the Nile; and may be allowed, perhaps, to give my own. Mrs. S. used frequently to say that, although she had traveled in France, Switzerland, Germany, Italy, and Sicily, she had never enjoyed a journey so much before, and was always afraid that it would end too soon. Another lady's sentiments, expressed in my hearing, were just the contrary. For myself, being alone, and not in very good health, I had some heavy moments; but I have no hesitation in saying that, with a friend, a good boat well fitted up, books, guns, plenty of time, and a cook like Michel, a voyage on the Nile would exceed any traveling within my experience. The perfect freedom from all restraint, and from the conventional trammels of civilized society, form an episode in a man's life that is vastly agreeable and exciting. Think of not shaving for two months, of washing your shirts in the Nile, and wearing them without being ironed. True, these things are not absolutely necessary; but who would go to

Egypt to travel as he does in Europe? "Away with all fantasies and fetters" is the motto of the tourist. We throw aside pretty much everything except our pantaloons; and a generous rivalry in long beards and soiled linen is kept up with exceeding spirit. You may go ashore whenever you like, and stroll through the little villages, and be stared at by the Arabs, or walk along the banks of the river till darkness covers the earth; shooting pigeons, and sometimes pheasants and hares, besides the odd shots from the deck of your boat at geese, crocodiles, and pelicans. And then it is so ridiculously cheap an amusement. You get your boat with ten men for thirty or forty dollars a month, fowls for three piasters (about a shilling) a pair, a sheep for half or three-quarters of a dollar and eggs almost for the asking. You sail under your own country's banner; and, when you walk along the river, if the Arabs look particularly black and truculent, you proudly feel that there is safety in its folds. From time to time you hear that a French or English flag has passed so many days before you, and you meet your fellow-voyagers with a freedom and cordiality which exist nowhere but on the Nile.

These are the little everyday items in the voyage, without referring to the great and interesting objects which are the traveler's principal inducements and rewards, the ruined cities on its banks, the mighty temples and tombs, and all the wonderful monuments of Egypt's departed greatness. Of them I will barely say, that their great antiquity, the mystery that overhangs them, and their extraordinary preservation amid the surrounding desolation, make Egypt perhaps the most interesting country in the world. In the words of an old traveler, "Time sadly overcometh all things, and is now dominant, and sitteth upon a sphinx and looketh into Memphis and old Thebes, while his sister Oblivion reclineth semisominous on a pyramid, gloriously triumphing and turning old glories into dreams. History sinketh beneath her cloud."[7]

Egypt became a popular destination for the package tourist long before jetliners made even remote archaeological sites accessible. The railroad and the steamship brought the Nile within easy reach of European capitals. Hundreds of British visitors passed through Cairo on their way to India via the newly constructed Suez Canal. Then, as now, the remains of the exotic civilization of ancient Egypt exercised a profound fascination on even the casual visitor.

Chapter Nine
Maya and Inca

And when we saw all those towns and villages built in the water, and other great towns on dry land, and that straight and level causeway leading to Mexico, we were astounded. These great towns . . . and buildings rising from the water, all made of stone, seemed like an enchanted vision. . . . Indeed some of our soldiers asked whether it was all not a dream. . . . It was all so wonderful that I do not know how to describe this first glimpse of things never heard of, seen, or dreamed of before.

Bernal Diaz de Castillo
on the Aztec capital, Tenochtitlán

CHAPTER NINE

Maya and Inca

Bernal Diaz de Castillo was a young soldier serving under Hernán Cortés on that memorable day in November 1519 when a small detachment of conquistadors gazed down at the city of Tenochtitlán, the spectacular capital of the Aztec civilization. Diaz wrote these words when he was in his seventies, the experiences of the Spanish conquest etched in his memory so clearly that it was as if they had happened a week before. The conquistadors gaped in amazement at a native American metropolis larger than Seville, then Spain's most populous city, and certainly better planned than many chaotically organized European capitals. Diaz relished his memories, but then added an almost melancholy footnote: "Today all that I then saw is overthrown and destroyed . . . nothing is left standing."

Nothing is left standing. Diaz wrote the literal truth. Today, the architectural, cultural, and material legacy of the Aztecs lies buried under the urban sprawl of Mexico City. Cortés himself hastened the disappearance, ordering the construction of an imposing Catholic cathedral atop the central precincts of Tenochtitlán, where temples to the sun and rain god reeked with the blood of human sacrifice. The conquistadors wandered through an enormous market attended by more than 20,000 people a day. There one could buy gold and tropical feathers, jade and chocolate, every valuable and commodity possible, at the heart of a sprawling city of single-story houses, terraced pyramids, canals, and well-defined ethnic neighborhoods. More than 200,000 people lived in Tenochtitlán in 1519. Two years later, the city was a smoking ruin. Within a century, the native population of the former Aztec domains was less than a fifth of what it had been a century earlier. Measles, smallpox, and other infectious diseases decimated the people. The population of the Basin of Mexico declined from an estimated 1.5 million to about 325,000 between 1519 and 1570. By that point, it was almost as if Aztec civilization had never existed.

Those who had survived had been forcibly converted to Catholicism—the old beliefs, customs, and oral traditions destroyed by church decree.

The Almost-forgotten Maya

Cortés had first made landfall near Cozumel on the Yucatán Peninsula before fighting and sailing his way on to Veracruz, the base for his journey into the highlands to the west. There he found a marooned Spaniard, Jeronimo de Aguilar, who had traveled for eight years among the local Maya people and learned their language. The Maya lived in villages and ceremonial centers adorned with pyramids, but the conquistadors soon lost interest in the villages when they discovered that the few gold objects in the temples came from the highlands. The lack of precious metals in the steamy Maya lowlands condemned the region to becoming a poor colonial backwater, but the people did not escape the reach of the Catholic Church. The process of conversion began with the arrival of Franciscan friars in 1545–1549, among them an austere zealous missionary, Diego de Landa. The friars found themselves surrounded by an abundance of impressive ceremonial centers and lavishly adorned temples, evidence of rich religious traditions. Landa was a strange contradiction. On the one hand, he forcibly converted entire villages and tortured backsliders. On the other, he displayed a lively interest in ancient Maya sites and institutions. He was, in a sense, Central America's first archaeological traveler. "There are in Yucatan," he wrote, "many beautiful buildings. . . . They are all of stone very well hewn, although there is no metal in this country with which they could have worked." He went on to add perceptively: "These buildings have not been constructed by other nations than the Indians; and this is seen from the naked stone men made modest by long girdles which they called in their language *ex* as well as from other devices which the Indians wear."[1] Landa traveled to several sites, among them Izamal, east of Merida, where the temples were being quarried for building stone. He also studied Maya codices, which he called "lies of the devil" and destroyed by the dozen with such efficiency that only four survive. Nevertheless, Landa also studied the intricate Maya script and managed to decipher several glyphs with some accuracy.

Diego de Landa's travels lay forgotten in the Franciscan archives at Merida until 1864. By then, the ancient Maya had vanished into oblivion. Their great ceremonial centers and temples disappeared under dense forest. Only the occasional priest or government official stumbled across "curious stone houses" near remote colonial settlements. It was not until 1773 that an artillery officer, Captain Antonio del Rio, accompanied by an artist traveled deep into the rain forest from what is now Guatemala City. He hacked his way through dense brush and trees to the Maya city at Palenque, where the undergrowth was so thick that people were invisible a mere two meters away. Rio rounded up 79 local Maya and set them to work clearing brush from the ruins. Two weeks later, he stood in the midst of a complicated maze of rooms and courtyards. Nearby was what he called a palace, its walls covered with "uncouth" stucco decoration. He returned to base with a handful of artifacts and some drawings, and wrote a report that was forwarded to the royal archives in Spain. The document languished, until by chance a copy traveled to England and was published in 1822—to a deafening critical silence.

For more than three centuries, Maya civilization remained where the ecclesiastical authorities of sixteenth-century Mexico had intended it to be—in near physical and intellectual obscurity. The same was true of Aztec civilization, its major temples buried under the streets of Mexico City. Only the spectacular ruins of nearby Teotihuacán, with its vast pyramids of the Sun and Moon, attracted the attention of the occasional European visitor, who reported that the local Indians still revered the site. Built by an earlier civilization, Teotihuacán was the place where the Aztecs

9-1 The pyramid of the Sun at Teotihuacán, Mexico—one of the great cities of ancient Mesoamerica—lies on one side of the so-called Avenue of the Dead, lined by nobles' houses.

believed their world and cosmos came into being, a belief that lingered long after the conquest.

John Lloyd Stephens Reveals the Maya

The 1830s and 1840s were a time of fervent archaeological discovery and adventure, a time numerous long-vanished civilizations still awaited discovery. These were the years when the Frenchman Emile Botta and the Englishman Austen Henry Layard unearthed the biblical Assyrians—and when a New York lawyer turned traveler, John Lloyd Stephens, became a best-selling travel writer because of his journeys to Russia and Egypt, and, above all, because of his lyrical descriptions of Petra.

Stephens returned to New York in 1837, where he met a Scottish artist, Frederick Catherwood, who shared his passion for ancient civilizations. Catherwood shared with him rumors—then circulating in New York and European capitals—of lost cities in the Central American rain forest. The rumors were little more than will-o'-the-wisps based on the travels of a handful of people who had followed Rio, among them an intrepid Frenchman, Guillermo Dupaix, who visited Palenque and other nearby sites in 1804. His reports were ignored. So were those of Juan Galindo, a politician appointed governor of the Petén, who reached not only Palenque, but the overgrown city of Copán as well, where he admired plazas, pyramids, and grotesque human figures carved on stelae. His reports were ignored in academic circles, partly because of his extravagant claims that hailed Guatemala as the center of an early civilization, and also for the simple reason that no one was interested.

Both Dupaix and Galindo were travelers rather than archaeologists. So was another delightfully eccentric character, Jean Frédéric Waldeck, artist, socialite, and amateur archaeologist, who spent weeks sketching glyphs and reliefs at Palenque in 1832. Perennially short of money, Waldeck later traveled to Uxmal in the northern Yucatán before leaving Mexico and writing a short book about his experiences, which titillated rather than informed:

> Prior to my expedition, the ruins of Uxmal had been visited only by the owners of the neighboring farm, worthy people for whom a shattered city is not more than a quarry for building materials; but these ruins . . . are the remains of a powerful city, comparable in size with our greatest European capitals. . . . The structures . . . at Uxmal are of colossal dimensions, and are all constructed of dressed stone. Four great principal buildings, separated by open spaces, enclose an area of 57,672 square feet.[2]

Poor Waldeck! His book was far from a commercial success and laid a polite academic egg. Like all of his other schemes to get rich, his efforts to cash in on the Maya failed. His only major achievement in life was to live to an advanced age; he was said to be 109 when he died. Contrary to his hopes, only a few Spanish intellectuals from Europe or Mexico City had more than a passing interest.

Such, then, were the meager clues that Stephens and Catherwood had to work with when they set off on their journey to the Yucatán in 1839. Stephens used his impressive political connections to wrangle an appointment as American chargé d'affaires in Central America to give his expedition legitimacy. For the first time, truly experienced archaeological travelers would explore Maya civilization: a gifted writer and a brilliantly talented artist, both of them well known to large public audiences. They returned to New York ten months later, after traveling more than 2,000 kilometers through the rain forests of the Yucatán. *Incidents of Travel in Central America, Chiapas, and Yucatan* appeared in 1841 to rapturous acclaim. More than twenty thousand copies were sold in the first few months, an astounding number for the time. In what would be regarded as a classic of archaeological travel writing, John Lloyd Stephens revealed the glories of Maya civilization to an astounded world.

The two men sailed for Belize and traveled with five mules through rough country to the remote village of Copán, where they saw well-preserved walls across the river. The next day, they explored a vast, overgrown Maya city, silent except for monkeys moving through the tops of the trees. Stephens was moved to profound eloquence in one of the most memorable pieces of all archaeological travel writing:

> With an interest perhaps stronger than we had ever felt in wandering among the ruins of Egypt, we followed our guide, who, sometimes missing his way, with a constant and vigorous use of his machete conducted us through the thick forest, among half-buried fragments, to fourteen more monuments of the same character and appearance, some with more elegant designs, and some in workmanship equal to the finest monuments of the Egyptians. One, we found, had been displaced from its pedestal by enormous roots; another, locked in the close embrace of branches of trees, was almost lifted out of the earth; and still another had been hurled to the ground and bound down by huge vines and creepers. One with its altar before it stood in a grove of trees which grew around it, seemingly to shade and shroud it as a sacred thing; in the solemn stillness of the woods, it seemed a divinity mourning over a fallen people. The only sounds that disturbed the quiet of this buried city were the noise of monkeys moving among the tops of the trees and the cracking of dry branches broken by their weight. They moved over our heads in long and swift processions, forty or fifty at a time. Some with little ones wound in their long arms

walked out to the end of boughs and, holding on with their hind feet or a curl of the tail, sprang to a branch of the next tree; with a noise like a current of wind, they passed on into the depths of the forest. It was the first time we had seen these mockeries of humanity and, amid these strange monuments, they seemed like wandering spirits of the departed race guarding the ruins of their former habitations.

We returned to the base of the pyramidal structure and ascended by regular stone steps, which in some places had been forced apart by bushes and saplings and in others thrown down by the growth of large trees. In parts they were ornamented with sculptured figures and rows of death's heads. Climbing over the ruined top, we reached a terrace overgrown with trees and, crossing it, descended by stone steps into an area so covered with trees that at first we could not make out its form. When the machete had cleared the way, we saw that it was a square with steps on all the sides almost as perfect as those of the Roman amphitheatre. The steps were ornamented with sculpture, and on the south side, about halfway up, forced out of its place by roots, was a colossal head, again evidently a portrait. We ascended these steps and reached a broad terrace a hundred feet high overlooking the river and supported by the wall which we had seen from the opposite bank. The whole terrace was covered with trees, and even at this height were two gigantic ceibas (kapok trees), over twenty feet in circumference; their half-naked roots extended fifty or a hundred feet around, binding down the ruins and shading them with their wide-spreading branches.

We sat down on the very edge of the wall and strove in vain to penetrate the mystery by which we were surrounded. Who were the people that built this city? In the ruined cities of Egypt, even in the long-lost Petra, the stranger knows the story of the people whose vestiges he finds around him. America, say historians, was peopled by savages; but savages never reared these structures, savages never carved these stones. When we asked the Indians who had made them, their dull answer was "Quién sabe? (Who knows?)" There were no associations connected with this place, none of those stirring recollections which hallow Rome, Athens, and "The world's great mistress on the Egyptian plain." But architecture, sculpture, and painting, all the arts which embellish life, had flourished in this overgrown forest; orators, warriors, and statesmen, beauty, ambition, and glory had lived and passed away, and none knew that such things had been, or could tell of their past existence. Books, the records of knowledge, are silent on this theme.

The city was desolate. No remnant of this race hangs round the ruins, with traditions handed down from father to son and from generation to generation. It lay before us like a shattered bark in the midst of the ocean, her masts gone, her name effaced, her crew perished, and none to tell whence she came, to whom she belonged, how long on her voyage, or what caused her destruction—her lost people to be traced only by some fancied resemblance in the construction of the vessel, and, perhaps, never to be known at all. The place where we were sitting, was it a citadel from which an unknown people had sounded the trumpet of war? or a temple for the worship of the God of peace? or did the inhabitants worship idols made with their own hands and offer sacrifices on the stones before them? All was mystery, dark, impenetrable mystery, and every circumstance increased it. In Egypt the colossal skeletons of gigantic temples stand in unwatered sands in all the nakedness of desolation; but here an immense forest shrouds the ruins, hiding them from sight, heightening the impression and moral effect, and giving an intensity and almost wildness to the interest. . . .

Of the moral effect of the monuments themselves, standing as they do in the depths of a tropical forest, silent and solemn, strange in design, excellent in sculpture, rich in ornament, different from the works of any other people, their uses and purposes and whole history so entirely unknown, with hieroglyphics explaining all but being perfectly unintelligible, I shall not pretend to convey any idea. Often the imagination was pained in gazing at them. The tone which pervades the ruins is that of deep solemnity. An imaginative mind might be infected with superstitious feelings. From constantly calling them by that name in our intercourse with the Indians, we regarded these solemn memorials as idols—deified kings and heroes—objects of adoration and ceremonial worship. We did not find on either the monuments or sculptured fragments any delineations of human, or, in fact, any other kind of sacrifice, but we had no doubt that the large sculptured stone invariably found before each idol had been employed as a sacrificial altar. The form of sculpture most frequently met with was a death's head, sometimes the principal ornament and sometimes only accessory. There were whole rows of them on the outer wall, adding gloom to the mystery of the place, keeping death and the grave before the eyes of the living, presenting the idea of a holy city—the Mecca or Jerusalem of an unknown people.

In regard to the age of this desolate city I shall not at present offer any conjecture. Some idea might perhaps be formed from the accumulations of earth and the gigantic trees growing on the top of the ruined structures, but it would be uncertain and unsatisfactory. Nor shall I at this moment offer any conjecture in regard to the people who built it; or to the time when or the means by which it was depopulated to become a desolation and ruin; or as to whether it fell by the sword, or famine, or pestilence. The trees which shroud it may have sprung from the blood of its slaughtered inhabitants; they may have perished howling with hunger; or pestilence, like the cholera, may have piled its streets with the dead and driven forever the feeble remnants from their homes. Of such dire calamities to other cities we have authentic accounts, in eras both prior and subsequent to the discovery of the country by the Spaniards. One thing I believe: its history is graven on its monuments. No Champollion has yet brought to them the energies of his inquiring mind. Who shall read them?

Chaos of ruins! who shall trace the void,
O'er the dim fragments cast a lunar light,
And say "here was or is," where all is doubly night?[3]

From Copán, the two friends traveled to Guatemala City, and eventually traveled overland northeastward for more than 1,000 kilometers to Palenque over dirt trails and forest paths through the heart of country controlled by rebel bands. Palenque also cast a memorable spell, but Stephens's account gives us telling insights into the rough conditions suffered by the early rain forest traveler. There were no layered waterproof jackets, no anti-malaria pills or insect repellents. Most of the time, you ate what the local people ate. For days on end you suffered from fever and usually emerged from the forest emaciated and weak. Here is Stephens's recounting of conditions at Palenque, and of magical moments with fireflies:

> We had reached the end of our long and toilsome journey, and the first glance indemnified us for our toil. For the first time we were in a building erected by the aboriginal inhabitants, standing before the Europeans knew of the existence of this continent, and we prepared to take up our abode under its roof. We selected the front corridor as our dwelling, turned turkey and fowls loose in the courtyard, which was so overgrown with trees that we could barely see across it; and as there was no pasture for the mules except the leaves of the trees, and we could not turn them loose into the woods, we brought them up the steps through the palace, and turned them into the courtyard also. At one end of the corridor Juan built a kitchen, which operation consisted in laying three stones anglewise, so as to have room for a fire between them. Our luggage was stowed away or hung on poles reaching across the corridor. Pawling mounted a stone about four feet long on stone legs for a table, and with the Indians cut a number of poles, which they fastened together with bark strings, and laid them on stones at the head and foot for beds. We cut down the branches that entered the palace, and some of the trees on the terrace, and from the floor of the palace overlooked the top of an immense forest stretching off to the Gulf of Mexico. . . .
>
> While we were making our observations, Juan was engaged in a business that his soul loved. As with all the mozos of that country, it was his pride and ambition to servir a mano. He scorned the manly occupation of a muleteer, and aspired to that of a menial servant. He was anxious to be left at the village, and did not like the idea of stopping at the ruins, but was reconciled to it by being allowed to devote himself exclusively to cookery. At four o'clock we sat down to our first dinner. The tablecloth was two broad leaves, each about two feet long, plucked from a tree on the terrace before the door. Our saltcellar stood like a pyramid, being a case made of husks of corn put together lengthwise, and holding four or five pounds, in lumps from the size of a pea to that of a hen's egg. Juan was as happy as if he had prepared the dinner exclusively for his own eating; and all went merry as a marriage-bell, when the sky became overcast, and a sharp thunder-clap heralded the afternoon's storm. From the elevation of the terrace, the floor of the palace commanded a view of the top of the forest, and we could see the trees bent down by the force of the wind; very soon a fierce blast swept through the open doors, which was followed instantaneously by heavy rain. The table was cleared by the wind, and, before we could make our escape, was drenched by the rain. We snatched away our plates, and finished our meal as we could.

The rain continued, with heavy thunder and lighting, all the afternoon. In the absolute necessity of taking up our abode among the ruins, we had hardly thought of our exposure to the elements until it was forced upon us. At night we could not light a candle, but the darkness of the palace was lighted up by fireflies of extraordinary size and brilliancy, shooting through the corridors and stationary on the walls, forming a beautiful and striking spectacle. They were of the description with those we saw at Nopa, known by the name of shining beetles, and are mentioned by the early Spaniards, among the wonders of a world where all was new, "as showing the way to those who travel at night." The historian describes them as "somewhat smaller than Sparrows, having two stars close by their Eyes, and two more under their Wings, which gave so great a Light that by it they could spin, weave, write, and paint; and the Spaniards went by night to hunt the Utios or little Rabbits of that country; and a-fishing, carrying these Animals tied to their great Toes or Thumbs: and they called them Locuyos, being also of use to save them from the Gnats, which are there very troublesome. They took them in the Night with Firebrands, because they made to the Light, and came when called by their Name; and they are so unwieldy that when they fall they cannot rise again; and the Men stroaking their Faces and Hands with a sort of Moisture that is in those Stars, seemed to be afire as long as it lasted."

It always gave us high pleasure to realize the romantic and seemingly half-fabulous accounts of the chroniclers of the conquest. Very often we found their quaint descriptions so vivid and faithful as to infuse the spirit that breathed through their pages. We caught several of these beetles, not, however, by calling them by their names, but with a hat, as schoolboys used to catch fireflies, or, less poetically, lightning-bugs, at home. They are more than half an inch long, and have a sharp movable horn on the head; when laid on the back they cannot turn over except by pressing this horn against a membrane upon the front. Behind the eyes are two round transparent substances full of luminous matter, about as large as the head of a pin, and underneath is a larger membrane containing the same luminous substance. Four of them together threw a brilliant light for several yards around, and by the light of a single one we read distinctly the finely-printed pages of an American newspaper. It was one of a packet, full of debates in Congress, which I had as yet barely glanced over, and it seemed stranger than any incident of my journey to be reading by the light of beetles, in the ruined palace of Palenque, the sayings and doings of great men at home. In the midst of it Mr. Catherwood, in emptying the capacious pocket of a shooting-jacket, handed me a Broadway omnibus ticket:

"Good to the bearer for a ride,

"A. Brower."

These things brought up vivid recollections of home, and among the familiar images present were the good beds into which our friends were about that time turning. Ours were set up in the back corridor, fronting the courtyard. This corridor consisted of open doors and pilasters alternately. The wind and rain were sweeping through, and, unfortunately, our beds were not out of reach of the spray.

They had been set up with some labour on four piles of stones each, and we could not then change their position. We had no spare articles to put up as screens; but, happily, two umbrellas, tied up with measuring rods and wrapped in a piece of matting, had survived the wreck of the mountain-roads. These Mr. C. and I secured at the head of our beds. Pawling swung a hammock across the corridor so high that the sweep of the rain only touched the foot; and so passed our first night at Palenque. In the morning, umbrellas, bedclothes, wearing apparel, and hammocks were wet through, and there was not a dry place to stand on. Already we considered ourselves booked for a rheumatism. We had looked to our residence at Palenque as the end of troubles, and for comfort and pleasure, but all we could do was to change the location of our beds to places which promised a better shelter for the next night.

A good breakfast would have done much to restore our equanimity; but, unhappily, we found that the tortillas which we had brought out the day before, probably made of half-mouldy corn, by the excessive dampness were matted together, sour, and spoiled. We went through our beans, eggs, and chocolate without any substitute for bread, and, as often before in time of trouble, composed ourselves with a cigar. Blessed be the man who invented smoking, the soother and composer of a troubled spirit, allayer of angry passions, a comfort under the loss of breakfast. . . .

In regard to the extent of these ruins. Even in this practical age the imagination of man delights in wonders. The Indians and the people of Palenque say that they cover a space of sixty miles; in a series of well-written articles in our own country they have been set down as ten times larger than New York; and lately I have seen an article in some of the newspapers, referring to our expedition, which represents this city, *discovered* by us, as having been three times as large as London! It is not in my nature to discredit any marvellous story. I am slow to disbelieve, and would rather sustain all such inventions; but it has been my unhappy lot to find marvels fade away as I approached them; even the Dead Sea lost its mysterious charm; and besides, as a traveller and "writer of a book," I know that if I go wrong, those who come after me will not fail to set me right. Under these considerations, not from any wish of my own, and with many thanks to my friends of the press, I am obliged to say that the Indians and people of Palenque really know nothing of the ruins personally, and the other accounts do not rest upon any sufficient foundation. . . .

I repeat what I stated in the beginning, there may be more buildings, but, after a close examination of the vague reports current in the village, we are satisfied that no more have ever been discovered; and from repeated inquiries of Indians who had traversed the forest in every direction in the dry season, we are induced to believe that no more exist. The whole extent of ground covered by those as yet known, as appears by the plan, is not larger than our Park or Battery. In stating this fact I am very far from wishing to detract from the importance or interest of the subject. I give our opinion, with the grounds of it, and the reader will judge for himself how far these are entitled to consideration. It is proper to add, however, that, considering the space now occupied by the ruins as the site of palaces, temples, and public buildings, and supposing the houses of the inhabitants to have been, like those of the Egyptians and the present race of Indians, of frail and perishable materials, and, as at Memphis and Thebes, to have disappeared altogether, the city may have covered an immense extent.

There was no necessity for assigning to the ruined city an immense extent, or an antiquity coeval with that of the Egyptians or of any other ancient and known people. What we had before our eyes was grand, curious, and remarkable enough. Here were the remains of a cultivated, polished, and peculiar people, who had passed through all the stages incident to the rise and fall of nations; reached their golden age, and perished, entirely unknown. The links which connected them with the human family were severed and lost, and these were the only memorials of their footsteps upon earth. We lived in the ruined palace of their kings; we went up to their desolate temples and fallen altars; and wherever we moved we saw the evidences of their taste, their skill in arts, their wealth and power. In the midst of desolation and ruin we looked back to the past, cleared away the gloomy forest, and fancied every building perfect, with its terraces and pyramids, its sculptured and painted ornaments, grand, lofty, and imposing, and overlooking an immense inhabited plain; we called back into life the strange people who gazed at us in sadness from the walls; pictured them, in fanciful costumes and adorned with plumes of feathers, ascending the terraces of the palace and the steps leading to the temples; and often we imagined a scene of unique and gorgeous beauty and magnificence, realizing the creations of Oriental poets, the very spot which fancy would have selected for the "Happy Valley" of Rasselas. In the romance of the world's history nothing ever impressed me more forcibly than the spectacle of this once great and lovely city, overturned, desolate, and lost; discovered by accident, overgrown with trees for miles around, and without even a name to distinguish it. Apart from everything else, it was a mourning witness to the world's mutations.[4]

Copán and Palenque are among the largest and most imposing of Maya cities, something quite unexpected deep in dense tropical wilderness inhabited by peasant villagers. Like many of his contemporaries, Stephens could have attributed the ruins to the ancient Egyptians or some other foreign civilization and few people would have argued with him. But, like many perceptive travelers, Stephens looked closely at local culture and decided that the cities were built by the Maya. All subsequent research on the ancient Maya has been based on this logical assumption.

There is, then, no resemblance in these remains to those of the Egyptians; and, failing here, we look elsewhere in vain. They are different from the works of any other known people, of a new order, and entirely and absolutely anomalous: they stand alone.

I invite to this subject the special attention of those familiar with the arts of other countries; for, unless I am wrong, we have a conclusion far more interesting and wonderful than that of connecting the builders of these cities with the Egyptians or any other people. It is the spectacle of a people skilled in architecture, sculpture, and drawing, and, beyond doubt, other more perishable arts, and possessing the cultivation and refinement attendant upon these, not derived from the Old World, but originating and growing up here, without models or masters, having a distinct, separate, independent existence; like the plants and fruits of the soil, indigenous. . . .

It perhaps destroys much of the interest that hangs over these ruins to assign to them a modern date; but we live in an age whose spirit is to discard phantasms and arrive at truth, and the interest lost in one particular is supplied in another scarcely inferior; for, the nearer we can bring the builders of these cities to our own times, the greater is our chance of knowing all. Throughout the country the convents are rich in manuscripts and documents written by the early fathers, caciques, and Indians, who very soon acquired the knowledge of Spanish and the art of writing. These have never been examined with the slightest reference to this subject; and I cannot help thinking that some precious memorial is now mouldering in the library of a neighbouring convent, which would determine the history of some one of these ruined cities; moreover, I cannot help believing that the tablets of hieroglyphics will yet be read. No strong curiosity has hitherto been directed to them; vigour and acuteness of intellect, knowledge and learning, have never been expended upon them. For centuries the hieroglyphics of Egypt were inscrutable, and, though not perhaps in our day, I feel persuaded that a key surer than that of the Rosetta stone will be discovered. And if only three centuries have elapsed since any one of these unknown cities was inhabited, the race of the inhabitants is not extinct. Their descendants are still in the land, scattered, perhaps, and retired, like our own Indians, into wildernesses which have never yet been penetrated by a white man, but not lost; living as their fathers did, erecting the same buildings of "lime and stone," "with ornaments of sculpture and plastered," "large courts," and "lofty towers with high ranges of steps," and still carving on tablets of stone the same mysterious hieroglyphics. If, in consideration that I have not often indulged in speculative conjecture, the reader will allow one flight, I turn to that vast and unknown region, untraversed by a single road, wherein fancy pictures that mysterious city seen from the topmost range of the Cordilleras, of unconquered, unvisited, and unsought aboriginal inhabitants.

In conclusion, I am at a loss to determine which would be the greatest enterprise, an attempt to reach this mysterious city, to decipher the tablets of hieroglyphics, or to wade through the accumulated manuscripts of three centuries in the libraries of the convents.

Stephens and Catherwood returned on a second trip to Maya country in 1841, visiting Uxmal and Chichén Itzá in the northeastern Yucatán, where Stephens described the ball courts and the ancient game played in them. His second best-seller on the Maya, *Incidents of Travel in Yucatan*, appeared in 1843. In it, he reaffirmed his belief that Maya civilization was an indigenous development. "I leave them with all their mystery around them," he wrote, setting the stage for contemporary Maya research. Unfortunately, Stephens himself never returned to the Maya lowlands. He died of complications from tropical fever while involved in a project to build a trans-Panama railroad in 1852.

The *Incidents* books appeared in print as the New England historian William Prescott was writing one of the immortal books of American history, *The Conquest of Mexico*, which appeared in 1843. His account of the Spanish conquest read like a romantic, swashbuckling adventure, but was also remarkable for its generally accurate accounts of the Aztecs, the Maya, and other early indigenous American societies. Prescott based some of his material on Stephens's travels.

For decades after Stephens and Catherwood's journeys, the Maya lowlands remained off the beaten track even for serious visitors. Political uncertainties, distrustful local officials, and the logistical difficulties of rain forest travel tended to deter casual tourists until well into the twentieth century. But the spell that the Maya cast over John Lloyd Stephens echoes in his writings. Scrambling between ancient foundations and monkeys moving overhead in the dry branches, Stephens, in few words, described

9-2 Like the Maya ruins at Copán in Honduras, or Tikal in Guatemala, Tulum, Mexico is now a popular destination for travelers, partly because of its scenic location on the east coast of the Yucatán peninsula.

the essence of a lost city overgrown by clinging forest. Today, Copán—lovingly restored, with the grass and forest cut back—receives thousands of visitors a year. It is more difficult to evoke the spirit of its former inhabitants. If you look far enough and wander off well-worn paths, you can still experience a deserted Maya city as it must have appeared to pioneering explorers. Some years ago, I was lucky enough to visit a virtually unexplored site, Naranjo, in Guatemala's Petén in the southern Yucatán, near the well-known city of Tikal. Like Copán, Naranjo lay silent, its pyramids and plazas masked under a dense canopy of branches. We climbed the overgrown steps of a pyramid, slipping and sliding on the dusty slopes. Suddenly, we emerged into bright sunlight, above the forest canopy, looking across a sea of green foliage. The experience was eerily reminiscent of John Lloyd Stephens's experience of Copán, except that there were no longer monkeys moving overhead.

Ephraim Squier and Inca Civilization

It was not long before sunset, when the van of the royal procession entered the gates of the city. . . . Elevated high above his vassals came the Inca Atahualpa, borne on a sedan or open litter, on which was a sort of throne made of massive gold of inestimable value. The palanquin was lined with the richly colored plumes of tropical birds, and studded with shining plates of gold and silver. . . . The bearing of the Inca was sedate and dignified, and from his lofty station he looked down on the multitudes below with an air of composure, like one accustomed to command.[5]

Drawing on eyewitness Spanish accounts, the historian William Prescott vividly recreated the Inca Atahualpa's entrance into Cajamarca, Peru, in November 1532. Here, Atahualpa met face-to-face with Francisco Pizarro and his motley band of conquistadors. Seven months later, Pizarro killed Atahualpa and soon afterward laid waste to the Inca capital at Cuzco, high in the Andes. Within less than half a century, one of native America's greatest civilizations had effectively vanished, remembered only by elderly survivors, and by the network of dirt and stone roads that once linked every corner of the huge Inca empire. Unlike the Aztec, whose material legacy soon dissolved, the Inca left ample signs of their once great power—densely terraced hillsides on steep mountainsides from Bolivia to Ecuador, the jigsawlike patterns of their enduring masonry at Cuzco and elsewhere. But as their cultures melted into historical obscurity, their rich history was kept alive by a handful of native chronicles and contemporary histories.

Many early travelers visited Inca country and Lake Titicaca, among them the priest Bernabe Cobo (1583–1657), who in 1616 visited the Island of the Sun in the lake, one of the most sacred places in the Andean universe, the place where the sun god Viracocha created the Inca world. Cobo wrote:

> The Inca had many buildings constructed in order to enlarge and lend more authority to this shrine. The former temple was augmented with new and impressive buildings. In addition, it was ordered that other buildings be constructed for other purposes; these included a convent for *mamaconas* [chosen women] which was placed here, many magnificent lodgings and rooms to serve as a dwelling place for the priest and attendants, and one quarter of a league before one reaches the temple, there was an impressive *tambo* or inn for the pilgrims to stay in. . . . The ruins of these storehouses remain to this day, and I have seen them myself.[6]

The Boston historian William Prescott brought Inca civilization to international attention with the publication of his *History of the Conquest of Peru* in 1847. Like his Mexico volume, *Peru* rapidly became a best-seller, written like a lush, romantic adventure story. But the Andes were remote of access for most travelers, and U.S. visitors to South America in particular were either diplomats or transitory sightseers sailing down the coast. Thus it was that Ephraim Squier, archaeologist, diplomat, and journalist, journeyed through Inca domains in 1864–1865. Squier was a man of many parts and an ardent traveler. He began his career as a journalist in Connecticut and Ohio. While still in his twenties, a "mere youth," as he admitted, Squier collaborated with the physician Edwin Davis on an archaeological survey of the ancient mounds and earthworks of the Midwest. *Ancient Monuments of the Mississippi Valley* was published by the Smithsonian Institution in 1847 and was the first systematic description of these important, and at the time little understood, sites. Many of the earthworks described by Squier and Davis have now vanished, so their research conducted "with limited resources but an earnest purpose" are of inestimable value today.

Squier's mound-builder research brought him to the attention of William Prescott, and the two men became friends. Prescott used his considerable influence to secure a diplomatic appointment for his protégé. Squier duly became United States Commissioner to Peru from 1863 to 1865. He was charged with settling various reparations claims between the United States and the adolescent nation of Peru, a task that he completed promptly while taking what he called a "change of scene and occupation" when threatened by blindness that was brought about by job stress. The cure was rapid and complete. He discharged his obligations in a mere six months, then embarked on an ambitious eighteen-month journey in search of sites and other traces of the Andean past. His travels took him to the Inca shrine at Pachamacac south of Lima, to the great Chimu capital at Chan Chan, and to the Moche Valley, now well known for the spectacular burials of the warrior priests of Sipán in the nearby Lambayeque Valley. While on the north coast of Peru, Squier observed the remarkable abundance of the anchovy fishery that had sustained the ancient Moche and Chan Chan. He saw men and women using baskets to scoop up thousands of the small fish.

From the north coast, Squier traveled high in the Andes foothills, traveling the length of highland Peru southward to the heart of the ancient Inca empire, and as far south as the shores of Lake Titicaca. There he admired the spectacular ruins of Tiwanaku, the "Stonehenge of America," with its exotic Gateway of the Sun God, and the Akapana temple with its terraces and sunken courts. A visitor in A.D. 650 would have marveled at a city of palaces, plazas, and brightly colored temples shimmering with gold-covered bas-reliefs that reflected the bright sunlight. Tiwanaku was a shrine to the sun god Viracocha, personified by the city's rulers. Each rainy season, water would cascade out of the sunken court of the Akapana onto the surrounding terraces and into the temple, then into a moat that surrounded the ceremonial precincts. For much of the first millennium A.D., the powerful but anonymous rulers of the city created a trading empire based on Tiwanaku that stretched from the highlands and Lake Titicaca to the deserts of Peru's south coast. Their capital was a prosperous city, fed by many hectares of irrigated fields, a trading center, and an important shrine devoted to the sun god Viracocha. The central precincts, with their high platform and sunken courts, commemorated the power of the god and Tiwanaku's conquest of surrounding, lesser kingdoms. This remarkable state and its capital collapsed in about A.D. 1000, in part because of drought conditions around Lake Titicaca.

From Tiwanaku, Squier journeyed to Cuzco, then a little-known highland town, where he described the remains of the Temple of the Sun, the fine Inca masonry, and the brooding Sachsahuaman fortress. The fort is famous for its superb Inca masonry, huge blocks fitted together so tightly that a business card will often not slide into the joins. Squier also visited the Ollantaytambo fortress, a massive citadel and sacred place with a sun temple constructed of huge boulders and monoliths. At every turn, he described not only minute details of Inca sites and their superb masonry—details that were better preserved than they are today—but also the challenges and hazards of traveling by horse and mule in arduous terrain. Squier's archaeological explorations were no picnic: they required resourcefulness, a good measure of courage, and a sense of humor. His description of the Inca rope bridge over the Apurimac River epitomizes the unique challenges of nineteenth-century archaeological discovery in remote lands.

High mountain-ranges and broad and frigid deserts, swept by fierce, cold winds, are not the sole obstacles to intercommunication in the Altos of Peru, and among those snow-crowned monarchs of the Andes and Cordilleras. There are deep valleys, gorges, and ravines among these mountains, or cut deep in the plains that alternate with them, in which flow swelling rivers or rapid torrents, fed by the melting snows in the dry season, and swollen by the rains in the wet season. They are often unfordable; but still they must somehow be passed by the traveller. A few bridges of stone were constructed by the Spaniards, some after the Conquest, and a few others have been erected by their descendants; but, as a rule, the rivers and mountain torrents are passed to-day by the aid of devices the same as were resorted to by the Incas, and at points which they selected. Had the principle of the arch been well understood by the ancient inhabitants, who have left some of the finest stone-cutting and masonry to be found in the world, there is no doubt the interior of Peru would have abounded in bridges rivalling those of Rome in extent and beauty. As it was, occupying a country destitute of timber, they resorted to suspension-bridges, no doubt precisely like those now constructed by their descendants and successors—bridges formed of cables of braided withes, stretched from bank to bank, and called *puentes de mimbres* (bridges of withes). Where the banks are high, or where the streams are compressed between steep or precipitous rocks, these cables are anchored to piers of stone. In other places they are approached by inclined causeways, raised to give them the necessary elevation above the water. Three or four cables form the floor and the principal support of the bridge, over which small sticks, sometimes only sections of cane or bamboo, are laid transversely, and fastened to the cables by vines, cords, or thongs of raw hide. Two smaller cables are sometimes stretched on each side, as a guard or hand-rail. Over these frail and swaying structures pass men and animals, the latter frequently with their loads on their backs.

Each bridge is usually kept up by the municipality of the nearest village; and as it requires renewal every two or three years, the Indians are obliged at stated periods to bring to the spot a certain number of withes of peculiar kinds of tough wood, generally of that variety called ioke, which are braided by experts, and then stretched across the stream or river by the united exertions of the inhabitants. Some of the larger and most important structures of this kind are kept up by the Government, and all passengers and merchandise pay a fixed toll. Such is the case with the great bridge over the Apurimac, on the main road from the ancient Guamanga (now Ayacucho) to Cuzco.

The Apurimac is one of the head-waters of the Amazon, a large and rapid stream, flowing in a deep valley, or, rather, gigantic ravine, shut in by high and precipitous mountains. Throughout its length it is crossed at only a single point, between two enormous cliffs, which rise dizzily on both sides, and from the summits of which the traveller looks down into a dark gulf. At the bottom gleams a white line of water, whence struggles up a dull but heavy roar, giving to the river its name, *Apu-rimac*, signifying, in the Quichua tongue, "the great speaker." From above, the bridge, looking like a mere thread, is reached by a path which on one side traces a thin, white line on the face of the mountain, and down which the boldest traveller may hesitate to venture. This path, on the other side, at once disappears from a rocky shelf, where there is just room enough to hold the hut of the bridge-keeper, and then runs through a dark tunnel cut in the rock, from which it emerges to trace its line of many a steep and weary zigzag up the face of the mountain. It is usual for the traveller to time his day's journey so as to reach this bridge in the morning, before the strong wind sets in; for, during the greater part of the day, it sweeps up the cañon of the Apurimac with great force, and then the bridge sways like a gigantic hammock, and crossing is next to impossible.

It was a memorable incident in my travelling experiences, the crossing of this great swinging bridge of the Apurimac. I shall never forget it, even if it were not associated with a circumstance which, for the time, gave me much uneasiness and pain. The fame of the bridge over the Apurimac is coextensive with Peru, and every one we met who had crossed it was full of frightful reminiscences of his passage: how the frail structure swayed at a dizzy height between gigantic cliffs over a dark abyss, filled with the deep, hoarse roar of the river, and how his eyes grew dim, his heart grew faint, and his feet unsteady as he struggled across it, not daring to cast a look on either hand.

Our road to the bridge was circuitous and precipitous, leading down the steeper side of the ridge of La Banca, where it seemed hardly possible for a goat to find foothold. It was a succession of abrupt zigzags, here and there interrupted by a stretch of horizontal pathway. To see our cavalcade it was necessary to look up or down, not before or behind. It was like descending the coils of a flattened corkscrew. In places the rocks encroached on the trail, so that it was necessary to crouch low on the saddle-bow to pass beneath them, or else throw the weight of the body upon the stirrup overhanging the declivity of the mountain, to avoid a collision. The most dangerous parts, however, were where land-slips had occurred, and where it was impossible to construct a pathway not liable at any moment to glide away beneath the feet of our animals. The gorge narrowed as we descended, until it was literally shut in by precipices of stratified rock strangely contorted; while huge masses of stone, rent and splintered as from some terrible convulsion of nature, rose sheer before us, apparently preventing all exit from the sunless and threatening ravine, at the bottom of which a considerable stream struggled, with a hoarse roar, among the black boulders.

There was foothold for neither tree nor shrub; and our mules picked their way warily, with head and ears pointed downwards, among the broken and angular masses. The occasional shouts of the arrieros sounded here sharp and percussive, and seemed to smite themselves to death against the adamantine walls. There was no room for echo. Finally the ravine became so narrowed between the precipitous mountain-sides as barely to afford room for the stream and our scant party. Here a roar, deeper, stronger, and sterner than that of the stream which we had followed, reached our ears, and we knew it was the voice of "the Great Speaker." A little farther on, we came in view of the river and two or three low huts built on the circumscribed space, where the two streams come together. Our muleteers were already busy in unloading the baggage, preparatory to its being carried across the bridge on the cicatrized backs of the occupants of the huts.

To the left of the huts, swinging high in a graceful curve, between the precipices on either side, looking wonderfully frail and gossamer-like, was the famed bridge of the Apurimac. A steep, narrow path, following for some distance a natural shelf, formed by the stratification of the rock, and for the rest of the way hewn in its face, led up, for a hundred feet, to a little platform, also cut in the rock, where were fastened the cables supporting the bridge. On the opposite bank was another and rather larger platform partly roofed by the rock, where was the windlass for making the cables taut, and where, perched like goats on some mountain shelf, lived the custodians of the bridge. The path could barely be discovered, turning sharp around a rocky projection to the left of this perch, then reappearing high above it, and then, after many a zigzag, losing itself in the dark mouth of a tunnel.

My companions and myself lost no time in extracting the measuring-tapes and sounding-lines from our *alforjas*, and hurriedly scrambled up the rocky pathway to the bridge. It was in bad condition. The cables had slacked so that the centre of the bridge hung from twelve to fifteen feet lower than its ends, and, then, the cables had not stretched evenly, so that one side was considerably lower than the other. The cables on either hand, intended to answer the double purpose of stays and parapets, had not sunk with the bridge, and were so high up that they could not be reached without difficulty; and many of the lines dropping from them to the floor, originally placed widely apart, had been broken, so that practically they were useful neither for security, nor for inspiring confidence.

Travelling in the Andes soon cures one of any nervousness about heights and depths, and is a specific against dizziness. Nevertheless, we all gave a rather apprehensive glance at the frail structure before us, but we had no difficulty in crossing and recrossing—as we did several times—except on approaching the ends, to which our weight transferred the sag of the cables, and made the last few yards rather steep. A stiff breeze swept up the cañon of the river, and caused a vibration of the bridge from side to side of at least six feet. The motion, however, inspired no sense of danger.

We carefully measured the length and altitude of the bridge, and found it to be, from fastening to fastening, 148 feet long, and at its lowest part 118 feet above the river. Mr. Markham, who crossed it in 1855, estimated the length at 90 feet and the height at 300 feet. Lieutenant Gibbon, who crossed it in 1857, estimated the length 324 feet and the height 150 feet. Our measurements, however, are exact. The height may be increased perhaps ten feet when the cables are made taut. They are five in number, twisted from the fibres of the cabuya, or maguey plant, and are about four inches thick. The floor is of small sticks and canes, fastened transversely with raw-hide strings. The Indians coming from Andahuaylas and other districts, where the cabuya grows, generally bring a quantity of leaves with them, wherewith to pay their toll. These are prepared and made into rope by the custodians of the bridge, who must be glad of some occupation in their lone and lofty eyrie.

Our baggage was carried over the bridge, and the animals were then led across one by one, loaded and started up the mountain. The space is too limited to receive more than two loaded mules at a time, and instances are known of their having been toppled off the precipice from overcrowding. We led our horses over without difficulty, except in getting them on the bridge. But once fairly on the swaying structure, they were as composed as if moving on the solid ground. Perhaps even to the lowest animal intelligence it must be apparent that the centre of the bridge of the Apurimac is not the place for antics, equine or asinine.[7]

Squier published his *Incidents of Travel and Exploration in the Land of the Incas* in 1877. Eloquent but verbose, the book became a classic of its day. Archaeology was the central theme, but we also learn a great deal about the Peru of the day, of an attack by a condor at Pachamacac, and brushes with bandits, grave robbers, and languid aristocrats. Squier's archaeology was very much descriptive and a product of his time, but his overview of Inca culture and earlier archaeology was the foundation of today's more modern Andean excavation methodology.

Hiram Bingham at Machu Picchu

By the end of the nineteenth century, Peru was familiar terrain to many tourists, even if the remote valleys of the Andes were still largely unexplored by Europeans. Visitors to Cuzco were stirred by the tragic story of Pizarro's ruthless defeat of the Inca and the thirty-year resistance that followed. This prompted a search for the secret capital of the Inca, the famous "lost city" of popular lore. In 1911, a flamboyant American traveler and academic, Hiram Bingham, followed the course of the Urubamba River upstream from Cuzco and discovered the spectacular ruins of Machu Picchu. Larger than life and given to exaggeration, Bingham claimed that he "found" a city that was, in fact, well known to the local population. He believed he had indeed discovered the "lost city of the Incas," but subsequent research has proved him wrong.

Bingham's fast-moving tale is a classic of archaeological travel and is often reprinted. I make no apologies for including it here.

The morning of July 24th dawned in a cold drizzle. Arteaga shivered and seemed inclined to stay in his hut. I offered to pay him well if he would show me the

9-3 This breathtaking view of Machu Picchu, Peru, is familiar to thousands of modern tourists. The Andean flora that covered the site when Hiram Bingham first saw it in 1911 has since been cleared to encourage sightseeing.

ruins. He demurred and said it was too hard a climb for such a wet day. But when he found that I was willing to pay him a *sol* (a Peruvian silver dollar, fifty cents, gold), three or four times the ordinary daily wage in this vicinity, he finally agreed to go. When asked just where the ruins were, he pointed straight up to the top of the mountain. No one supposed that they would be particularly interesting. And no one cared to go with me. The naturalist said there were "more butterflies near the river!" and he was reasonably certain he could collect some new varieties. The surgeon said he had to wash his clothes and mend them. Anyhow it was my job to investigate all reports of ruins and try to find the Inca capital.

So, accompanied only by Sergeant Carrasco I left camp at ten o'clock. Arteaga took us some distance upstream. On the road we passed a snake which had only just been killed. He said the region was the favorite haunt of "vipers." We later learned the lance-headed or yellow viper, commonly known as the fer-de-lance, a very venomous serpent, capable of making considerable springs when in pursuit of its prey, is common hereabouts.

After a walk of three-quarters of an hour Arteaga left the main road and plunged down through the jungle to the bank of the river. Here there was a primitive bridge which crossed the roaring rapids at its narrowest part, where the stream was forced to flow between two great bowlders. The "bridge" was made of half a dozen very slender logs, some of which were not long enough to span the distance between the bowlders, but had been spliced and lashed together with vines!

Arteaga and the sergeant took off their shoes and crept gingerly across, using their somewhat prehensile toes to keep from slipping. It was obvious that no one could live for an instant in the icy cold rapids, but would immediately be dashed to pieces against the rocks. I am frank to confess that I got down on my hands and knees and crawled across, six inches at a time. Even after we reached the other side I could not help wondering what would happen to the "bridge" if a particularly heavy shower should fall in the valley above. A light rain had fallen during the night and the river had risen so that the bridge was already threatened by the foaming rapids. It would not take much more to wash it away entirely. If this should happen during the day it might be very awkward. As a matter of fact, it did happen a few days later and when the next visitors attempted to cross the river at this point they found only one slender log remaining.

Leaving the stream, we now struggled up the bank through dense jungle, and in a few minutes reached the bottom of a very precipitous slope. For an hour and twenty minutes we had a hard climb. A good part of the distance we went on all fours, sometimes holding on by our fingernails. Here and there, a primitive ladder made from the roughly notched trunk of a small tree was placed in such a way as to help one over what might otherwise have proved to be an impassable cliff. In another place the slope was covered with slippery grass where it was hard to find either handholds or footholds. Arteaga groaned and said that there were lots of snakes here. Sergeant Carrasco said nothing but was glad he had good military shoes. The humidity was great. We were in the belt of maximum precipitation in eastern Peru. The heat was excessive; and I was not in training! There were no ruins or *andenes* of any kind in sight. I began to think my companions had chosen the better part.

Shortly after noon, just as we were completely exhausted, we reached a little grass-covered hut two thousand feet above the river where several good-natured Indians, pleasantly surprised at our unexpected arrival, welcomed us with dripping gourds full of cool, delicious water. Then they set before us a few cooked sweet potatoes. It seems that two Indian farmers, Richarte and Alvarez, had recently chosen this eagles' nest for their home. They said they had found plenty of terraces here on which to grow their crops. Laughingly they admitted they enjoyed being free from undesirable visitors, officials looking for army "volunteers" or collecting taxes.

Richarte told us that they had been living here four years. It seems probable that, owing to its inaccessibility, the canyon had been unoccupied for several centuries, but with the completion of the new government road, settlers began once more to occupy this region. In time somebody clambered up the precipices and found on these slopes at an elevation of nine thousand feet above the sea, an abundance of rich soil conveniently situated on artificial terraces, in a fine climate. Here the Indians had finally cleared off and burned over a few terraces and planted crops of maize, sweet and white potatoes, sugar cane, beans, peppers, tree tomatoes, and gooseberries.

They said there were two paths to the outside world. Of one we had already had a taste; the other was "even more difficult," a perilous path down the face of a rocky precipice on the other side of the ridge. It was their only means of egress in the wet season when the primitive bridge over which we had come could not be maintained. I was not surprised to learn that they went away from home "only about once a month."

Through Sergeant Carrasco I learned that the ruins were "a little further along." In this country one never can tell whether such a report is worthy of credence. "He may have been lying" is a good footnote to affix to all hearsay evidence. Accordingly, I was not unduly excited, nor in a great hurry to move. The heat was still great, the water from the Indians' spring was cool and delicious, and the rustic wooden bench, hospitably covered immediately after my arrival with a soft woolen poncho, seemed most comfortable. Furthermore, the view was simply enchanting. Tremendous green precipices fell away to the white rapids of the Urubamba below. Immediately in front, on the north side of the valley, was a great granite cliff rising two thousand feet sheer. To the left was the solitary peak of Huayna Picchu, surrounded by seemingly inaccessible precipices. On all sides were rocky cliffs. Beyond them cloud-capped snow-covered mountains rose thousands of feet above us.

We continued to enjoy the wonderful view of the canyon, but all the ruins we could see from our cool shelter were a few terraces.

Without the slightest expectation of finding anything more interesting than the ruins of two or three stone houses such as we had encountered at various places on the road between Ollantaytambo and Torontoy, I finally left the cool shade of the pleasant little hut and climbed farther up the ridge and around a slight promontory. Melchor Arteaga had "been there once before," so he decided to rest and gossip with Richarte and Alvarez. They sent a small boy with me as a "guide." The sergeant was in duty bound to follow, but I think he may have been a little curious to see what there was to see.

Hardly had we left the hut and rounded the promontory than we were confronted with an unexpected sight, a great flight of beautifully constructed stone-faced terraces, perhaps a hundred of them, each hundreds of feet long and ten feet high. They had been recently rescued from the jungle by the Indians. A veritable forest of large trees which had been growing on them for centuries had been chopped down and partly burned to make a clearing for agricultural purposes. The task was too great for the two Indians so the tree trunks had been allowed to lie as they fell and only the smaller branches removed. But the ancient soil, carefully put in place by the Incas, was still capable of producing rich crops of maize and potatoes.

However, there was nothing to be excited about. Similar flights of well-made terraces are to be seen in the upper Urubamba Valley at Pisac and Ollantaytambo, as well as opposite Torontoy. So we patiently followed the little guide along one of the widest terraces where there had once been a small conduit and made our way into an untouched forest beyond. Suddenly I found myself confronted with the walls of ruined houses built of the finest quality of Inca stonework. It was hard to see them for they were partly covered with trees and moss, the growth of centuries, but in the dense shadow, hiding in bamboo thickets and tangled vines, appeared here and there walls of white granite ashlars carefully cut and exquisitely fitted together. We scrambled along through the dense undergrowth, climbing over terrace walls and in bamboo thickets where our guide found it easier going than I did. Suddenly without any warning, under a huge overhanging ledge the boy showed me a cave beautifully lined with the finest cut stone. It had evidently been a Royal Mausoleum. On top of this particular ledge was a semi-circular building whose outer wall, gently sloping and slightly curved bore a striking resemblance to the famous Temple of the Sun in Cuzco. This might also be a Temple of the Sun. It followed the natural curvature of the rock and was keyed to it by one of the finest examples of masonry I had ever seen. Furthermore it was tied into another beautiful wall, made of very carefully matched ashlars of pure white granite, especially selected for its fine grain. Clearly, it was the work of a master artist. The interior surface of the wall was broken by niches and square stone-pegs. The exterior surface was perfectly simple and unadorned. The lower courses, of particularly large ashlars, gave it a look of solidity. The upper courses, diminishing in size toward the top, lent grace and delicacy to the structure. The flowing lines, the symmetrical arrangement of the ashlars, and the gradual gradation of the courses, combined to produce a wonderful effect, softer and more pleasing than that of the marble temples of the Old World. Owing to the absence of mortar, there were no ugly spaces between the rocks. They might have grown together. On account of the beauty of the white granite this structure surpassed in attractiveness the best Inca walls in Cuzco which had caused visitors to marvel for four centuries. It seemed like an unbelievable dream. Dimly, I began to realize that this wall and its adjoining semicircular temple over the cave were as fine as the finest stonework in the world.

It fairly took my breath away. What could this place be? Why had no one given us any idea of it? Even Melchor Arteaga was only moderately interested and had no appreciation of the importance of the ruins which Richarte and Alvarez had adopted for their little farm. Perhaps after all this was an isolated small place which had escaped notice because it was inaccessible.

Then the little boy urged us to climb up a steep hill over what seemed to be a flight of stone steps. Surprise followed surprise in bewildering succession. We came to a great stairway of large granite blocks. Then we walked along a path to a clearing where the Indians had planted a small vegetable garden. Suddenly we found ourselves standing in front of the ruins of two of the finest and most interesting structures in ancient America. Made of beautiful white granite, the walls contained blocks of Cyclopean size, higher than a man. The sight held me spellbound.

Each building had only three walls and was entirely open on one side. The principal temple had walls twelve feet high which were lined with exquisitely made niches, five, high up at each end, and seven on the back. There were seven courses of ashlars in the end walls. Under the seven rear niches was a rectangular block fourteen feet long, possibly a sacrificial altar, but more probably a throne for the mummies of departed Incas, brought out to be worshipped. The building did not look as though it ever had a roof. The top course of beautifully smooth ashlars was not intended to be covered, so the sun could be welcomed here by priests and mummies. I could scarcely believe my senses as I examined the larger blocks in the lower course and estimated that they must weigh from ten to fifteen tons each. Would anyone believe what I had found? Fortunately, in this land where accuracy in reporting what one has seen is not a prevailing characteristic of travelers, I had a good camera and the sun was shining.

The principal temple faces the south where there is a small plaza or courtyard. On the east side of the plaza was another amazing structure, the ruins of a temple containing three great windows looking out over the canyon to the rising sun. Like its neighbor, it is unique among Inca ruins. Nothing just like them in design and execution has ever been found. Its three conspicuously large windows, obviously too large to serve any useful purpose, were most beautifully made with the greatest care and solidity. This was clearly a ceremonial edifice of peculiar significance. Nowhere else in Peru, so far as I know, is there a similar structure conspicuous for being "a masonry wall with three windows." It will be remembered that Salcamayhua, the Peruvian who wrote an account of the antiquities of Peru in 1620, said that the first Inca, Manco the Great, ordered "works to be executed at the place of his birth, consisting of a masonry wall with three windows." Was that what I had found? If it was, then this was not the capital of the last Inca but the birthplace of the first. It did not occur to me that it might be both. To be sure the region was one which could fit in with the requirements of Tampu Tocco, the place of refuge of the civilized folk who fled from the southern barbarian tribes after the battle of La Raya and brought with them the body of their king Pachacutec who was slain by an arrow. He might have been buried in the stone-lined cave under the semi-circular temple.

Could this be "the principal city" of Manco and his sons, that Vilcapampa where was the "University of Idolatry" which Friar Marcos and Friar Diego had tried to reach? It behooved us to find out as much about it as we could.[8]

> Fifteen years ago, one winter night, I fell asleep before my desk in the old tower of the Smithsonian Institution. I dreamed that I was far away in a country I had never seen or heard of. There the sun was brighter, the air clearer; the valleys, vast and twilit, were like cracks down to the foundation rocks of the world.
>
> FRANK CUSHING
> "Life in Zuñi" (1890), a lecture

CHAPTER TEN

The World of the Pueblos

The search for El Dorado, the fabled land of gold, brought Spanish conquistadors north from New Spain into the harsh deserts of the North American Southwest. They were searching for the Seven Lost Cities of Cibola, cities said to have been founded as long ago as the eighth century by a legendary bishop who had fled west from Lisbon, Portugal, in fear of the Moors and Islam. When a Franciscan friar, Fray Marcos of Niza, returned to Mexico City from a preliminary expedition in 1539 with stories of a "faire citie with many houses builded in order" and gold and silver in abundance, the viceroy of New Spain quickly organized a major expedition under Francisco Coronado. The expedition ranged widely over the Southwest and far into the interior plains from 1540 to 1542. The disappointed Spaniards found no gold, however, just crowded pueblos "looking as if [they] had been crumpled all up together." Coronado and his men visited Zuñi pueblos, as well as Pecos in what is now northern New Mexico, where the pueblo was "square, situated on a rock, with a large court or yard in the middle, containing the steam rooms. The houses are all alike, four stories high. One can go over the whole village without there being a street to hinder."[1] Coronado returned to Mexico City empty-handed from a seemingly desolate and unproductive land. The pueblos were largely forgotten until a sparse population of Catholic friars and then colonists moved northward into the arid lands about a century later. By the early nineteenth century, the great pueblos of Chaco Canyon and Mesa Verde were but vague memories, except to the Native Americans who claimed ancestry from them, and were never visited by outsiders.

Chaco Canyon

In 1823, José Antonio Vizcarra, governor of the Mexican province of New Mexico, rode through Chaco Canyon with a small military party during a campaign against the local Navajo. He was in a hurry and contented himself with the observation that the great houses were built by unknown people. Sixteen years later, an American government expedition against the Navajo descended into the Chaco Canyon drainage and sighted "a conspicuous ruin" on a low hill. The expedition's Mexican guide called it Pueblo Pintado, "painted village," its name to this day. The pueblo formed a single structure and was "built of tabular pieces, of hard, fine-grained compact grey sandstone . . . to which the atmosphere has imparted a greyish tinge." Lieutenant James Hervey Simpson, a surveyor with the expedition, wrote these words; he admired the masonry, which he felt to be superior to anything built by modern-day Indians. After the expedition pitched camp in the heart of Chaco Canyon, Simpson and the artist Robert Kern received permission to travel farther down the canyon while the troops took a more circuitous route. The two men found themselves surrounded by ruined pueblos and the remains of much smaller settlements. At Chetro Ketl pueblo, called Chettro Kettle by their guide, Simpson counted at least 124 rooms on the ground floor, with walled-up windows, six kivas (subterranean chambers), and at least four stories of rooms stacked one upon the other. One room was remarkably well preserved. "The stone walls still have their plaster upon them . . . The ceiling showed two main beams, laid transversely; on these, longitudinally, were a number of smaller ones in juxtaposition, the ends being tied together by a species of wooden fibre, and the interstices chinked in with small stones; on these again, transversely, in close contact, was a kind of lathing of the odor and appearance of cedar."[2] Several short lengths of rope, perhaps for looms, hung from the beams.

Only a few hundred yards downstream was yet another large pueblo, destined to become the most famous of all the Chacoan great houses. This was Pueblo Bonito (beautiful village), the best preserved of Chaco's pueblos. Simpson had a passion for accurate measurement. He counted 139 rooms on the ground floor, but estimated that there had once been as many as 200. He located four kivas, dug deep into the ground and neatly walled with thin blocks of tabular stone. The masonry in many of the rooms was skillfully wrought with "alternate beds of large and small stones, the regularity of the combination producing a very pleasing effect."[3]

William Henry Jackson and the Pueblos

At the time—the early nineteenth century—the Southwest was far off the beaten track of trade routes and wagon trails, and much of it was still unexplored. After the Civil War, a number of civilian and military surveys traversed the West, one of their objectives being to study the native American peoples "in their natural state." The geologist Ferdinand Vandiveer Hayden oversaw a series of important surveys in Nebraska and Colorado between 1871 and 1878; his party included a teamster and stock driver turned photographer who became a celebrated chronicler of the West.

William Henry Jackson was an early photographer of the American West and a gifted visual artist. He learned his craft in various studios before the Civil War, then traveled west along the Oregon-California trail in 1866–1867. After serving as a bushwhacker, he set up a photographic studio in Omaha, Nebraska, where he photographed scenes along the new Union Pacific Railroad. His work came to the attention of Ferdinand Hayden, who was organizing an expedition to explore the unfamiliar region known as Yellowstone. He hired Jackson, providing him with food and equipment and allowing him to retain any profits from his photographs. Hayden was well aware of the publicity value in Congress—where his funding came from—of good pictures. Jackson was the first photographer to record Yellowstone's natural wonders on film. His photographs played an important part in convincing Congress to make Yellowstone the first U.S. National Park in 1872.

For the next few years, Jackson accompanied other geological surveys of the West and Southwest, including the Tetons in Wyoming and the Mesa Verde region of Colorado. As Hayden's parties spread through what is now southern Colorado, they heard rumors of "cliff dwellings," long-abandoned Indian ruins in remote canyons. Curious, Jackson led a separate photographic party that included his own assistant and a mule dedicated to carrying his heavy wet-plate camera equipment. The party also included Ernest Ingersoll, a naturalist and an "occasional correspondent" for the *New York Tribune*. In September 1874, Jackson's party traveled to Mancos Canyon in the northern San Juan region, which cuts through the northeastern part of Mesa Verde. The party's guide was John Moss, a miner who had firsthand knowledge of the cliff dwellings known to exist in the area. They traveled by mule to the Mancos Valley, then into the deepest part of the canyon of that name, where Jackson takes up the story.

Late on September 9 we arrived within rifle shot of the ruins. As we were riding through the deepest part of Mancos Canyon with the Mesa Verde eight hundred feet above us, Moss suddenly pointed toward the top of the plateau and said, "There it is."

"I see it," was the instant answer of Steve, the packer; and in a moment all of us had managed to pick out something that looked like a house, with spots suggesting

10-1 Famed Yellowstone photographer William Henry Jackson (1843–1942) also documented Colorado's Mancos Canyon, as seen in this example that he titled *Our First Discovery—The Two-Story Cliff House in Mancos Canyon, with John Moss and Ernest Ingersoll.*

windows and a door, sandwiched between two strata of sandstone almost at the top. Abruptly all of us forgot the day's long ride. Only the top would do, and at once.

For the first 600 feet or so we had a stiff climb but not a difficult one. Then we found ourselves facing a flat, vertical wall rising some 200 feet above the ledge on which we were standing. Fifty feet above our heads, in a shallow cave, was a two-story house. But how to reach it?

At that point everybody but Ingersoll and me decided to leave all problems until morning. We two, however, were determined to look for the way up at once. And it was not wholly the zeal of the inexperienced which pushed us on. Ingersoll was a newspaper man, and I was a photographer. Even in those days men of our callings got their stories.

We made it, too. After Moss and the others had gone down we found an old dead tree which we propped up and used to reach some ancient handholds and footholds cut in the rock. Invisible in the twilight, they served our need, and up we went to the house. It was worth everything I possessed to stand there and to know that, with Ernest Ingersoll, I was surely the first white man who had ever looked down into the canyon from this dwelling in the cliff.

And now I want Ernest Ingersoll to take up the story. When we returned to Denver he sent the full account of our preliminary discoveries to his newspaper, and the *New York Tribune* thus was the first to publish, November 3, 1874, a description of the ruins which subsequent explorations established as the most remarkable in this country:

". . . We came down abundantly satisfied, and next morning carried up our photographic kit and got some superb negatives. There, seven hundred measured feet above the valley, perched on a little ledge only just large enough to hold it, was a two-story house made of finely cut sandstone, each block about 14 by 6 inches, accurately fitted and set in mortar now harder than the stone itself. The floor was the ledge upon which it rested, and the roof the overhanging rock. There were three rooms upon the ground floor, each one 6 by 9 feet, with partition walls of faced stone. Between the stories was originally a wood floor, traces of which still remained, as did also the cedar sticks set in the wall over the windows and door . . . Each of the stories was six feet in height, and all the rooms, upstairs and down, were nicely plastered and painted what now looks a dull brick-red color, with a white band along the floor like a base-board. There was a low doorway from the ledge into the lower story, and another above, showing that the upper chamber was entered from without. The windows were large, square apertures, with no indication of any glazing or shutters. They commanded a view of the whole valley for many miles. Near the house several convenient little niches in the rock were built into better shape, as though they had been used as cupboards or caches; and behind it a semicircular wall inclosing the angle of the house and cliff formed a water-reservoir holding two and a half hogsheads . . .

INNUMERABLE GROUPS OF DESTROYED EDIFICES

Searching further in this vicinity we found remains of many houses on the same ledge, and some perfect ones above it quite inaccessible. The rocks also bore some inscriptions—unintelligible hieroglyphics for the most part . . . All these facts were carefully photographed and recorded.

Leaving here we soon came upon traces of houses in the bottom of the valley in the greatest profusion, nearly all of which were entirely destroyed, and broken pottery everywhere abounded. The majority of the buildings were square, but many round, and one sort of ruin always showed two square buildings with very deep cellars under them and a round tower between them, seemingly for watch and defense . . . Another isolated ruin that attracted our attention particularly consisted of two perfectly circular walls of cut stone, one within the other. The diameter of the inner circle was twenty-two feet and of the outer thirty-three feet. The walls were thick and were perforated apparently by three equidistant doorways. Was this a temple?

. . . A little cave high up from the ground was found, which had been utilized as a homestead by being built full of low houses communicating with one another, some of which were intact and had been appropriated by wild animals. About these dwellings were more hieroglyphics scratched on the wall, and plenty of pottery, but no implements. Further on were similar but rather ruder structures on a rocky bluff, but so strongly were they put together that the tooth of time had found them hard gnawing; and in one instance, while that portion of the cliff upon which a certain house rested had cracked off and fallen away some distance without rolling, the house itself had remained solid and upright. Traces of the trails to many of these dwellings, and the steps cut in the rock, were still visible, and were useful indications of the proximity of buildings otherwise unnoticed.

A STREET A THOUSAND FEET DEEP

We were now getting fairly away from the mountains and approaching the great, sandy, alkaline plains of the San Juan River. Our Valley of the Mancos was gradually widening, but still on either side rose the perpendicular sides of the mesa, composed of horizontal strata of red and white sandstone . . . Imagine East River one thousand or twelve hundred feet deep, the piers and slips on both sides made of red sandstone and extending down to that depth, and yourself at the bottom, gazing up for human habitations far above you . . .

Keeping close under the mesa on the western side—you never find houses on the eastern cliff of a canyon, where the morning sun, which they adored, could not strike them full with its first beams—one of us espied what he thought to be a house on the face of a particularly high and smooth portion of the precipice . . . Fired with the hope of finding some valuable relics, the Captain [Moss] and Bob started for the top . . . After a while an inarticulate sound floated down to us, anal looking up we beheld the Captain, diminished to the size of a cricket . . . He had got where [as it appeared to us below] he could not retreat, and it seemed equally impossible to go ahead.

A TRAGIC INCIDENT

There was a moment of suspense, then came a cry that stopped the beating of our hearts as we watched with bated breath a dark object, no larger than a cricket, whirling, spinning, dropping through the awful space. . . .

The Captain had thrown down his boots.

He was still there, crawling carefully along, clinging to the wall like a lizard; till finally a broader ledge was reached; and, having the nerve of an athlete, he got safely to the house. He found it perfect, almost semicircular in shape, of the finest workmanship yet seen . . .

Photographs and sketches completed, we pushed on, rode twenty miles or more, and camped just over the Utah line, two miles beyond Aztec Springs . . .

Our next day's march was westerly . . . The road was an interesting one intellectually, but not at all physically—dry, hot, dusty, long and wearisome. We passed a number of quite perfect houses, perched high up on rocky bluffs, and many other remains . . ."

This was the end of our season's work. From the eastern edge of Utah we returned through Baker's Park to Denver, and by the beginning of November I was back in Washington.[4]

Subsequently, the group traveled to Aztec Springs, down McElmo Creek, and into Hovenweep Canyon in southwestern Utah, where they saw what Jackson described as "watchtowers," tower kivas. Jackson's brief report, "Ancient Ruins in Southwestern Colorado," published in the *Bulletin of the US Geological and Geographical Survey of the Territories* in 1875, provided a brief summary of what he saw, but again it was his vivid photographs that had the greatest impact on the public at large. Hayden sent him back to the Four Corners in 1875, where Jackson photographed ruins of villages, as well as modern living Hopi villages, and drafted plans and maps of various ruins to serve as the basis for models of the pueblos to be exhibited at the Philadelphia Centennial Exhibition of 1876. Hung in the large exhibit halls, Jackson's large-scale photographs caused a sensation.

Jackson later traveled to Chaco Canyon, New Mexico, where he recorded a set of rock-cut steps behind Chetro Ketl pueblo that bear his name today. Jackson did not realize it, but the steps formed part of an extensive road system centered on Chaco Canyon. Until the first use of aerial photography in the 1920s—and, in the 1980s, the first use of infrared film—no one had any idea that the Chaco roads covered such a large area. They extend from the vicinity of Aztec Ruins on the St. Juan River in the north to southern New Mexico, and far east and west from the canyon. But the roads remain a mystery, for they are discontinuous, sometimes ending nowhere. Many experts believe that they were symbolic roads that helped define sacred places on the Chaco landscape. Others argue that they were processional ways, which brought people from outlying communities to the canyon for major ceremonies such as the summer and winter solstices. The debate over the roads is unresolved.

In later life, Jackson established a successful photography studio in Denver, where he photographed mountain railroads and a view of the Mount of the Holy Cross in one of his most famous images. He also embarked on an ambitious world tour in 1895 that took him across Siberia, to Japan, and through Africa. He never returned to Mesa Verde, where a rancher, Richard Wetherill, stumbled across the Cliff Palace and other spectacular pueblos in 1888. But Jackson's magnificent prints of ancient pueblo ruins brought the Southwest into the public consciousness a generation before Congress passed the Antiquities Act of 1906 and preserved many of them for posterity.

Frank Cushing, "1st War Chief of the Zuñi, U.S. Assistant Ethnologist"

In late September 1879, a young anthropologist, Frank Cushing, arrived at the Zuñi pueblo on a mule. He was a member of a Smithsonian

Institution–sponsored expedition under Colonel James Stevenson, sent out to collect masks, pottery, textiles, and other Native American artifacts as part of field research for the newly founded Bureau of Ethnology. Cushing had worked at the Smithsonian for five years and had been deeply involved in the 1876 Centennial Exhibition at Philadelphia, where he had learned of the Pueblo Indians of New Mexico. Their art and artifacts, along with Jackson's pictures, were a major feature of the exposition. When Cushing was invited to join Stevenson's expedition, he was told to find out as much as he could about a single Pueblo Indian group, using "your own methods." Young Cushing leapt at the opportunity.

From the beginning, Cushing was captivated by Zuñi. His first approach to the pueblo was uniquely memorable, for he arrived alone, having ridden far ahead of the rest of his party:

> Thus it happened that, on a sultry afternoon in late September, by no means firmly seated in the first saddle I had ever bestridden, I was belaboring a lazy Government mule just at the entrance of a pass between two great banded red-and-gray sandstone mesas, in the midst of a waterless wilderness. I had ridden from Las Vegas, then the southern terminus of the railway across New Mexico, to

10-2 Frank Cushing spent more than four years with the Zuñi people, and his written accounts and sketches (his *Zuñi Terrace in Mid-Summer* is shown here) together give one of the earliest cultural accounts of pueblo life.

Fort Wingate, and over a spur of the Sierra Madres, until here I was far in advance of our little caravan, and nearer the close of my long journey than I had dreamed. Beyond the pass I followed the winding road up a series of cedar-clad sand-hills to where they abruptly terminated in a black lava descent of nearly two hundred feet.

Below and beyond me was suddenly revealed a great red and yellow sand-plain. It merged into long stretches of gray, indistinct hill-lands in the western distance, distorted by mirages and sand-clouds, and overshadowed toward the north by two grand, solitary buttes of rock. From the bases of the latter to a spire-encircled, bare-faced promontory to the right, stretched a succession of cañon-seamed, brown, sandstone mesas, which, with their mantle of piñon and cedar, formed a high, dark boundary for the entire northern side of the basin.

To the left, a mile or two away, crowning numberless red foot-hills, rose a huge rock-mountain, a thousand feet high and at least two miles in length along its flat top, which showed, even in the distance, fanciful chiselings by wind, sand, and weather. Beyond its column-sentineled western end the low sand-basin spread far away to the foot-hills of the gray-and-white southern mesas, which, broken by deep cañons, stretched, cliff after cliff, westward to the hills of the horizon.

Out from the middle of the rock-wall and line of sand-hills on which I stood, through a gate of its own opening, flowed a little rivulet. Emerging from a succession of low mounds beneath me, it wound, like a long whip-lash or the track of an earth-worm, westward through the middle of the sandy plain and out almost to the horizon, where, just midway between the northern buttes and the opposite gray mesas, it was lost in the southern shadows of a terraced hill.

Down behind this hill the sun was sinking, transforming it into a jagged pyramid of silhouette, crowned with a brilliant halo, whence a seeming midnight aurora burst forth through broken clouds, bordering each misty blue island with crimson and gold, then blazing upward in widening lines of light, as if to repeat in the high heavens its earthly splendor.

A banner of smoke, as though fed from a thousand craterfires, balanced over this seeming volcano, floating off, in many a circle and surge, on the evening breeze. But I did not realize that this hill, so strange and picturesque, was a city of the habitations of men, until I saw, on the topmost terrace, little specks of black and red moving about against the sky. It seemed still a little island of mesas, one upon the other, smaller and smaller, reared from a sea of sand, in mock rivalry of the surrounding grander mesas of Nature's rearing.

Descending, I chanced to meet, over toward the river, an Indian. He was bareheaded, his hair banged even with his eyebrows in front, and done up in a neat knot behind, with long locks hanging down either side. He wore a red shirt and white cotton pantalets, slitted at the sides from the knees down so as to expose his bare legs, and raw-hide soled moccasins. Strings of shell-beads around his neck, and a leather belt around his waist, into which were stuck a boomerang or two, completed his costume. Knitting-work in hand, he left his band of dirty white and black sheep and snuffling goats in charge of a wise-looking, grizzled-faced, bob-tailed mongrel cur, and came, with a sort of shuffling dog-trot, toward the road, calling out, "Hai! hai!" and extending his hand with a most good-natured smile.

I shook the proffered hand warmly, and said, "Zuñi?"

"E!" exlaimed the Indian, as he reverentially breathed on my hand and from his own, and then, with a nod of his head and a fling of his chin toward the still distant smoky terraces, made his exclamation more intelligible.

I hastened on with all the speed I could scourge out of my obstinate, kicking mule, down the road to where the rivulet crossed it, and up again, nearer and nearer to the strange structures.

Imagine numberless long, box-shaped, adobe ranches, connected with one another in extended rows and squares, with others, less and less numerous, piled up on them lengthwise and crosswise, in two, three, even six stories, each receding from the one below it like the steps of a broken stairflight—as it were, a gigantic pyramidal mud honey-comb with far outstretching base,—and you can gain a fair conception of the architecture of Zuñi.

Everywhere this structure bristled with ladder-poles, chimneys, and rafters. The ladders were heavy and long, with carved slab cross-pieces at the tops, and leaned at all angles against the roofs. The chimneys looked more like huge bamboo-joints than anything else I can compare them with, for they were made of bottomless earthen pots, set one upon the other and cemented together with mud, so that they stood up, like many-lobed, oriental spires, from every roof-top. Wonderfully like the holes in an ant-hill seemed the little windows and door-ways which everywhere pierced the walls of this gigantic habitation; and like ant-hills themselves seemed the curious little round-topped ovens which stood here and there along these walls or on the terrace edges.

All round the town could be seen irregular, large and small adobe or dried-mud fences, inclosing gardens in which melon, pumpkin and squash vines, pepper plants and onions were most conspicuous. Forming an almost impregnable belt nearer the village were numerous stock corrals of bare cedar posts and sticks. In some of these, burros, or little gray, white-nosed, black-shouldered donkeys, were kept; while many others, with front legs tied closely together, were nosing about over the refuse heaps. Bob-tailed curs of all sizes, a few swift-footed, worried-looking black hogs, some scrawny chickens, and many eagles—the latter confined in wattled stick cages, diminutive corrals, in the corners and on the house-tops—made up the visible life about the place.[5]

He had arrived in the middle of a ceremonial dance. Cushing dismounted and made his way up to the top of the pueblo, where the inhabitants were gazing intently down into the plaza. The people angrily gestured that he should leave, but he breathed on an old man's hand and grasped it, apparently an appropriate greeting, and was allowed to stay. His description of the scene is a classic of southwestern travel narratives:

Not an Indian was to be seen, save on the topmost terraces of this strange city. There hundreds of them were congregated, gazing so intently down into one of the plazas beyond that none of them observed my approach, until I had hastily dismounted, tied my mule to a corral post, climbed the refuse-strewn hill and two or three ladders leading up to the house-tops. The regular *thud, thud* of rattles and drum, the cadence of rude music which sounded more like the soughing of a storm wind amid the forests of a mountain than the accompaniment of a dance, urged me forward, until I was suddenly confronted by forty or fifty of the men . . . .

A priest, with plumed head and trailing whiter buckskin mantle, gravely stepped in through a tunnel under the houses, scattering on the ground, as he came, sacred meal from a vessel which he held in one hand, while with the other he waved a beautiful wand of macaw plumes. He was followed by some twenty dancers elaborately costumed from head to foot. Close-fitting plumed wigs covered their heads, and black, long-bearded, yellow-eyed masks, with huge rows of teeth from ear to ear, red tongues lolling out between them, gave frightful grinning expressions to their faces. Their half nude bodies were painted black and yellow, while badges of buckskin were crossed over their shoulders, and skirts of the same material, secured at the waists with elaborately embroidered and fringed sashes, depended to the ankles. Their feet were incased in green and red buckskins, and to the legs were bound clanging rattles of tortoise-shell and deer-hoofs. . . . Each carried in his right hand a painted gourd rattle, in his left bow, arrows and long wands of yucca.

As the leader sounded his rattle, they all fell into a semicircular line across the plaza and began stepping rapidly up and down, swaying from side to side, facing first one way, then the other, in perfect unison, and in exact time to their rattles and strange measures of wild music.

Sprawling on the ground in front of and behind the row of dancers, in attitudes grotesque yet graceful, I observed for the first time ten most ludicrous characters, nude save for their skirts and neck-cloths of black tattered clothing, their heads entirely covered with flexible, round, warty masks. Both masks and persons were smeared over with pink mud, giving them the appearance of reptiles in human form that had ascended from the bottom of some muddy pool. . . .

One of them seated himself a little way off and began pounding with a short, knotty war-club a buffalo-skin bale, which he held between his knees, while the others, motionless save for their heads, which they were continually twisting and screwing about, or nodding in time to the drummer's strokes, kept up a series of comments and banterings which sometimes convulsed the whole throng of spectators with laughter.

In a few moments the leader shook his rattle again, and the dancers ceased as promptly as they had begun, breaking up irregularly and bellowing out large war-cries, brandishing their weapons, and retiring, as they had entered, one by one in the wake of the priest, through the tunnel. Suddenly the motionless, warty-headed figures sprang up, running against one another, crying out in loud tones, and motioning wildly with their long, naked arms. One moment they would all gather around one of their number, as if intensely interested in something he was saying, then as suddenly they would run confusedly about. They would catch up balls and pelt one another most vehemently, such as were struck making great ado about it. . . . Their antics were cut short by a renewal of the dance. While one commenced the drumming, another whirled a whizzing stick, and as soon as the others had arranged the costumes of some of the dancers, and had seen them fairly in line, they resumed their sprawling attitudes on the ground.[6]

Meanwhile, the rest of the party had arrived and set up camp near the mission, about a quarter of a mile (half a kilometer) from the pueblo. There were some ladies in the group who wanted to explore the pueblo, and they followed the anthropologist into the maze of mud-brick buildings. "We attempted to penetrate a narrow street or two, to enter one of the strange, terrace-bound courts, but the myriad dogs, with barks and howls in concert, created such a yelping pandemonium that the ladies were frightened, and we returned to camp."[7]

The next morning, Cushing returned to explore the pueblo on his own:

The next morning I climbed to the top of the pueblo. As I passed terrace after terrace the little children scampered for sundry sky-holes, through which long ladder-arms protruded, and disappeared down the black apertures like frightened prairie dogs; while the women, unaccustomed to the sound of shoes on their roofs, as suddenly appeared head and shoulders through the openings, gazed a moment, and then dropped out of sight. Five long flights passed, I stood on the topmost roof.

Spread out below us were the blocks of smoothly plastered, flat-roofed, adobe cells, red and yellow as the miles of plain from which they rose, pierced by many a black sky-hole, and ladder-poles and smoke-bannered chimneys were everywhere to be seen. In abrupt steps they descended toward the west, north, and central plaza, while eastward they were spread out in broad flats, broken here and there by deep courts. The whole mass was threaded through and through by narrow, often crooked, passage-ways or streets, more of them lengthwise than crosswise, and some, like tunnels leading under the houses from court to court or street to street.

The view extended grandly from the outlying, flat lower terraces, miles away to the encircling mesa boundaries north, east, and south, while westward a long, slanting notch in the low hills was invaded to the horizon by the sand-plain through which, like molten silver, the little river ran.

Every school-boy sketches a map of the Zuñi basin when he attempts with uncertain stroke to draw on his slate a cart-wheel. The city itself represents the jagged hub, whence the radiating, wavering trails form the spokes, and the surrounding mesas and hills, the rim. Let some crack across the slate and through the middle of the picture indicate the river, and your map is complete.

In and out, on the diverging trails, the Indians were passing to and from their distant fields, some on foot, some on burro-back, with others of the little beasts loaded from tail to ears with wood, blankets full of melons, pumpkins and corn, or great panniers of peaches. A series of them away out on the bare plain, mere moving specks in the distance, appeared like a caravan crossing a desert waste. Occasionally a half-nude rider, mounted on a swift-footed pony would come dashing in from the hills. Far away he seemed a black object with a long trail of golden dust behind, but his nearer approach revealed remarkable grace of motion and confusion of streaming hair and mane. There was an occasional heavily laden ox-cart, with urchins sprawling over the top, a driver on either side, and leading up the rear a mounted donkey or two; while away to one side, more picturesque than all this, a band of dust-shrouded sheep straggled over the slopes toward their mesa pastures, followed by their solitary herder and his dog.

Strangely out of keeping with the known characteristics of the Indian race were the busy scenes about the smoky pueblo. All over the terraces were women, some busy in the alleys or at the corners below, husking great heaps of many-colored corn, buried to their bushy, black bare heads in the golden husks, while children romped in, out, over and under the flaky piles; others, bringing the grain up the ladders in blankets strapped over their foreheads, spread it out on the terraced roofs to dry. Many, in little groups, were cutting up peaches and placing them on squares of white cloth, or slicing pumpkins into long spiral ropes to be suspended to dry from the protruding rafters.

One of these busy workers stopped, deposited her burden, and hailed a neighboring house-top. Almost immediately an answering echo issued from the red stony walls, and forthwith a pair of bare shoulders seem to shove a tangled head and expectant countenance up through an unsuspected sky-hole into the sunshine. In one place, with feet over-hanging the roof, a woman was gracefully decorating some newly made jars, and heaps of the rude, but exquisite bric-à-brac scattered around her,—while, over in a convenient shadow, sat an old blind man, busy spinning on his knee with a quaint bobbin-shaped spindle-whorl.

Out near the corrals old women were building round-topped heaps of dried sheep dung, and depositing therein with nice care their freshly painted pots and bowls for burning. Others, blankets in hand, were screening their already blazing kilns from the wind, or poking the fires until eddying columns of black pungent smoke half hid them from my view, and made them seem like the "witches and cauldrons" of child-lore.

Children were everywhere, chasing one another over the terraces, up and down ladders, through alleys, and out again into the sunlight. Some, with bows and arrows, sticks and stones, were persecuting in mock chase dogs and hogs alike, as attested by their wild shrieks of delight, or the respondent ceaseless yelps arising seemingly from all quarters of the town at once.

Along the muddy river below the long southern side of the pueblo, more of these youngsters were ducking one another, or playing at various games on the smooth, sandy banks. Women, too, were there engaged in washing wool or blankets on flat stones, or in cleansing great baskets of corn. I was attracted thither and observed that these primitive laundresses had to raise the water with little dams of sand. I smiled as the thought occurred that the first expedition of Americans to Zuñi had been sent here by Government to explore this self-same river, "relative to its navigability."[8]

After two months, Stevenson was ready to move on. But Cushing wanted to gain the confidence of the Zuñi and refused to leave. Stevenson left him with no provisions, so Cushing moved into the pueblo governor's house, where he became completely dependent on the generosity of the inhabitants. (The governor was a kin leader and head of the pueblo.) Cushing had originally intended to stay for only two months, but he ended up remaining at Zuñi for four and a half years, becoming a member of the tribe and achieving a high position in the Priesthood of the Bow. Having arrived as a mere traveler, Frank Cushing became a pioneer of what anthropologists call "participant observation." His health was none too good, and the winters nearly killed him, but he persisted, becoming a mediator between the people and an ever more intrusive outside world of prospectors and ranchers. Cushing was a flamboyant man who rejoiced in signing his letters "1st War Chief of the Zuñi, U.S. Assistant Ethnologist," and he was a shrewd observer and a superb writer. His articles, published in such journals as the *Century Illustrated Magazine*, were widely read and introduced a large public audience to the intricacies and sacred rites of Zuñi life. The members of the pueblo debated at length as to whether he should be allowed to record details of their ceremonies, and in particular the details of the *Keá-k' ok-shi,* the Sacred Dance. After he faced down the participants, he was allowed to watch it, a turning point in his relations with the Zuñi.

Next morning before I was awake, the herald and two or three *tinieutes* had come in, and, as I arose, were sitting along the side of the house. The old head chief had just prepared my morning meal, and gone out after something. I greeted all pleasantly and sat down to eat. Before I had half finished I heard the rattle and drum of the coming dance. I hastily jumped up, took my leather book-pouch from the antlers, and strapping it across my shoulder, started for the door. Two of the chiefs rushed ahead of me, caught me by the arms, and quietly remarked that it would be well for me to finish my breakfast. I asked them if the dance was coming. They said they didn't know. I replied that I did, and that I was going out to see it.

"Leave your books and pencils behind, then," said they.

"No, I must carry them wherever I go."

"If you put the shadows of the great dance down on the leaves of your books to-day, we shall cut them to pieces," they threatened.

Suddenly wrenching away from them, I pulled a knife out from the bottom of my pouch, and, bracing up against the wall, brandished it, and said that whatever hand grabbed my arm again would be cut off, that whoever cut my books to pieces would only cut himself to pieces with my knife. It was a doubtful game of bluff, but the chiefs fell back a little, and I darted through the door. Although they followed me throughout the whole day, they did not again offer to molest me, but the people gathered so closely around me that I could scarcely find opportunity for sketching.

As the month of November approached, the cold rains began to fall. Frost destroyed the corn-plants and vines. Ice formed over the river by night to linger a little while in the morning, then be chased away by the midday sun. Not in the least did these forerunners of a severe winter cause the dance ceremonials to abate. The Indians were, to some extent reassured when on the occasion of the next dance, which happened to be a repetition of the first, I did little or no sketching. At another dance, however, I resumed the hated practice, which made matters worse than before. A second council was called. Of this, however, I knew nothing, until afterward told by the old chief. It seems that it was a secret. It discussed various plans for either disposing of me, or compelling me to desist. Among others was the proposal that I be thrown off the great mesa, as were the two "children of the angry waters," but it was urged that should this be done, "*Wa-sin-tona*" might visit my death on the whole nation. In order to avoid this difficulty, others suggested that I be *há-thli-kw'ïsh-k'ia* (condemned of sorcery) and executed. They claimed that sorcery was such a heinous crime that my execution would be pardoned, if represented to the Americans as the consequence of it. But some of the councilors reminded the others that the Americans had no sorcerers among them, and were ignorant of witchcraft.

At last a plan was hit upon which the simple natives thought would free them from all their perplexities. Surely, no objection would be offered to the "death of a Navajo." Forthwith the Knife Dance was ordered, as it was thought possible that the appearance of this dance would be sufficient to intimidate me, without recourse to additional violence.

One morning thereafter, the old chief appeared graver and more affectionate toward me than usual. He told me the "*Ho-mah-tchi* was coming,—a very *sa-mu* (ill-natured) dance," and suggested that "it would be well for me not to sketch it." Unaware either of the council or of the functions of the angry dance, I persisted. The old man, a little vexed, exclaimed, "Oh, well, of course, a fool always makes a fool of himself." But he said no more, and I assigned, as the cause of his remarks, superstitious reasons, rather than any solicitude for my safety.

When the great dance appeared, the governor seemed desirous of keeping me at home. During most of the morning I humored him in this. At last, however, fearing I would miss some important ceremonial, I stole out across the house-tops and took a position on one of the terraces of the dance court.

The dancers filed in through the covered way, preceded by a priest, and arranged themselves in a line across the court. Their costumes were not unlike those of the first dance I had witnessed, save that the masks were flatter and smeared with blood, and the beards and hair were long and streaming. In their right hands the performers carried huge, leaf-shaped, blood-stained knives of stone, which, during the movements of the dance, they brandished wildly in the air, in time and accompaniment to their wild song and regular steps, often pointing them toward me.

As the day advanced, spectators began to throng the terraces and court, few, however, approaching to where I was sitting; and the masked clowns made their appearance.

I had been busy with memoranda and had succeeded in sketching three or four of the costumes, when there dashed into the court two remarkable characters. Their bodies, nude save for short breech-clouts, were painted with ashes. Skull-caps, tufted with split corn-husks, and heavy streaks of black under their eyes and over their mouths, gave them a most ghastly and ferocious appearance. Each wore around his neck a short, twisted rope of black fiber, and each was armed with a war-club or ladder-round.

A brief intermission in the dance was the signal for a loud and excited harangue on the part of the two, which, at first greeted with laughter, was soon received with absolute silence, even by the children. Soon they began to point wildly at me with their clubs. Unable as I was to understand all they had been saying, I at first regarded it all as a joke, like those of the *Keó-yi-mo-shi*, until one shouted out to the other, "Kill him! kill him!" and the women and children excitedly rising rushed for the doorways or gathered closer to one another. Instantly, the larger one approached the ladder near the top of which I sat, brandishing his war-club at me. Savagely striking the rounds and poles, he began to ascend. A few Indians had collected behind me, and a host of them stood all around in front. Therefore, I realized that in case of violence, escape would be impossible.

I forced a laugh, quickly drew my hunting-knife from the bottom of the pouch, waved it two or three times in the air so that it flashed in the sunlight, and laid it conspicuously in front of me. Still smiling, I carefully placed my book—open—by the side of the pouch and laid a stone on it to show that I intended to resume the sketching. Then I half rose, clinging to the ladder-pole with one hand, and holding the other in readiness to clutch the knife. The one below suddenly grabbed the skirt of the other and shouted, "Hold on, he is a *kí-he!* a *kí-he!* We have been mistaken. This is no Navajo." Jumping down to the ground, the one thus addressed glanced up at me for an instant, waved his war-club in the air, breathed from it, and echoed the words of his companion, while the spectators wildly shouted applause. The two held a hurried conference. They swore they must "kill a Navajo," and dashed through the crowd and passage-way out of the court.

The *Keó-yi-mo-shi* freed from their restraint, rushed about with incessant jabber, and turned their warty eyes constantly in my direction. As I replaced my knife and resumed the sketching, the eyes of nearly the whole assemblage were turned toward me, and the applause, mingled with loud remarks, was redoubled. Some of the old men even came up and patted me on the head, or breathed on my hands and from their own.

> Presently a prolonged howl outside the court attracted the attention of all, and the frantic pair rushed in through the covered way, dragging by the tail and hind legs a big, yelping, snapping, shaggy yellow dog. "We have found a Navajo," exclaimed one, as they threw the dog violently against the ground. While he was cringing before them, they began an erratic dance, wildly gesticulating and brandishing their clubs, and interjecting their snatches of song with short speeches. Suddenly, one of them struck the brute across the muzzle with his war-club, and a well-directed blow from the other broke its back. While it was yet gasping and struggling, the smaller one of the two rushed about frantically, yelling, "A knife, a knife." One was thrown down to him. Snatching it up, he grabbed the animal and made a gash in its viscera. The scene which followed was too disgusting for description.[9]

Cushing left the Zuñi in 1884 and never returned. Plagued by ill health, he died at the age of forty-three by choking on a fish bone. His legacy as a traveler and observer is sometimes underrated, but his legacy as an anthropologist has endured, although the Zuñi soon became weary of the scholars who followed him and resentful of the secrets he had revealed. But from the traveler's perspective, Frank Cushing revealed the deep cultural roots of pueblo society. His experiences at Zuñi have enriched archaeological travelers to the Southwest ever since.

Early Tourists

As a cattle rancher, Richard Wetherill spent many days exploring the remote vastnesses of southern Colorado. He collected blankets and jewelry, herded his livestock, and acquired artifacts from dozens of pueblos. The Wetherill homestead became a mecca for visitors to the Southwest, who now arrived in much larger numbers, thanks to the railroad line to Denver. In late 1888, Richard and his cousin Charlie Mason came across the Cliff Palace, widely regarded as the most spectacular of all the Mesa Verde ruins. Jackson and his party had missed this huge complex of more than 200 rooms and 23 kivas. Wetherill and Mason also found the nearby Spruce Tree and Square Tower House ruins, formed a partnership to dig in them, and sold for large sums several collections of pottery, textiles, and weapons. Wetherill needed the money, for his ranch was heavily mortgaged. He generated significant income by selling artifacts and guiding tourists to the cliff dwellings at Mesa Verde. As word spread, the numbers of tourists rose rapidly, with about 1,000 people visiting the Wetherill ranch and the cliff dwellings between 1880 and 1901. Among Wetherill's clients was a twenty-three-year-old Swede, Gustaf Nils Adolf Nordenskiöld, who produced the first scientific account of the pueblos. In his *Cliff*

10-3 The Cliff Palace at Mesa Verde, Colorado, has survived the depredations of the cattle rancher Richard Wetherill and others, and is now protected by the National Park Service.

Dwellings of the Mesa Verde, published in 1893, he made a point of stressing the close links between the ancient pueblos and the living Native Americans.

Richard Wetherill was a controversial figure, excoriated by many for ravaging ancient pueblos for artifacts to sell. His heyday was during the early days of the Santa Fe Railway, which reached Santa Fe in 1880. Until then, the West had been seen as a wild, even dangerous place. Now it was possible to visit the pueblos in comfort. The railroad and the associated Fred Harvey Company began to market the region as a place to be savored and admired—"the Land of Enchantment." Among other attractions was a "weekend exposure to the primitive world." A popular writer, Lilian Whiting, wrote a book called *The Land of Enchantment: From Pike's Peak to the Pacific* (1906), which described New Mexico as a place of mystery. "The ancient Indian pueblos are still largely inhabited, and strange ruins of unknown civilization add to their atmosphere of mystery," she wrote, adding that the state abounded in "cliffs and communal buildings . . . older than any other ruins on the American continent, and probably in the world."[10]

The Fred Harvey Company played an important role in the development of tourism in the Southwest. By 1890, the company had entered an already thriving Indian arts and crafts market, decorating its hotels in Albuquerque, and later Gallup, New Mexico, with Native American motifs. An arcade connected the Alvarado Hotel in Albuquerque to the Indian Building, where artifacts were for sale and craftspeople were at work. The visitor entered a kind of living museum of Native American material culture: "See patient Navajo squaws weaving blankets, their men engaged in fashioning showy bracelets, rings, and trinkets; Indians from Acoma and Laguna making pottery; skillful squaws plaiting blankets . . . undisturbed by the eager gaze of the tourist, the stoic works on as unconcernedly as though in his reservation home."[11]

The Indians were marketed as a quaint curiosity, poor but happy. The tourist saw them at work in stores and on side trips by automobile and motor coach. But this growing industry offered more. In 1925, Harvey Detours, a subsidiary of the Fred Harvey Company, organized trips to various well-known archaeological sites, where tour guides hastily trained by archaeologists and anthropologists escorted visitors from across the

10-4 Interior view of the Indian Building in Albuquerque, New Mexico, 1903, with crafts displayed for sale.

country. Sometimes a lecture at the museum in Santa Fe was part of the entertainment.

The commoditization of archaeological travel began earlier in the Southwest than it did in many parts of the world, thanks to the railroad and the relatively easy travel conditions leading away from the railheads. Many visitors came to the Southwest in search of artifacts, to satisfy their curiosity and interest in native peoples, and sometimes looking for the "life forces" that were thought to emanate from "natural" people like the Native Americans. In 1930, New Mexico–born Harvey Fergusson wrote a biting satire of Taos and Santa Fe. In *Footloose McGarnigal*, an artist tells the hero that the Indian "can't come into your world and you can't go into his. Here in Taos, we paint them and patronize them, and crowd around all their sacred ceremonies like boys writing a dog fight, and to them we simply aren't there except to the extent that we're a minor nuisance." Fergusson also wrote of those seeking spiritual awakenings: "All these queer lost souls that hang around the Indians . . . What really fascinates them is the perfect peaceful rhythm of the Indian life, going on as it has for a thousand years without missing a beat."[12]

Today, tens of thousands of people visit the Southwest every year. In 2004 alone, 76,756 of them ventured down the well-maintained gravel road that links Chaco Canyon with the outside world. The once mysterious realm of the pueblos has become another facet of mainstream, mass-market tourism, albeit with the difference that people can visit on their own, by automobile, and take their time savoring the past. Chaco Canyon is especially compelling if you can camp in the canyon and walk there at sunset. I will never forget my own experience:

> I walked upstream along the floor of the great canyon as the cool of evening settled over Chaco. The sun cast the steep cliffs in deep relief. Pueblo Bonito's weathered ruins glowed with a roseate orange as massing clouds towered high above, dwarfing outcrop and site alike. As the shadows lengthened, I gazed upward at the wide bowl of the heavens and imagined the canyon nine hundred years ago. A chill wind sloughed at my back as I sat down to enjoy the spectacular sunset. Chaco came alive; I sensed the acrid scent of wood smoke carried on the evening breeze, dogs barking at the setting sun. Flickering hearths and blazing firebrands highlight dark windows and doorways on the terraces of the great house that is Pueblo Bonito. People move between light and shadow, dark silhouettes against the flames. The shrill cries of children playing in the shadows, the quiet talk of men leaning against sun-baked walls—the past comes alive in the gloaming. So does the most pervasive sound of all: the scrape, scrape of dozens of grinders against dozens of milling stones as the women prepare the evening meal.

The image faded as darkness fell, leaving Chaco in intense silence. The brightly clothed visitors from our own world had long departed in their cars. A few stars twinkled in the heavens overhead, but the dark and stillness settled around me so tangibly that past and present seemed to merge. The ancient inhabitants of the canyon surrounded me and entered my consciousness, ancestral guardians of a once sacred place. They enticed me into their long-vanished world, into long winter nights where the dancers would perform underground in great kivas now open to the sky, wood smoke swirling from the fire as the chants and singing reached a crescendo. . . . I could imagine the nights when the fires at Pueblo Bonito and Chetro Ketl burned high and the chants of the dancers echoed off the precipitous cliffs.

I sat for more than an hour in the dark as the past softly assaulted me with a vivid immediacy that I have rarely experienced during a lifetime as an archaeologist. Then I shivered in the chill and the spell was broken.

Next morning, I returned to my wandering, but the past was remote, almost beyond reach, a silent record of crumbling rooms and kivas open to the sky. It was as if no one had ever lived in the canyon. The ancient Chacoans had vanished on the wind, leaving only empty buildings behind them. I was reminded of the Victorian archaeologist Austen Henry Layard's memorable remark about his excavations of Assyrian cities in Mesopotamia: "The great tide of civilization has long since ebbed, leaving these scattered wrecks on the solitary shore. . . . We

10-5 Pueblo Bonito in Chaco Canyon, New Mexico, is now a popular destination of tourists in the American Southwest, but it was in a more ruinous state when first visited in the nineteenth century.

wanderers were seeking what they had left behind, as children gather up the coloured shells on the deserted sands."[13]

No longer sheltered from outside influence by geography and obscurity, the Southwest nevertheless is still a place where you can evoke the past and commune with it in solitude.

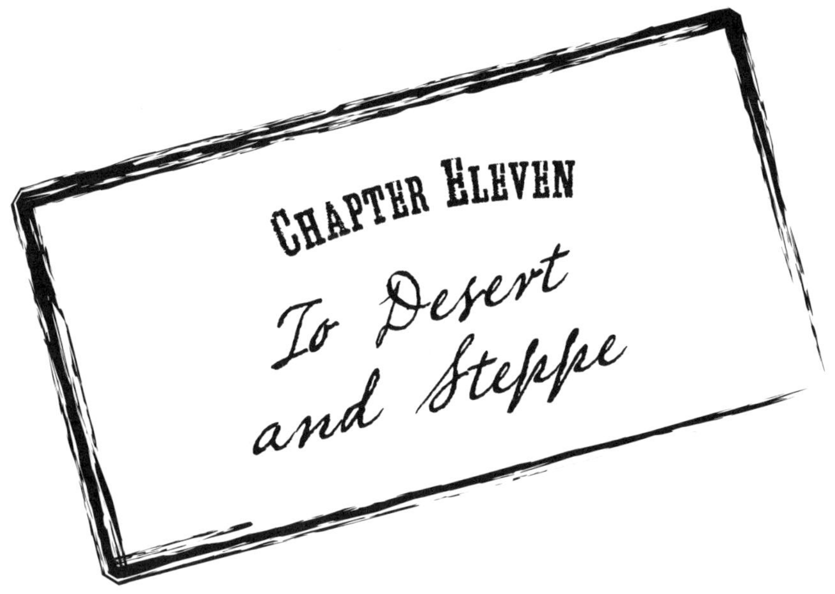

Chapter Eleven

To Desert and Steppe

There is neither water nor vegetation, but a hot wind often rises, which takes away the breath of man, horse, and beast, and not seldom is the cause of sickness. You hear almost always shrill whistlings, or loud shouts; and when you try to discover whence they come, you are terrified at seeing nothing.... After four hundred li, you come to the ancient kingdom of Tu-ho-lo. It is a long time since that country was changed into a desert. All its towns lie in ruins and are overgrown with wild plants.

An anonymous Chinese traveler of the Tang Dynasty on the area north of Khotan, seventh century A.D.[1]

CHAPTER ELEVEN

To Desert and Steppe

The vast reaches of central Asia are redolent with history, with stirring tales of Marco Polo's epic journeys and all the romance of the Silk Road, an arduous caravan route that connected Asia and the West for hundreds of years. The archaeology of both central Asia and the Silk Road has yet to reveal all their secrets, for the area presents formidable obstacles for even the most experienced researchers and travelers. A century ago, the obstacles were even more severe—no rail lines, no roads beyond caravan tracks and horse trails, and endemic political instability, to say nothing of harsh deserts and high mountain passes. Despite these obstacles, Afghanistan, Tibet, and other countries along the Silk Road were the arena for what became known in the nineteenth century as the "great game," the hide-and-seek struggle between Russia and Britain for control of a strategically vital area north of British India. Here, archaeological travel was in the hands of explorers and truly dedicated scientists, and certainly was not the domain of tourists. The logistics and enormous distances ensured that anyone traveling in central Asia vanished from civilization for months, and more often for years.

During the nineteenth century, the occasional British army officer and political agent, and also French and German travelers, ventured widely through the region, although their concerns were predominantly military and strategic rather than scientific. The great game culminated in Colonel Francis Younghusband's military and diplomatic expedition for Britain into Tibet in 1904, prompted by rumors that Russia had its eye on the country. After Younghusband's return to India and because of his account of the fascinating, mountainous regions to the north, the rugged terrain that formed India's northern frontier became a place where solitary young officers went exploring, hunting, or climbing mountains for sport.

Sven Hedin, Explorer and Adventurer

During this period, only a handful of travelers penetrated central Asia with scientific objectives, among them the Swedish explorer Sven Hedin, who traveled via Russia and the Pamirs to China in 1893–1897. He nearly died crossing the western Taklimakan Desert in the Tarim Basin to reach the Khotan River. This huge basin was a melting pot of different religions and cultures, a bridge for silk caravans between East and West. On another expedition, in 1899–1902, Hedin floated alone with his local employees down the Tarim River until stopped by ice, and then explored much of the Silk Road before traveling south to India. Hedin wrote a stream of popular books in Swedish about his travels, some of which were translated into English, but his interests were predominantly geological and geographical, although he did visit archaeological sites like Persepolis. He was the first European traveler to see the desert ruins of Dandan-Uiliq ("the houses with ivory"), with its Buddhist shrines, in the Taklimakan Desert, as well as sites in the Karadong Oasis dating from the first to third centuries A.D. The town of Karadong was once a prosperous oasis settlement on the Silk Road because it skirted the south side of the Taklimakan

11-1 Dramatic and varied representations of Buddha were common finds along central Asia's Silk Road and continue to be popular photographic subjects.

Desert; it was a town where the inhabitants lived in wood-framed houses adorned with representations of Buddha and other divines. In its heyday, poplars lined the streets and citrus orchards flourished. Dandan-Uiliq was a caravan town, where elements of Chinese and Indian Buddhist culture mingled. The art has Indian Buddhist associations, and shows the Greek influence that became part of this tradition. Iranian artistic styles were also part of this cosmopolitan center's culture. Dandan-Uiliq was known to the Chinese as Li-sieh and flourished in the centuries before Islam, being abandoned to the desert in the eighth century A.D.

In December 1895, Hedin traveled along an ancient caravan route—marked by flattened clay pyramids that functioned as signposts—through eastern Turkestan and past Yamarkand, stopping at caravanserai (large inns built around courtyards to serve caravans) with enormously deep wells, many of them over 30 meters deep. Early in January, he arrived in Khotan itself, where he bought "antique relics," including Chinese coins and Buddhist manuscripts. After a stay of ten days, he traveled north to check out rumors of an ancient city buried in sand. He thought he would be away for a short time, but in fact he was away for four and a half months. Temperatures dropped far below zero at night and did not rise much higher by day, when fortunately the air was still. Hedin pulled his fur coat over his head to sleep and was rarely warm. The camels sank into the cold sand, making progress slow and tiring. But the main hardship was the unrelenting cold. It was so cold that the drinking water remained frozen in the goatskins even at midday. But the tough journey was worth it:

> On the fourth day, we camped in a hollow, where a dead, dried-up forest provided us with excellent fuel. The next day we went to the ruins of the ancient city, which our guides called Takla-makan, or Dandan-uilik, the "Ivory Houses." Most of the houses were buried in the sand. But here and there, posts and wooden walls stuck out of the dunes; and on one of the walls, which was possibly three feet high, we discovered several figures, artistically executed in plaster. They represented Buddha and Buddhistic deities, some standing, some seated on lotus-leaves, all robed in ample draperies, their heads encircled by flaming aureoles. All these finds, and many other relics, were wrapped up carefully, and packed in my boxes; and the fullest possible notes on the ancient city, its location, sand-covered canals, dead-poplar avenues, and dried-up apricot-orchards were entered in my diary. I was not equipped to make a thorough excavation; and, besides, I was not an archaeologist. The scientific research I willingly left to the specialists. In a few years, they too would be sinking their spades into the loose sand. For me it was sufficient to have made the important discovery, and to have won, in the heart of the desert, a new field for archaeology. And now, at last, I felt rewarded and encouraged, after the preceding year's vain search for traces of a dead civilization.

The ancient Chinese geographers, as well as the present-day natives living on the edge of the desert, were now vindicated. My rejoicing over this first find, which was to be followed by similar discoveries in later years, is evident from notes made at the time.

"No explorer," I wrote, "had an inkling, hitherto, of the existence of this ancient city. Here I stand, like the prince in the enchanted wood, having wakened to new life the city which has slumbered for a thousand years."[2]

Hedin was hungry for celebrity and led four more expeditions to central Asia, accompanied by botanists, geologists, and other scientists from several European nations. He surveyed large areas of unmapped terrain and made two attempts to reach the holy city of Lhasa in Tibet, but he never located any more major archaeological discoveries.

Between 1927 and 1935, Hedin was the leader of an elaborate expedition that explored part of the Silk Road in an attempt to open routes for motor traffic. One of the sponsors of the expedition was Lufthansa, a company that was hoping to open air routes from inner Asia to China. In later life, Hedin became a controversial figure because of his racist, pro-Nazi views. As a result, many travelers regarded him with suspicion, suspecting him of exaggerating his discoveries. He was an expert, fluent writer, which meant that he gave his adventures a racy edge, which did not sit well with more sober contemporaries such as Aurel Stein, the doyen of Asian travelers at the time. These contemporaries preferred balanced, judicial descriptions of the lands and the people, their own adventures and hardships taking second place. In retrospect, however, Hedin's travels were of considerable importance, if only because they helped to open up central Asia to Western science.

Sir Aurel Stein and the Caves of a Thousand Buddhas

The flamboyant Hedin was a very different type of traveler compared to one of his contemporaries, the British explorer, archaeologist, and traveler Sir Marc Aurel Stein, one of the last true pioneering archaeological travelers. Like those of his Swedish counterpart, Stein's journeys through little-known parts of central Asia provided the outside world with its first scientific glimpse of the Silk Road.

Aurel Stein was born into a Jewish family in Hungary, but his parents baptized him a Protestant so that he could attend a prestigious school in Germany. He soon showed impressive intellectual talents, but he also went through Hungarian military training, which gave him excellent surveying skills. After obtaining a doctorate in linguistics from the University of Tübingen in 1883, he carried out postdoctoral research in Asian languages at Oxford University. Stein has been described as "the great archaeologist who nearly never was." He easily could have taken—as many Asian specialists did at the time—a cozy academic position and never gone into the field. However, at an early age, Stein developed a fascination with the Asian expeditions of Alexander the Great, to the point that he wanted to tread on the same ground. Thanks in large part to the influence of several senior retired Indian civil servants, Stein decided on a career in India. His strong language qualifications and surveying expertise ensured him a civil service career in the Indian Educational Service, starting in 1887. Eventually, he became principal of the Oriental College in Lahore, an appointment that suited him well, for he could travel far and wide during school vacations.

At first, Stein contented himself with investigating topographical conundrums and taking short excursions looking for the locations of historic Buddhist sites. From these activities it was a short step to organizing an expedition to Chinese Turkestan, the country between Mongolia and the Caspian Sea, which is now divided into several nations, including Turkmenistan, Uzbekistan, and Kazakhstan. Stein was relentless in pursuit of his field research. The day-to-day routines of teaching and administration bored him; he spent much of his time on special leaves—sometimes granted, one suspects, by a department head eager to get rid of him. Stein had no ambition for fame and fortune, just an obsessive fascination with geography, archaeology, and languages. Writing was hard for him, although he wrote academic articles and books constantly. His lecture style was long-winded and monotonous; in short, he droned. Stein was happiest in the desert, far from civilization, priding himself on his ability to walk as many as 100 kilometers a day and to write accurate descriptions of the lands, people, and archaeological sites he encountered and explored. He thrived on austere living conditions and climatic extremes.

Aurel Stein traveled with as few companions and as little baggage as possible. He was a walker and surveyor, not an excavator, spending no more than two or three weeks in one place. Apart from his valuable archaeological discoveries, he mapped thousands of square kilometers of country that had been a blank on most European maps.

Stein's first serious expedition was in 1900–1901, when he explored remote areas on the Chinese and Indian borders, where he made a study of the little-known Khotan Empire. Khotan was an early center for the spread of Buddhism from India to China, but fell to the Arab invaders in the eighth century A.D.; meanwhile, though, Khotan had grown rich from the caravan trade in silk and other luxuries along the Silk Route. Stein's primary objective on this first expedition was to examine the trade in artifacts and sacred books that were being sold to European collectors at the time. In December 1900, his camels reached Dandan-Uiliq—already visited by Sven Hedin—now little more than desolate clusters of modest buildings, wall stumps, and dead trees that had once lined cultivated fields. The outlines of houses could be discerned from wooden posts sticking above the dunes. Here he discovered important evidence of Greco-Buddhist art, and used the site as a laboratory to learn the ground plans and other features of houses and shrines buried in the sand. Having stumbled over the library of a Buddhist monastery, he also found Brahmi manuscripts, written on paper preserved by the arid environment. (Paper was invented in China as early as 140 B.C.) Stein's writings reveal that he was deeply moved by what he found:

> It was with mixed feelings that I said farewell to the silent sand-dunes amidst which I had worked for the last three weeks. They had yielded up enough to answer most of the questions which arise about the strange ruins which they have helped to preserve. . . . I have grown almost fond of their simple scenery. Dandan-Uiliq was to lapse once more into that solitude which for a thousand years had probably never been disturbed so long as during my visit . . . The recollection of this fascinating site will ever suggest the bracing air and the unsullied peace and purity of the wintry desert.

Stein was among the first Western travelers to visit Khotan, and he returned with important collections and the material for two books, the second of which, *Ancient Khotan* (1907), aroused considerable interest in scholarly circles.

With his Khotan expeditions, Stein established a pattern of archaeological travel that he was to maintain for the rest of his life: traveling alone except for his servants, taking copious notes, surveying his route, and collecting artifacts and manuscripts wherever he could. His interests were omnivorous, his energy astounding. The extent of his travels was staggering, especially if one remembers that he was venturing into largely unknown, often politically volatile territory hundreds of kilometers from the security of British India. He traveled on horseback, by mule, by camel, or on foot, often vanishing into the unknown for months on end.

By 1910, at age forty-eight, his teaching days were over. He transferred to the staff of the Indian Archaeological Service in that year, where his reputation as a traveler, and more especially as a successful collector, gave him virtual carte blanche. Seldom has an archaeological organization made a better hire. Stein was a bachelor and very much a loner, which made him the ideal person for the kind of all-consuming archaeological travel that central Asia demanded. He was never happier than when in the field, surrounded by his faithful staff and accompanied by a succession of fox terriers named Dash.

Between 1906 and 1913, Aurel Stein traveled deep into central Asia on a long journey that took him into the least accessible parts of China. It was on this journey that he visited the Caves of the Thousand Buddhas near Dunhuang in the far western part of the country. Four hundred and ninety two caves carved into the local sandstone contain elaborate Buddhist artworks of every kind. Almost all the shrines housed a huge seated Buddha with divine attendants, and painted frescoes covered the cavern walls. Chinese monks had founded the earliest shrine in these caves in A.D. 366, forming important religious communities in the region, which was an important stop on the Silk Road.

Stein arrived on March 12, 1907, in a cold sandstorm, but managed to secure fairly comfortable living quarters about a mile from the walled city of Dunhuang. There he wrestled with the expedition's accounts, which had to be submitted to the Indian government on the correct forms, with the expenditures incurred strictly according to government guidelines. Each evening he took walks with Dash, where he observed that the people

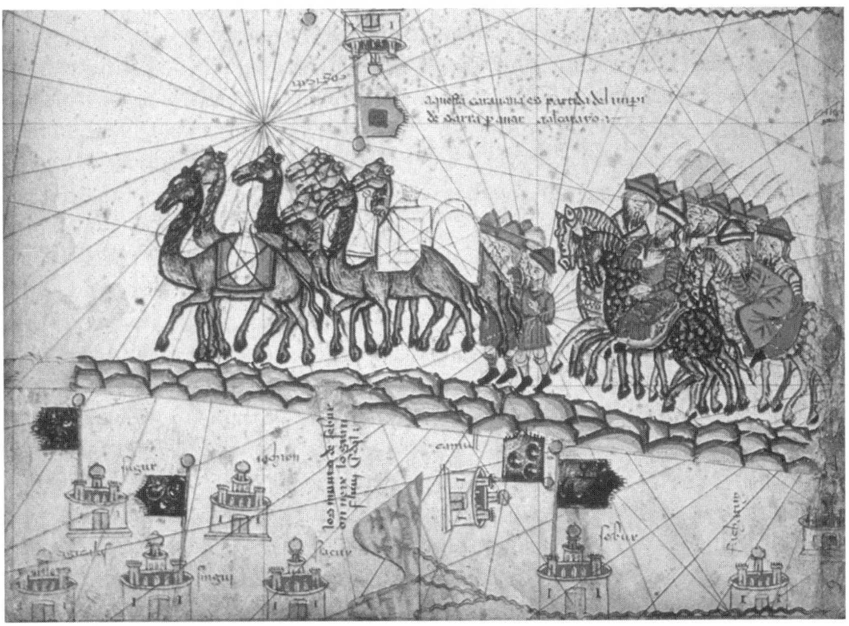

11-2 This detail of a map from the fourteenth-century Catalan Atlas shows a caravan crossing the famous Silk Road.

"are still as pious as in Marco's day [Marco Polo's]; curious Buddhist temples with coloured woodwork & frescoes are scattered throughout the hamlet & the half-deserted big city enclosure. I was eager to pay my preliminary visit to the Grottos of the 'Thousand Buddhas' which had first attracted my eyes to this region."[3]

As one of the first Westerners to marvel at the caves, Stein was not disappointed:

> On the almost perpendicular conglomerate cliffs a multitude of dark cavities, mostly small, was seen here honeycombing the somber rock faces in irregular tiers from the foot of the cliffs where the stream almost washed them, to the top of the precipice. . . . The whole strangely recalled fancy pictures of troglodyte dwellings of anchorites such as I remembered having seen long, long ago in early Italian paintings. . . . But the illusion did not last long. I recrossed the broad but thin ice sheet [of the stream] to the lowest point, where the rows of grottoes did not rise straight above the rubble bed but had a narrow strip of fertile alluvium in front of them and at once I noticed that fresco paintings covered the walls of all the grottoes. . . . The 'Caves of the Thousand Buddhas' were indeed tenanted not by Buddhist recluses, however holy, but by images of the Enlightened One himself. All this host of grottoes represented shrines. . . .
>
> The fine avenue of trees, apparently elms, which extended along the foot of the honeycombed cliffs, and the distant view of some dwellings farther up where the river bank widened, were evidence that the cave-temples had still their resident guardians. Yet there was no human being about to receive us, no guides to distract one's attention. In bewildering multitude and closeness the lines of the grottoes presented their faces, some high, some low, perched one above the other without any order or arrangement. In front of many were open verandah-like porches carved out of the soft rock with walls and ceilings bearing faded frescoes. Rough stairs cut into the cliff and still rougher wooden galleries served as approaches to the higher caves. . . .
>
> As I passed rapidly from one cella to another my eyes could scarcely take in more than the general type of frescoes and certain technical features of the stucco sculptures. The former, in composition and style, showed the closest affinity to the remains of Buddhist pictorial art transplanted from India to Eastern Turkestan, and already familiar from the ruined shrines I had excavated at Dandan-Uiliq and other old sites about Khotan. But in the representation of figures and faces the influence of Chinese taste made itself felt distinctly, and instead of the thin outlines and equally thin colouring there appeared often a perfect exuberance of strong but well-harmonized colours. Where deep blues and greens predominated there was something in the effect distinctly recalling Tibetan work. . . .
>
> Within the cella was ordinarily to be found a group of images occupying either an elevated platform or else placed in a kind of alcove facing the entrance. All the wall faces were covered with plaster bearing frescoes. . . . But whether the wall decoration showed pious compositions, or only that infinite multiplication of

Bodhisattvas and saints in which Buddhist piety revels, all details in the drawing and grouping of the divine figures bore the impress of Indian models. . . . In the subject of the friezes and side panels, which often apparently reproduced scenes from the daily life of monks and other mundane worshippers; in the design of the rich floral borders, the Chinese artists seemed to have given free expression to their love for the ornate landscape backgrounds, graceful curves, and bold movement. But no local taste had presumed to transform the dignified serenity of the features, the simple yet expressive gestures, the graceful richness of folds with which classical art, as transplanted to the Indus, had endowed the bodily presence of Tathagata [Buddha] and his many epiphanies. . . .

Of the sculptural remains it was more difficult to form a rapid impression; for much of this statuary in friable stucco had suffered badly through decay of its material, mere soft clay, and even more from the hands of iconoclasts and the zeal of pious restorers. In almost all the shrines I visited, a seated Buddha, sometimes of colossal proportions, was the presiding image; but by his side there appeared regularly groups of standing Bodhisattvas and divine attendants more or less numerous. I readily recognize representations of Dvarapalas, the celestial 'Guardian of the Quarters,' . . . But from the first I realized that prolonged study and competent priestly guidance would be needed. . . . It was pleasing to note the entire absence of those many-headed and many-armed monstrosities which the Mahayana Buddhism of the Far East shares with the later development of that cult in Tibet and the border mountains of Northern India.[4]

Touring the shrines with his Chinese secretary Chiang-ssu-yeh, Stein kept his eyes open for a recess in which, it was said, a huge hoard of ancient manuscripts had accidentally come to light. A young Taoist priest in charge of the sanctuary brought him one such manuscript that he had borrowed to adorn, and to add sanctity to, the private chapel of his spiritual guide, a Tibetan monk. Ancient manuscripts were considered sacred documents of great spiritual authority. To possess one in your chapel was a sign of piety.

It was a beautifully preserved roll of paper, about a foot high and perhaps fifteen yards long, which I unfolded with Chiang in front of the original hiding-place. The writing was, indeed, Chinese; but my learned secretary frankly acknowledged that to him the characters conveyed no sense whatsoever. Was this evidence of a non-Chinese language, or merely an indication of how utterly strange the phraseology of Chinese Buddhism is? . . .

It was a novel experience to find these shrines, notwithstanding all apparent decay, still frequented as places of actual worship. . . . I reflected with some apprehension upon the difficulties which this continued sanctity of the site might raise against archaeological exploitation. . . . Only experience and time could show. Meanwhile I was glad enough to propitiate the young Buddhist priest with an appropriate offering. I always like to be liberal. . . . But, unlike the attitude usually taken up by my Indian Pandit friends on such occasions, when they could—

vicariously—gain 'spiritual merit' for themselves, Chiang in his worldly wisdom advised moderation. A present too generous might arouse speculations about ulterior motives.

This remarkable document, obtained for almost nothing, was enough to whet Stein's always acquisitive appetite.

Dunhuang offered far more than sacred caves. It lay near a great intersection on the Silk Road as it passed from east to west, an intersection with another caravan trail leading from Mongolia to India and Tibet. The cool weather of spring offered a chance to explore the old Chinese frontier wall in the vicinity. Stein recruited a small party of workers and soon located the ancient *Pao-t' ais*, or watchtowers, that once lined the road, each made of solid clay and standing some 6 to 9 meters high. He examined small buildings near the towers, and also refuse heaps, and soon recovered wooden tablets bearing records from as early as A.D. 36. This had been a desolate but busy frontier, where the soldiers had to deal with political unrest in their homeland, as well as with raids by Huns from the north. There were records of detachments starving because their rations did not arrive. This field research would have satisfied many scholars, but the watchtowers were but the overture for what followed. Back at Dunhuang's caves, Stein found two dwellings,

unoccupied save for a fat jovial Tibetan Lama who had sought shelter here after long wanderings among the Mongols of the Mountains. In one of the courts my Indians found rooms to spread themselves in, and the Naik a convenient place to turn into a dark-room. In the other my Muhammadan followers secured shelter . . . while a hall possessed of a door and trellised windows, was reserved as a safe and discreet place of deposit for my collection of antiques. Chiang himself had a delightfully cool room at the very feet of a colossal seated Buddha reaching through three stories and with his innate sense of neatness promptly turned it into a quite cozy den with his camp rugs. My tent could be pitched under the shade of some fruit trees on the one little plot, grass-covered, offered on the narrow strip of cultivation extending in front of the caves for about half a mile.

Stein was now obsessed with finding the larger cache:

[I] asked to be shown over his restored cave-temple. It was the pride and mainstay of his Tun-huang existence, and my request was fulfilled with alacrity. As he took me through the lofty antechapel with its substantial woodwork, all new and lavishly gilt and painted . . . I could not help glancing to the right where an ugly patch of unplastered brickwork still masked the door of the hidden chapel. This was not the time to ask questions . . . but rather to display my interest in what his zeal had accomplished. Pride not greed would prove the avenue to access.

The manuscript hoard lay in a place that was bricked up as a precaution against tampering by pilgrims. After prolonged negotiations, which convinced Wang, the young priest, of Stein's devotion to the memory of the ancient Chinese traveler Hsüan-tsang, the wall was removed. Chiang caught a glimpse of a room crammed to the ceiling with manuscript bundles, and Stein hastened to the shrine.

Wang now summoned up the courage to open before me the rough door. . . . The sight of the small room disclosed was one to make my eyes open wide. Heaped up in layers, but without perfect order, there appeared in the dim light of the priest's little lamp a solid mass of manuscript bundles rising to a height of nearly ten feet, and filling, as subsequent measurement showed, close on 500 cubic feet. The area left clear within the room was just sufficient for two people to stand in. . . . In this 'black hole' no examination of the manuscripts would be possible. . . .

Nowhere could I trace the slightest effect of moisture. And, in fact, what better place for preserving such relics could be imagined than a chamber carved in the live rock of these terribly barren hills, and hermetically shut off from what moisture, if any, the atmosphere of this desert valley ever contained? Not in the driest soil could relics of a ruined site have so completely escaped injury as they had here in a carefully selected rock chamber where, hidden behind a brick wall and protected by accumulated drift sand, these masses of manuscripts had lain undisturbed for centuries . . . when, on opening a large packet wrapped in a stout sheet of coloured canvas, I found it full of paintings on fine gauze-like silk and on linen, ex-votos of all kinds of silks and brocades, with a mass of miscellaneous fragments of painted papers and cloth materials. Most . . . were narrow pieces from two to three feet in length, and proved by their floating streamers and the triangular tops provided with strings for fastening, to have served as temple banners. Many were in excellent condition . . . and showed when unfurled beautifully painted figures of Buddhas and Bodhisattvas almost Indian in style, or else scenes from Buddhist legend. The silk . . . was almost invariably a transparent gauze of remarkable fineness . . . allowing a good deal of light to pass through—very important since these paintings to be properly seen would have to be hung across or near the porches through which the cellas of the temples receive their only lighting. For the same reason of transparency most of the banners appeared to have been painted on both sides. Some had undergone damage [while still used] in the temples as proved by the care with which rents had been repaired. There were also silk paintings much larger in size . . . up to six feet or more. Closely and often carelessly folded up at the time of their deposition and much creased in consequence, . . . any attempt to open them out would have implied obvious risk to the material. . . . But by lifting a fold here and there, I could see that the scenes represented were almost as elaborate as the fresco panels on the walls.

[Some of the manuscripts] consisted of thick rolls of paper about one foot high . . . in excellent preservation, [they] showed in paper, arrangement, and other

> details unmistakable signs of great age. The joined strips of strongly made and remarkably tough and smooth yellowish paper, often ten yards or more long, were neatly rolled up after the fashion of Greek papyri, over small sticks of hard wood. . . . All showed signs of having been much read and handled; often the protecting outer folds, with the silk tape which had served for tying up the bundles, had got torn off. Where these covering folds were intact, it was easy for Chiang to read off the title of the Sutra, the chapter number, etc.

After five days of strenuous work carefully removing the priceless documents, Stein examined the collection, which contained manuscript rolls of Buddhist writings and canonical texts. In the end he was able to spirit seven cases of manuscripts and five cases of paintings and embroideries out of China. Had he taken the lot, he would have needed a "procession of carts" that would have caused suspicion among the local people. Stein was unrepentant. He felt that he was performing a "pious act" in rescuing the manuscripts for Western scholarship. Later, he acquired by stealth even more manuscripts, for the earlier removal was still a secret. Stein acquired the so-called Thousand Buddha manuscripts—more than 3,000 manuscript rolls—for about £150, which was, of course, worth much more than it is today, but was still a ludicrous bargain. The manuscripts and artwork currently adorn the British Museum. While the Chinese and many Western experts now condemn Stein's methods as unethical robbery, one must view them in the context of their time. His behavior was unethical, but it is an open question whether the manuscripts would have survived for posterity had not Stein passed them into expert hands. The British Raj left him in no doubt of its approval: Stein was knighted. He also received the prestigious Founder's Medal of the Royal Geographical Society in London.

From 1913 to 1916, Stein again returned to central Asia. But this time he faced stiff competition from French, German, and Russian archaeologists, who had moved into the field as a result of the news—which appeared in academic journals throughout Europe—of his remarkable discoveries. He now penetrated deep into Mongolia and traced unknown segments of the Silk Road, acquiring artifacts of all kinds at every turn. Word of his previous activities had spread to local officials, who had become more suspicious and much harder to deal with. Nevertheless, Stein negotiated adeptly and returned with many intact manuscripts, magnificent jade ornaments, and fine pottery. He remained very much a traveler and not an excavator, preferring to buy specimens for as low a price as possible, sometimes neglecting to take note of their cultural and historical contexts. He also collected artifacts himself from the surface of deserted archaeological sites, something that is now generally considered unethical for the archaeological traveler.

For the rest of his career, Stein continued to lead small-scale expeditions far into central Asia, and was encouraged by the Indian government, who saw Stein's expeditions as a cheap way of acquiring both geographical and foreign intelligence information. Many of his forays took him deep into the arid wastes of Persia and Iraq, where he searched for links with India's early civilizations, like the Harappan cities of the Indus Valley, now in Pakistan. In 1932, he crossed the ancient province of Gedrosia in what is now southwestern Pakistan, an area covered by Alexander the Great in 325 B.C. Even in his sixties and seventies, he kept a punishing schedule; he wrote of himself, "I am hard at work daily from 7:00 a.m. to 6:00 p.m., pushing on as well as my poor pen, and my inveterate claim at critical soundness, permit the account . . . of my expedition."[5] When he was well into his seventies, he explored central Iran, mapping the remote frontiers of the Roman Empire.

Almost single-handedly, and sometimes in the face of intense rivalries from archaeologists of other nations, Stein traveled most of the Silk Road long before motor vehicles arrived in central Asia, oblivious of hardship and obsessed with the archaeology of a vast, unknown region of the world. The British archaeologist Leonard Woolley of Ur fame, himself an expert on overcoming adversity in the field, once remarked that Stein's journeys were the most daring and adventurous raid on the ancient world that anyone had ever undertaken.

> The trouble about making journeys nowadays is that they are easy to make but difficult to justify. The earth, which once danced and spun before us as alluringly as a celluloid ball on top of a fountain in a rifle-range, is now a dull and vulnerable target. All along the line we have been forestalled, and forestalled by better men than we. Only the born tourist—happy, goggling ruminant—can follow in their tracks with the conviction that he is not wasting his time.
>
> PETER FLEMING
> *News from Tartary* (1936)

CHAPTER TWELVE

Individualists

The French-speaking Swiss traveler Ella Maillart (1903–1997) was a remarkable personality. By age thirty, she had taught French in a Welsh school, sailed in the Olympics for the Swiss team, acted on the Parisian stage, captained the Swiss women's field hockey team, assisted on an excavation in Crete, studied film production in Moscow, published a book about a north-south walk through the Caucasus, and ridden a camel across the Kizil Kum Desert in present-day Kazakhstan and Uzbekistan, southeast of the Aral Sea—in midwinter. No one knows why she had such a penchant for adventure and variety: perhaps she was rebelling against the staid and thoroughly conventional family life of her childhood. The freedom and self-assertion taken for granted by many women today could then be achieved only by being unconventional and heading off into the unknown.

At the age of twenty-eight, Maillart gazed on China for the first time. "In 1932, having gone east from Moscow, I climbed a mountain nearly 17,000 feet high on foot, and succeeded in reaching the eastern frontier of Russian Turkestan. There, at least, from the heights of the Celestial Mountains I could decry, on a plain far away and still further to the east, the yellow dust of the Takla Makan desert. It was China, the fabulous country of which, since my childhood, I had dreamed. There the caravan trails that were as old as the world, still wound. Long ago, Marco Polo followed them as far as Peking."[1] But she was unable to obtain a visa to enter Chinese Turkestan, which, like Outer Mongolia, was virtually isolated from the world by political turmoil. "Sadly," she wrote, "I retraced my steps, turning my back on the limitless unknown that beckoned."

Maillart and Fleming

Maillart traveled in romantic lands whose very names evoke adventure—Pingliang, Yarkand, Kashgar. For centuries, the Silk Road was synonymous with danger, mystery, and high adventure beyond the frontiers of the Western world. The men and women who explored this remote and unfamiliar realm had no illusions about the dangers and political disorder that awaited them, but they would have been quietly horrified to hear their travels described as adventures. Today, perilous journeys to remote parts of the world or across rough Antarctic seaways are a matter of technology, publicity, and sponsors. Modern communications link all parts of the world, even the South Pole and the summit of Mount Everest. Three-quarters of a century ago, Aurel Stein vanished into the limbo of central Asia for months and sometimes years at a time. When, in 1935, Ella Maillart and the English journalist Peter Fleming took a (technically illegal) 3,500-mile (5,600-kilometer) journey from Beijing to Kashgar and India through some of the most inhospitable terrain on earth, they did so without fuss and with the minimum of equipment. They did not possess any less ego than their contemporaries; they simply had different standards of comfort, diet, and hygiene. Fleming, the elder brother of Ian Fleming, the creator of James Bond, was very much a go-getter, and a very different personality from Maillart, who was at ease with people from different cultures and rolled with the punches when confronted with the frustrations and discomforts of central Asia. She

12-1 Ella Maillart was known for her friendly relations with local people. Here she shows residents of China's Ts'ing Hai (or Qinghai) province Owen Lattimore's book *The Desert Road to Turkestan.*

was receptive, tolerant, curious, and interested, perfect qualities for an archaeological traveler far from anywhere familiar.

Maillart was only casually interested in archaeology, but her attitude toward travel in remote, uncomfortable places was shared by many other young wanderers between 1900 and 1950, a new era of classic archaeological travel. The travels of these wanderers were as much a literary movement as an attempt to explore the exotica of the world outside New York, London, Paris, and other familiar stamping grounds. Some excellent books resulted, among them Peter Fleming's *News from Tartary* and Maillart's *Forbidden Journey*, books that should be read together because the two authors traveled together. But they were two travelers of very different mien, the one (Fleming) always in a hurry, the other content to go with the flow—a wiser strategy in the topsy-turvy world of central Asia as it was three-quarters of a century ago, where little had changed since the days when the great game pitted Russia against Great Britain in Afghanistan. "For much of the time we were in country very little known—country where even the collated wisdom represented by our maps was sometimes at fault and seldom comprehensive," wrote Fleming.[2] He described their travels as "monotonous, unheroic, but a strange existence."

Together, Fleming and Maillart stepped back centuries:

> There were days . . . when we rode or walked for hours, singly or together, filled with contentment at our lot. The sun shone, the mountains were alluring on our left, and we remembered the virtues of desolation and felt keenly the compensations of a nomad's life. Each march, each camp, differed very slightly from the one before; but they did differ, and we appreciated the slight but ever present freshness of our experience as much as we appreciated the tiny changes in the flavour of our food. . . .
>
> We were traveling in Asia at Asia's pace. . . . We had left the twentieth century behind with the lorries at Lanchow, and now we were up against the immemorial obstacles, the things which had bothered Alexander and worried the men who rose with Chinghis Khan—lack of beasts, lack of water, lack of grazing. We were doing the same stages every day that Marco Polo would have done if he had branched south from the Silk Road into the mountains.[3]

Fleming and Maillart had little interest in the past; they were more concerned with surviving the present. But occasionally they saw life as it had unfolded for many centuries. They visited the great monastery at Kumbum in Tibet, one of the richest in the country. As they approached the monastery, Fleming described the sensation of journeying backward in time:

Here was something altogether more dour, more self sufficient and aloof than pliant, conciliatory China; something that Time had hardly touched, that the West had not touched at all; something that had not yet faced, perhaps would never face, the necessity to prove itself adaptable, to change certain of its spots; something for better or worse immutable. . . . We crossed a little bridge, passed the chortens [commemorative monuments] and turned left into a maze of buildings whose small trapezoid windows, wider at the top than at the bottom, seemed to frown down on us from under lowering brows. . . . The cart drew up at the gateway of a large, clean pink-walled building and we walked through it into the central courtyard.

All around us lamas with shaven heads, in red robes or in yellow, paced and squatted in the courtyards. Others, inside the temples, seated rank upon rank in semi-darkness, endlessly intoned their prayers, sending up waves of rhythmic, hypnotizing sound to beat upon the scarlet pillars and the hangings between which a dull gleam betrayed the smiling and gigantic god. Here, in the greatest temple, looking down from a high gallery upon the huddled, chanting figures, I caught for a moment, and for the first time, something of that dark and powerful glamour with which Western superstition endows the sacred places of the East. I have been, as every traveler has, in many kinds of temples; never before in one where I had that tight, chill, tingling feeling which I suppose is something between spiritual awe and physical fear.[4]

"As travelers and travel writers, the English are special," remarks University of Pennsylvania English literature professor Paul Fussell in a study of British literary traveling between the two world wars.[5] Fussell notes that these travelers, often eccentric and larger than life, tended to be individualists who set off for remote places on their own, or with only one or two companions. The result was a distinctive literary genre to which many modern readers return again and again. Fussell has been criticized for his nostalgia for a less complicated, more literary age, but I believe that he is right: the 1920s and 1930s were a special time for travel. More than a few larger-than-life personalities and some true eccentrics wrote entertaining and sometimes truly engrossing accounts of their wanderings. Among them was the novelist Evelyn Waugh, who remarked that the end of World War II marked the close of the golden age of travel writing. They were wonderful days when "Mr. Peter Fleming went to the Gobi desert, Mr. Graham Greene to the Liberian hinterland . . . [and] Mr. Robert Byron . . . to the ruins of Persia."[6] This did not stop Waugh from writing a preface to Eric Newby's *A Short Walk in the Hindu Kush*, which appeared in 1958. Waugh called Newby the last of a "whimsical tradition," but Newby himself lamented that he had been born a century too late: the forces of modern technology had spoiled the pleasures of the ruin-seeking traveler. "Whimsical" Newby indeed was, for he injected his tellings of his travels with self-deprecating humor, catering as he was to a refined middle-class audience.

A growing academic literature now surrounds travel writing, much of it concerned with such topics as travel writing's role as a mode of colonialist discourse that reinforces Western stereotypes. The debates in this proliferating literature also identify English gentlemen travelers as a distinctive breed of the early twentieth century and before. These gentlemen were indeed individualists and remarkable travelers, usually with no interest in science or archaeology. There were, however, a few exceptions, the best known of them being the eccentric and outspoken Robert Byron.

Byron in Oxiana

Robert Byron (1905–1941) was born into a wealthy English landowning family and received an education to match at Eton and at Merton College, Oxford. He studied history and emerged with an undistinguished degree and a reputation for outspoken eccentricity. He liked, for example, to attend London parties dressed as Queen Victoria, whom he imagined that he resembled. Travel was more than an interest with his contemporaries: it was a near-obsession. Like his friends, Byron was quick-witted and hungry for excitement, finding Britain after World War I a narrow, puritanical place. "I might have been a dentist, or a public man," he remarked after an encounter with Italy at the impressionable age of eighteen exposed him to a much wider world.[7]

By the time Byron was twenty, he had traveled through Greece and Hungary and discovered a talent for writing. In Greece, he became entranced with Byzantine mosaics and turned his back on classical sculpture, which he classified as "inert stone bodies which already bar persons of artistic sensibility from entering half the museums of Europe."[8] He returned several times to this engaging country and spent time with the monks on Mount Athos, where he helped a young Scottish art historian, David Talbot Rice, photograph the frescoes in the chapels and monasteries. Byron's resulting book, *The Byzantine Achievement*, published in 1929, was a serious study of Byzantine history that gave him a reputation as an impressive independent scholar. At the same time, he developed a style of travel writing that was at once learned, comic, and satirical, while sympathetic to people from very different cultures.

From Byzantium, Byron moved even further afield to India, Tibet, and the Soviet Union, writing two books that railed against the complacency of the British Raj and dwelt on "that most difficult of all lessons for the

Englishman, the tolerance and understanding of the customs and mentalities of foreigners."[9] In *First Russia, Then Tibet*, published in 1933, Byron remarked that travel was a serious endeavor, despite the existence of other ways of experiencing the world. "The traveler is a slave to his senses; his grasp of a fact can only be complete when reinforced by sensory evidence; he can know the world, in fact, only when he sees, hears, and smells it."[10] A better rationale for being an archaeological traveler cannot be imagined. One has not truly experienced the past until one has sensed it, perhaps atop a Bronze Age burial mound in southern England in the full drift of a southwesterly gale, or standing in New Mexico's semiarid San Juan Basin, watching the dark clouds of an afternoon thunderstorm mass over Chaco Canyon.

Between 1933 and 1934, Byron and his friend Christopher Sykes wandered through Persia, Afghanistan, and on to India, in a vague search for particularly tall brick towers in Persia that Byron had heard about in India. This was an interesting period to visit Persia, for the mosques were opened to nonbelievers only in 1931. From this trip came Byron's most famous book, *The Road to Oxiana*, which appeared in 1937. Byron still traveled occasionally after his Persian adventure, but he became increasingly preoccupied with the dangers of Nazism. A ship carrying him to an intelligence and newspaper assignment in Meshed, Iran, was sunk in February 1941, and Byron was lost.

Oxiana is the country surrounding the Oxus River, part of the frontier between the former Soviet Union and Afghanistan. At the time of Byron's journey, Oxiana was a very remote place indeed for Westerners, a place of volatile politics and constant violence. Byron's objective was to find the Gumbad-i-Kabus (Gondbad-e Qabus), a brick tower built by Qabus, ruler of Gurgan, as his mausoleum, and where Qabus's body was said to be suspended in a glass casket atop the tower. To resist such a spectacular challenge was impossible for Byron. He started in Venice, and was supposed to be transported to Persia by two young English friends who were both, separately, driving a charcoal-powered Rolls Royce across Asia Minor as a publicity stunt. The charcoal behemoth failed to appear, so Byron and Sykes traveled to Jerusalem, Baghdad, and Persia on their own, relying on buses, trucks, and even horses. Upon reaching Persia, they came under deep suspicion, since the shah was paranoid about foreign travelers, especially those arriving with cameras and sketchpads.

There is a wonderful gusto about Byron's writing, which produced a travel book that has, rather than a seamless narrative, a haphazard collage of diary entries and other materials, including fictional dialogues that mimicked reality. *The Road to Oxiana* captures the immediacy of Byron's life on the road and among the ruins in a way few authors achieve. He had the ability to define the experience in a few sentences:

> The traveler of old was one who went in search of knowledge and whom the indigenes were proud to entertain with their local interests. In Europe this attitude of reciprocal appreciation has long evaporated. But there at least the "tourist" is no longer a phenomenon. He is part of the landscape, and in nine cases out of ten has little money to spend beyond what he had paid for his tour. Here, he is still an aberration. If you can come from London to Syria on business, you must be rich. No one cares if you like the place, or hate it, or why. You are simply a tourist, as a skunk is a skunk, a parasitic version of the human species, which exists to be tapped like a milch cow or a gum tree.[11]

Byron started his journey with a visit to the spectacular ruins at Baalbek before they became a package-tour destination. At first, the experience was frustrating. He argued over the five-shilling admission fee to the ruins and got it reduced (by how much he does not tell us) by telephoning the authorities in Beirut. He complained when the old man at the gate took ten minutes to write out each ticket. "After that we escaped from these trivialities into the glory of Antiquity," he wrote, glad to escape momentarily a modern world in which the local people hated the British only slightly less than they hated the French who ruled over them. At Baalbek, he found serenity and a site worthy of unbounded admiration.

> Baalbek is the triumph of stone; of lapidary magnificence on a scale whose language, being still the language of the eye, dwarfs New York into a home of ants. The stone is peach-coloured, and is marked in ruddy gold as the columns of St. Martin-in-the-Fields are marked in soot. It has a marmoreal texture, not transparent, but faintly powdered, like bloom on a plum. Dawn is the time to see it, to look up at the Six Columns, when peach-gold and blue air shine with equal radiance, and even the empty bases that uphold no columns have a living, sun-blest identity against the violet deeps of the firmament. Look up, look up; up this quarried flesh, these thrice-enormous shafts, to the broken capitals and the cornice as big as a house, all floating in the blue. Look over the walls, to the green groves of white-stemmed poplars; and over them to the distant Lebanon, a shimmer of mauve and blue and gold and rose. Look along the mountains to the void: the desert, that stony, empty sea. Drink the high air. Stroke the stone with your own soft hands. Say goodbye to the West if you own it. And then turn, *tourist*, to the East.
>
> We did, when the ruins closed. It was dusk. Ladies and gentlemen in separate parties were picnicking on a grass meadow, beside a stream. Some sat on chairs by marble fountains, drawing at their hubble-bubbles; others on the grass beneath occasional trees, eating by their own lanterns. The stars came out and the

mountain slopes grew black. I felt the peace of Islam. And if I mention this commonplace experience, it is because in Egypt and Turkey that peace is now denied; while in India Islam appears, like everything else, uniquely and exclusively Indian. In a sense it is so; for neither man nor institution can meet that overpowering environment without a change of identity. But I will say this for my own sense: that when travelling in Mohammedan India without previous knowledge of Persia, I compared myself to an Indian observing European classicism, who had started on the shores of the Baltic instead of the Mediterranean.[12]

And turn to the east he did. Now Byron depended on public transport and the hospitality of "that admirable institution, the Persian caravanserai":

Garages are everywhere certainly. But they reproduce the old plan. This consists of a quadrangle, as big as an Oxford college, and defended by huge doors. Near the doors, beside the arched entrance, are rooms for cooking, eating, communal sleeping, and the transaction of business. Round the other three sides are rows of smaller rooms, which resemble monastic cells, and accommodation for horses and motors. Comfort varies. Here, in the Garage Massis, I have a spring bed, a carpet, and a stove. At Damghan there was no furniture at all, and the food was lumps of tepid rice.[13]

Nor was the transport necessarily reliable, as Byron also described.

It was nine o'clock before I found a seat on a British Bedford pilgrim bus. . . . That vehicle was carrying twice its proper number of passengers and their luggage as well. Exhilarated at the prospect of his journey's end the driver tore downhill at forty miles an hour, lurched across a stream-bed, and had just rebounded against the opposite slope, when to my great surprise the off front wheel ran back towards me, buckling the running board with a crunch, and escaped into the desert. "Are you English," asked the driver in disgust. "Look at that." An inch of British steel had broken clean through.

It took an hour and a half to fit another joint. The pilgrims huddled down with their backs to the wind, men beneath their yellow sheepskins, women veiled in black shrouds. Three chickens, tied to each other by the leg, enjoyed a temporary freedom. But their clucking boded little hope. When we started again, the driver was seized with a palsy of caution. He proceeded at five miles an hour, stopping at every caravanserai to refresh his nerves with tea; till at least we reached a small pass and a new view.[14]

But the archaeological rewards of his peregrinations were spectacular. The town of Herat in northwestern Afghanistan lay in the heart of the Mongolian conqueror Timur's domains. Timur the Lame, or Tamerlane, forged a large state based around Samarkand, and campaigned as far south as Delhi, devastated Baghdad, and clashed with the Ming emperors of China. More than a warrior king, he was also a noteworthy patron of the arts and adorned his capital with fine architecture. At the time of Byron's arrival, Herat's Friday mosque, built by the Ghorid sultan Ghiyasuddin in 1200, was in a poor state of repair (it is now being restored). The nearby Musalla ("prayer ground" in Arabic) was commissioned in about 1417, with a Friday mosque, madrassa (school), and the mausoleum of Gohar Shad, wife of Shah Rukh, son of Tamerlane, decorated with elaborate tile work and thirty minarets. Unfortunately, the British dynamited much of the Musalla to gain artillery sightlines against a possible Russian advance in 1885. Only Gohar Shad's mausoleum, six minarets, and a smaller madrassa survived. They were further damaged by an earthquake in 1931. In Byron's day, Herat was far off the beaten track for most travelers. So he used accounts written by nineteenth-century British officers as his guide. He visited the Friday mosque and the remains of the Musalla, a group of religious buildings with six minarets, between November 23 and 26, 1935.

Herat, November 23rd.—Keeping my two guides in my head, I walked up the northern of the four New Town roads in the direction of a gigantic mound, about 600 yards long, which appears to be artificial and must resemble, from all accounts, the mounds in the neighbourhood of Balkh. Hence one can climb up

12-2 Unlike many historical minarets in the region, those shown here at the central portal of Masjid-i Jameh in Herat, Afghanistan, stand intact.

on to another wall, an outwork of the town's defences, and survey the lie of the Musalla. This is the popular name for the whole of the seven minarets and the Mausoleum. But actually they were part of separate buildings built at different times, some in the reign of Shah Rukh, one in that of Hussein Baikara.

All the minarets are between 100 and 130 feet high. They lean at various angles; their tops are broken, their bases twisted and eaten away. The furthest distance between them, stretching from west-south-west to east-north-east is about a quarter of a mile. The two on the west are fatter than the others, but like the four on the east have one balcony each. The middle one, which stands by itself, has two balconies. The Mausoleum lies between the two on the west, but to the north of them. It is only half their height, but from a distance seems less.

This array of blue towers rising haphazard from a patchwork of brown fields and yellow orchards has a most unnatural look. The monarchs of Islam in early days had a habit of putting up isolated minarets, singly or in pairs: witness the Kutb at Delhi and the base of its fellow. But this did not extend till the fifteenth century, and never to such a number as seven. However, it can be seen from the insides of these minarets, where the tile-work stops short some forty feet from the ground, that they were originally joined by walls or arches and must have formed part of a series of mosques or colleges. What has happened to these buildings? Things on this scale may fall down, but they leave some ruin. They don't vanish of their own accord without trace or clue, as these have done.

It is a miserable story. Even Yate, who saw it happen, betrays an unsoldierly sigh. Ferrier thought these buildings, ruined as they then were, the finest in Asia. The other travellers concur in their extraordinary beauty, the radiance of their mosaic and the magnificence of their gilt inscriptions. Conolly, if I remember right, speaks of twenty or thirty minarets. In fact, allowing for the difference between English prose and Persian, his description is not unlike Khondemir's of the buildings in their prime.

In the seventies and eighties Herat was incessantly on English lips. It even crops up in Queen Victoria's letters. If the Russians took it, as they were expected to do, the low-lying Kandahar road would be theirs for a railway to the Indian border. In 1885 the Panjdeh incident occurred. Though St. Petersburg had already agreed to the joint Boundary Commission, Russian troops attacked the Afghans south-east of Merv and drove them back. An advance on Herat was expected any day, and the Emir Abdurrahman sent orders that the town was to be placed in a state of defence. The Russians would approach from the north. All buildings, therefore, that might give them cover on this side of the town must be demolished. For years officers of the Indian Army had been advising on such measures. I suspect this particular order was of British inspiration; though proof must wait till the archives of Delhi and the War Office give up their dead. In any case the most glorious productions of Mohammadan architecture in the fifteenth century, having survived the barbarism of four centuries, were now rased to the ground under the eyes, and with the approval, of the English Commissioners. Nine minarets and the Mausoleum escaped.

Even this epitaph of an epitaph is insecure. Two minarets have already disappeared since Niedermayer was here. They fell during an earthquake in 1931, which also destroyed a second domed mausoleum photographed by him. I saw the site of it yesterday, near the fork of the roads to Kushk and the Persian frontier: a mound of rubble. Unless repairs are done and foundations strengthened, the other monuments will soon be rubble too.

However, there is enough left, and enough information, to show how the buildings stood up to 1885.

The minarets that fell down the year before last were a pair to the two fat ones on the west. Together, the four marked the corners of a mosque. This was the real Musalla. According to an inscription on one of the minarets, which Niedermayer photographed and which must have perished in the earthquake, it was built, at her private expense, by Gohar Shad Begum, the wife of Shah Rukh, son of Timur, between the years 1417 and 1437. The architect, in all probability, was Kavam-ad-Din of Shiraz, who served Shah Rukh in that capacity during the greater part of his reign, and is mentioned by the historian Daulat Shah as one of the four great lights of his court.

Diez, who knows the subject as well as anyone, and is not the slave of his journey's emotions like me, says these minarets are adorned with such "fabulous richness and subtle taste" (märchenhafter Pracht und subtilem Geschmack) that no others in Islam can equal them. He speaks from photographs only. But no photograph, nor any description, can convey their colour of grape-blue with an azure bloom, or the intricate convolutions that make it so deep and luminous. On the bases, whose eight sides are supported by white marble panels carved with a baroque Kufic, yellow, white, olive green and rusty red mingle with the two blues in a maze of flowers, arabesques and texts as fine as the pattern on a tea-cup. The shafts above are covered with small diamond-shaped lozenges filled with flowers, but still mainly grape-blue. Each of these is bordered with white faience in relief, so that the upper part of each minaret seems to be wrapped in a glittering net.

In point of decoration minarets are generally the least elaborate parts of a building. If the mosaic on the rest of the Musalla surpassed or even equalled what survives today, there was never such a mosque before or since.

Yet I don't know. Gohar Shad built another mosque, inside the Shrine at Meshed. This mosque is still intact. I must see it somehow if I come back this way.

Looked at in detail, the decoration of the Mausoleum is inferior to that of the two minarets. The drum of the dome is encircled with tall panels filled with hexagons of lilac mosaic combined with triangles of raised stucco. The dome itself is turquoise, and the ribs, like those of Timur's Mausoleum at Samarcand, are scattered with black and white diamonds. Each rib is three-quarters in the round and as fat as a 64-foot organ-pipe. The walls below are bare, but for a few glazed bricks and a peculiar three-windowed bay that reminds one of a villa in Clapham. But the quality of these separate elements, if sometimes coarse, is transcended by the goodness of their proportions and the solidity of the whole idea. Few architectural devices can equal a ribbed dome for blind, monumental ostentation.

This too seems to have been the work of Gohar Shad. Babur speaks of her three buildings: her Mosque, which is the Musalla; her Madrassa or College; and her Mausoleum. And Khondemir states several times that the Mausoleum was inside the College. She was certainly buried in the Mausoleum; Yate noted the inscription on her tombstone. He also noted those on five others, all of Timurid princes. Twenty-five years earlier Khanikov had noted nine altogether. Now there are only three, of a matt black stone, shaped like oblong boxes and carved with flower designs. One is smaller than the others.

Next, on the east of the Mausoleum, stands the solitary minaret with two balconies. The origin of this baffles me. Its ornament of blue lozenges, jewelled with flowers, but separated by plain brickwork, is not to be compared with that of the Musalla minarets. Perhaps it was part of Gohar Shad's College. A College would naturally be more sober than a mosque. Babur speaks as if College, Mosque, and Mausoleum were all close together.

I feel some curiosity about Gohar Shad, not on account of her piety in endowing religious foundations, but as a woman of artistic instinct. Either she had that instinct, or she knew how to employ people who had it. This shows character. And besides this, she was rich. Taste, character, and riches mean power, and powerful women, apart from charmers, are not common in Mohammadan history.

Four minarets remain, near the bridge over a winding canal. They too are girt with a white network; though their blue is brighter than that of the Musalla minarets, so that from close at hand it seems as if one saw the sky through a net of shining hair and as if it had been planted, suddenly, with flowers. These mark the corners of the College of Hussein Baikara, who ruled Herat from 1469 to 1506. His grandfather's tombstone, of the same type as those in the Mausoleum but known as the Stone of the Seven Pens from its more profuse carving, lies close by and is still revered as a popular shrine.

The lyrical and less stately beauty of these minarets reflects the reign that produced it. Unlike Gohar Shad, Hussein Baikara is more than a name. His body at least is familiar. Bihzad drew it. Babur described it, and his amusements as well. He had slant-eyes, a white beard, and a slender waist. He dressed in red and green. Ordinarily he wore a small lambskin cap. But on feast-days he would "sometimes set up a threefold turban, wound broad and badly, and stick a heron's plume in it and so go to prayers". This was the least he could do; for towards the end of his life he was so crippled with rheumatism that he could not perform the prayers properly. Like small people, he enjoyed flying pigeons, and matching fighting cocks and fighting rams. He was also a poet, but published his verses anonymously. To meet he was cheerful and pleasant, but immoderate in temper and loud-spoken. In love, orthodox and unorthodox, he was insatiable. He had innumerable concubines and children who destroyed the peace of the state and his old age. As a result "what happened with his sons, the soldiers and the town was that everyone pursued vice and pleasure to excess."

Babur was not a Puritan. But the parties in Herat obliged him to get drunk. And in explaining how this happened, for the first time in his life, he reveals the effect of such an atmosphere on a young man's equilibrium. Nevertheless, looking back to Herat when he himself had become great, he still writes with deference, as one has seen a great age, and having learned how to live, had seen it vanish—like Talleyrand. The humanism of that age was the model of his life. His achievement in history was to replant it, and leave descendants to cherish it, amid the drab heats and uncouth multitudes of Hindostan.[15]

Meshed, in what is now northeastern Iran, is regarded as the seventh most holy place of Islam. Thousands of pilgrims visit the tomb of the eighth imam, Reza, who died there in 818. The sacred precincts of the city form a perfect circle known as the Bast, and are off-limits to nonbelievers. Both the tomb of Imam Reza and the superb Grand Mosque of Gohar Shad, one of the masterpieces of Islamic architecture, lie within the Bast. Byron paid two visits to Meshed. On the first occasion, accompanied by a nervous police officer, he gazed at the shrine through binoculars from half a kilometer away.

Attended by an unhappy police officer, I spent the morning on various roofs examining the Shrine through field-glasses from the other side of the circular street. There are three main courts, each with four ivans (no other word will describe those huge open-fronted halls with pointed vaults and high façades, which are the special feature of Persian mosque architecture). Two of the courts point north and south, and are situated end to end, though not on the same axis; the tilework in these, from a distance, looks like chintz and must date from the seventeenth or eighteenth centuries. Between them rises a helm-shaped dome plated in gold, which marks the tomb of the Imam and was erected by Shah Abbas in 1607; Chardin, in 1672, saw plates being made at Isfahan to repair it after an earthquake. Beside it stands a gold minaret, and there is another such minaret to the east of the southern court.

The third court points west, at right angles to the north and south courts. This is the mosque which Gohar Shad built between 1405 and 1418. Above the sanctuary chamber at the end, which is flanked by two enormous minarets, rises the sea-blue dome, bulbous in shape, inscribed on the bulge with bold black Kufic, and festooned from the apex with thin yellow tendrils.

The mosaic of the whole court appears to be still intact. Even from a quarter of a mile away I could see the difference in quality of its colour from that of the other courts. Here is the clue to the vanished glories of Herat. I must and will penetrate this mosque before I leave Persia. But not now; I haven't the initiative. It must wait till the spring, by which time perhaps I shall have found out more about Gohar Shad.[16]

On his second visit, Byron was determined to enter the Bast and resorted to disguise. His fleeting, surreptitious glimpse of the religious district was a memorable experience.

Meshed, May 7th.—Last night, excusing ourselves from the Consulate, we dined at the hotel. Christopher observed that an up-to-date guide to Meshed might contain a sentence such as: "Visitors intending to inspect the Shrine of the Imam Riza usually dine and make up at the Hotel de Paris". We finished with vanilla ices, and primed ourselves with a miserable sour Caucasian burgundy. At eight o'clock, I had just applied the last shred of cork to the nape of Christopher's neck when our friend the schoolmaster arrived with an Armenian lady, who had come to see the heroes start. She saw them into a broken-down victoria. This drove to the main gate of the Shrine, where we dismounted, but instead of entering, turned to the right up the circular avenue. "Are you ready?" said the guide, and dived into a dark tunnel. We followed like rabbits, found ourselves in a little yard, scurried down a lighted bazaar full of booths and purchasers, and came out into the great court of the Mosque of Gohar Shad.

Amber lights twinkled in the void, glowing unseen from the mighty arch before the sanctuary, reflecting a soft blaze over the gilded entrance to the Tomb opposite, and revealing, as the eye adapted itself, a vast quadrilateral defined by ranks of arches. An upper tier rose out of reach of the lights, and, passing through a zone of invisibility, reappeared as a black parapet against the stars. Turbaned mullahs, white-robed Afghans, vanished like ghosts between the orbits of the lamps, gliding across the black pavement to prostrate themselves beneath the golden doorway. A sound of chanting was heard from the sanctuary, where a single tiny figure could be seen abased in the dimness, at the foot of its lustred mihrab.

Islam! Iran! Asia! Mystic, languid, inscrutable!!

One can hear a Frenchman saying that, the silly fool—as if it was an opium den in Marseilles. We felt the opposite; that is why I mention it. Every circumstance of sight, sound, and trespass conspired to swamp the intelligence. The message of a work of art overcame this conspiracy, forcing its way out of the shadows, insisting on structure and proportion, on the impress of superlative quality, and on the intellect behind them. How this message was conveyed is difficult to say. Glimpses of arabesques so liquid, so delicately interlaced, that they looked no more like mosaic than a carpet looks like stitches; of larger patterns lost in the murk above our heads; of vaults and friezes alive with calligraphy—these were its actual words. But the sense was larger. An epoch, the Timurids, Gohar Shad herself, and her architect Kavam-ad-Din, ruled the night.

"Please blow your nose," whispered our guide to Christopher. "Why?"

"I ask you, blow it, and continue to blow it. You must cover your beard."

Our guide was well known to the mullahs and policemen on duty. They greeted him without noticing the shabby plebeian at his side or the sneezing consumptive at his heels. We walked twice round the quadrangle, very slowly, bowing to the Tomb each time; then quickened our pace through the other two great courts, an ethereal vision of silver-white niches in double tiers.

"Now," hissed our guide, "we are coming to the main gate. I shall talk to you, Mr. Byron, when we go out. You, Mr. Sykes, please blow your nose and walk behind."

Guards, porters, and ecclesiastics stood up respectfully as they saw him come. He seemed entirely preoccupied with his own conversation, which took the form of a charwoman's monologue and sounded so remarkable in Persian that I had no need to simulate interest: "So I said to him rumble rumble rumble rumble Rumble he said rumble Rumble? I said I said and rumble rumble Rumble rumble he said to me I said Rumble! rumblerumblerumblerumble. . . ." Everyone bowed. Our guide cast an eye over his shoulder to see that Christopher was following, and we were out, got a cab, and were soon scrubbing our faces at the hotel before returning to the Consulate.

We thanked him profusely. But in the same breath I was obliged to tell him that having seen this much, no amount of gratitude could prevent my begging him to take me again by daylight. Noticing his reluctance, Christopher offered not to come, as his beard was evidently an embarrassment. This relieved our guide. He arranged to call for me at two o'clock today.

This morning, when I entered the hotel, the bedroom attendant brought me a plate of corks and charcoal without being asked for them. It was another thing to make up for daylight with these crude materials: my moustache looked green instead of black, and turned out brindled; my eyes were still blue, inside lashes semi-black and sore with scrubbing. But the costume was subtle: brown shoes with tight black trousers four inches too short; grey coat; gold stud instead of a tie; our servant's mackintosh; and a black Pahlevi hat which I aged by kicking it—these components created the perfect type of Marjoribanks's Persia. Alas! my work of art was hardly complete before a telephone message informed me that our guide had funked at the last minute.

Not daring to take a cab by myself, I had to walk the mile and a half to the Shrine. The sun was at my back; I sweated under the mackintosh as I invented a quick Persian-looking trot of short high steps that would prevent me from tripping over uneven paving-stones; but no one looked at me. The goal grew nearer. There was the main gate. There the little tunnel. Without looking round, I was in it, found the yard, realised there were trees there, and then saw that the further exit was completely blocked by a group of mullahs, my potential assaulters, who were discussing the wares of a small bookshop.

Everything depended on my pace. I was keyed to it, and by it. If it faltered, I was exposed. So I kept to it, and clove that group of mullahs as a torpedo cleaves the waves. By the time they noticed me, grumbling at such ill manners, there was only my back to notice.

I hastened down the dark bazaar, found the dome where I turned to the left, and was greeted, on coming out into the court, by such a fanfare of colour and light that I stopped a moment, half blinded. It was as if someone had switched on another sun.

The whole quadrangle was a garden of turquoise, pink, dark red, and dark blue, with touches of purple, green, and yellow, planted among paths of plain buff brick. Huge white arabesques whirled above the ivan arches. The ivans themselves hid other gardens, shadier, fritillary-coloured. The great minarets beside the sanctuary, rising from bases encircled with Kufic the size of a boy, were bedizened with a network of jewelled lozenges. The swollen sea-green dome adorned with yellow tendrils appeared between them. At the opposite end glinted the top of a gold minaret. But in all this variety, the principle of union, the life-spark of the whole blazing apparition, was kindled by two great texts: the one, a frieze of white *suls* writing powdered over a field of gentian blue along the skyline of the entire quadrangle; the other, a border of the same alphabet in daisy white and yellow on a sapphire field, interlaced with turquoise Kufic along its inner edge, and enclosing, in the form of a three-sided oblong, the arch of the main ivan between the minarets. The latter was actually designed, it says, by "Baisanghor, son of Shah Rukh, son of Timur Gurkani (Tamerlane), with hope in God, in the year 821 (A.D. 1418)". Baisanghor was a famous calligrapher; and being the son of Gohar Shad also, he celebrated his mother's munificence with an inscription whose glory explains for ever the joy felt by Islam in writing on the face of architecture.

This vision was a matter of seconds. Simultaneously, I began to feel insecure. I had intended to follow last night's plan of walking slowly round the court, but was prevented by two crowds, one listening to a preacher before the main ivan, one praying before the Tomb opposite; so that either way was threatened by religious etiquette. Other pilgrims were squatting along the walls, many of them Afghans, all quite different in clothes and manner from my lower middle-class Persian self, and eyeing me, so I imagined, with hawk-like scowls as I walked to and fro between the two crowds. At last it was no longer imagination: my gaping inquisitiveness attracted notice. I scuttled back into the bazaar. The mullahs were no longer in the passage. Out in the street stood Christopher, leering wantonly as I passed him with eyes averted. Now, on the way back, the sun was in my face, and people turned to look at me as I passed. There was something wrong. Whatever it was, Mrs. Gastrell did not jump to it. She was drying her hair by the fire, and was highly incensed when her privacy was abused by an unknown native.

I have learned what I wanted to know: first, that the use of coloured mosaic out of doors reached its climax at the Timurid Renascence; and second, that the beauty of it in the Shrine here is nevertheless surpassed on six of the seven minarets at Herat, whose remains have an even finer quality and purer colour, and are not interrupted by plain brickwork. The few travellers who have visited Samarcand and Bokhara as well as the Shrine of the Imam Riza, say that nothing in those two towns can equal the last. If they are right, the Mosque of Gohar Shad must be the greatest surviving monument of the period, while the ruins of Herat show that there was once a greater.

I tremble to think that of the four finest buildings in Persia, the Gumbad-i-Kabus, the small dome-chamber in the Friday Mosque at Isfahan, the Mosque of Gohar Shad here, and the Mosque of Sheikh Lutfullah at Isfahan, my acquaintance with two was postponed till my last fortnight in the country.[17]

As he traveled south, Byron paused at Persepolis, where he commented on the contrast between the experience of the visitor during earlier times and that of the modern traveler (see Chapter 6). He also added some brief comments on the architecture there, comments that represent the work of a truly observant visitor.

No one would have been more pleased than I to leave the brain idle in a dream of history and landscape and light and wind and other impalpable accidents. But if circumstances insist on showing me more than I want to see, it is no good telling lies about it.

The columns, therefore, can be disposed of in a word. They are surprising, as Sir Gilbert Scott's town-hall in Bombay is surprising because it combines Hindu themes with Gothic. Like mules, these crosses are infertile. They have no bearing on the general course of architecture, and hold no precepts for it. You may like them in a casual way, if they happen to agree with some current of contemporary fashion. The columns at Persepolis don't.

The columns jump to the eye first. Other architectural features are the stairs, the platform, and the palace doors. The stairs are fine because there are so many of them. The platform is fine because its massive blocks have posed, and solved, an engineering problem. Neither has any art. But the doorways have. They, and they alone, boast a gleam of true invention; they suggest ideas, they utter a comment, with regard to other doorways. Their proportions are narrow and thick, thus inviting a perpetual to and fro; whereas our doors ask the figure to pause and frame itself. Like the arches at Stonehenge, they are made of monoliths, one for each side and one on top. But their mouldings and angles are as sharp and delicate as if cut by a machine.

Then comes the decoration. Those reliefs hold a horrid shock for anyone who has known them in photographs. Where they have been exposed to the weather, their line and rhythm emerges poetically from the black-mottled stone. The ones inside the doorways, and the ones that Herzfeld has dug up, have exactly the same line and rhythm. But their stone, owing to its extreme hardness, has proved impervious to age; it remains a bright smooth grey, as slick as an aluminium saucepan. This cleanness reacts on the carving like sunlight on a fake old master; it reveals, instead of the genius one expected, a disconcerting void. I see only too well what Christopher meant when he said the sculptures were "unemotional without being intellectual". My involuntary thought, as Herzfeld showed me the new staircase, was: "How much did this cost? Was it made in a factory? No, it wasn't. Then how many workmen for how many years chiselled and polished these endless figures?" Certainly they are not mechanical figures; nor are they guilty of elaboration for its own sake; nor are they cheap in the sense of lacking technical skill. But they are what the French call *faux bons*. They have art, but not spontaneous art, and certainly not great art. Instead of mind or feeling, they exhale a soulless refinement, a veneer adopted by the Asiatic whose own artistic instinct has been fettered and devitalised by contact with the Mediterranean. To see what that instinct really was, and how it differs from this, one can look at the Assyrian reliefs in the British Museum.

A lesser shock is administered by the crenellations along the parapet and balustrades of the staircase. Herzfeld found them in almost perfect condition; each has three steps and looks as if it had been built from a child's box of bricks. These jagged excrescences adorned all the palaces; Krefter has reproduced them with care on his. They are ugly enough in themselves. But adjacent to the reliefs, their clumsy iteration and angular shadows spoil the delicacy of the carving as well. Herzfeld said: "They give it life". They do. But it isn't a pretty life and it kills everything else.[18]

But he reserved his most enthusiastic remarks for Isfahan (Esfahan), south of modern-day Tehran:

Isfahan, March 18th.—The beauty of Isfahan steals on the mind unawares. You drive about, under avenues of white tree-trunks and canopies of shining twigs; past domes of turquoise and spring yellow in a sky of liquid violet-blue; along the river patched with twisting shoals, catching that blue in its muddy silver, and lined with feathery groves where the sap calls; across bridges of pale toffee brick, tier on tier of arches breaking into piled pavilions; overlooked by lilac mountains, by the Kuh-i-Sufi shaped like Punch's hump and by other ranges receding to a line of snowy surf; and before you know how, Isfahan has become indelible, has insinuated its image into that gallery of places which everyone privately treasures.

I gave it no help in doing so. The monuments have kept me too busy.

One could explore for months without coming to the end of them. From the eleventh century, architects and craftsmen have recorded the fortunes of the town, its changes of taste, government, and belief. The buildings reflect these local circumstances; it is their charm, the charm of most old towns. But a few illustrate the heights of art independently, and rank Isfahan among those rarer places, like Athens or Rome, which are the common refreshment of humanity.

The two-dome chambers of the Friday Mosque point this distinction by their difference. Both were built about the same time, at the end of the eleventh century. In the larger, which is the main sanctuary of the mosque, twelve massive piers engage in a Promethean struggle with the weight of the dome. The struggle in fact obscures the victory: to perceive the latter demands a previous interest in mediaeval engineering or the character of the Seljuks. Contrast this with the smaller chamber, which is really a tomb-tower incorporated in the mosque. The inside is roughly thirty feet square and sixty high; its volume is perhaps one third of the other's. But while the larger lacked the experience necessary to its scale, the smaller embodies that precious moment between too little experience and too much, when the elements of construction have been refined of superfluous bulk, yet still withstand the allurements of superfluous grace; so that each element, like the muscles of a trained athlete, performs its function with winged precision, not concealing its effort, as over-refinement will do, but adjusting it to the highest degree of intellectual meaning. This is the perfection of architecture, attained not so much by the form of the elements—for this is a matter of convention—but by their chivalry of balance and proportion. And this small interior comes nearer to that perfection than I would have thought possible outside classical Europe.

The very material is a signal of economy: hard small bricks of mousy grey, which swallow up the ornament of Kufic texts and stucco inlay in their puritan singleness of purpose. In skeleton, the chamber is a system of arches, one broad in the middle of each wall, two narrow beside each corner, four miniature in each squinch, eight in the squinch zone, and sixteen above the squinches to receive the dome. The invention of Firuzabad has expanded; and will expand much further before Persian architecture dies in the eighteenth century. Here we catch it in the prime of youth and vigour. Even at this stage, the system is repeated or varied in many other buildings: the tomb-tower at Maragha for instance. But I doubt if there is another building in Persia, or in the whole of Islam, which offers so tense, so immediate an apparition of pure cubic form.

According to the inscription round the dome, the tomb-tower was built by Abul Ghanaim Marzuban, the Minister of Malek Shah, in 1088. One wonders what circumstance at that moment induced such a flight of genius. Was it the action of a new mind from Central Asia on the old civilisation of the plateau, a procreation by nomadic energy out of Persian aestheticism? The Seljuks were not the only conquerors of Persia to have this effect. The Ghaznavide dynasty before them, the Mongol and Timurid dynasties after them, all came from north of the Oxus, and each produced a new Renascence on Persian soil. Even the Safavids, who inspired the last and most languid phase of Persian art, were Turks originally.

It was this last phase which gave Isfahan the character it has today, and which produced, curiously enough, its other great masterpiece. In 1612, Shah Abbas was occupied with the Royal Mosque at the south-west end of the Maidan, whose huge blue bulk and huge acreage of coarse floral tilework form just that kind of "oriental" scenery, so dear to the Omar Khayam fiends—pretty, if you like, even magnificent, but not important in the general scale of things. In 1618, however, he built another mosque on the south-east side of the Maidan, which was called after his father-in-law Sheikh Lutfullah.

This building stands at the opposite pole of architectural virtue to the small dome-chamber in the Friday Mosque. The latter is remarkable because, apart from its unique merit, that merit is of a kind which most people have regarded as the exclusive property of the European mind. The Mosque of Sheikh Lutfullah is Persian in the fabulous sense: the Omar Khayam brigade, to whom rational form is as much anathema as rational action, can wallow in it to their hearts' content. For while the dome-chamber is form only, has no colour, and obliterates its ornament by the intentness of its construction, the Mosque of Sheikh Lutfullah hides any symptom of construction or dynamic form beneath a mirage of shallow curved surfaces, the multitudinous offspring of the original squinch. Form there is and must be; but how it is created, and what supports it, are questions of which the casual eye is unconscious, as it is meant to be, lest its attention should wander from the pageant of colour and pattern. Colour and pattern are a commonplace in Persian architecture. But here they have a quality which must astonish the European, not because they infringe what he thought was his own monopoly, but because he can previously have had no idea that abstract pattern was capable of so profound a splendour.

As though to announce these principles as soon as possible, the outside of the mosque is careless of symmetry to a grotesque degree. Only the dome and portal are seen from the front. But owing to the discrepancy between the axis of the mosque and that of the Ali Gapu opposite, the portal, instead of being immediately under the dome, is set slightly to one side of it. Yet such is the character of the dome, so unlike is it to any other dome in Persia or elsewhere, that this deformity is hardly noticeable. Round a flattened hemisphere made of tiny bricks and covered with prawn-coloured wash runs a bold branching rose-tree inlaid in black and white. Seen from close to, the design has a hint of William Morris, particularly in its thorns; but as a whole it is more formal than pre-raphaelite, more comparable to the design of a Genoese brocade immensely magnified. Here and there, at the junction of the branches or in the depths of the foliage, ornaments of ochre and dark blue mitigate the harshness of the black and white tracery, and bring it into harmony with the soft golden pink of the background: a process which is continued by a pervading under-foliage of faint light blue. But the genius of the effect is in the play of surfaces. The inlay is glazed. The stucco wash is not. Thus the sun strikes the dome with a *broken* highlight whose intermittent flash, moving with the time of day, adds a third texture to the pattern, mobile and unforeseen.

If the outside is lyric, the inside is Augustan. Here a still shallower dome, about seventy feet in diameter, swims above a ring of sixteen windows. From the floor to the base of the windows rise eight main arches, four enclosing right-angles, four flat wall-space, so that the boundaries of the floor form a square. The space between the tops of the arches is occupied by eight pendentives divided into planes like a bat's-wing.

The dome is inset with a network of lemon-shaped compartments, which increase in size as they descend from a formalised peacock at the apex and are surrounded by plain bricks; each is filled with a foliage pattern inlaid on plain stucco. The walls, bordered by broad white inscriptions on dark blue, are similarly inlaid with twirling arabesques or baroque squares on deep ochre stucco. The colours of all this inlay are dark blue, light greenish blue, and a tint of indefinite wealth like wine. Each arch is framed in turquoise corkscrews. The mihrab in the west wall is enamelled with tiny flowers on a deep blue meadow.

Each part of the design, each plane, each repetition, each separate branch or blossom has its own sombre beauty. But the beauty of the whole comes as you move. Again, the highlights are broken by the play of glazed and unglazed surfaces; so that with every step they rearrange themselves in countless shining patterns; while even the pattern of light through the thick window traceries is inconstant, owing to outer traceries which are several feet away and double the variety of each varying silhouette.

I have never encountered splendour of this kind before. Other interiors came into my mind as I stood there, to compare it with: Versailles, or the porcelain rooms at Schönbrunn, or the Doge's Palace, or St. Peter's. All are rich; but none so rich. Their richness is three-dimensional; it is attended by all the effort of shadow. In the Mosque of Sheikh Lutfullah, it is a richness of light and surface, of pattern and colour only. The architectural form is unimportant. It is not smothered, as in rococo; it is simply the instrument of a spectacle, as earth is the instrument of a garden. And then I suddenly thought of that unfortunate species, modern interior decorators, who imagine they can make a restaurant, or a cinema, or a plutocrat's drawing-room look rich if given money enough for gold leaf and looking-glass. They little know what amateurs they are. Nor, alas, do their clients.[19]

And, at last, he could lay eyes on Gumbad-i-Kabus, the ultimate objective of the entire journey, achieved by persistence and occasional cunning. He described the tower as one of the great buildings of the ancient world. The description of his small party's approach to the town is a superb example of evocative writing:

Even in the dark, we could perceive the steppe. The headlights died in space, finding nothing to reveal but a passing boar. There came a scent of sweet grass, as on a night in June at home before the hay is cut. At Asterabad the populace were celebrating Mohurram, marching through the streets behind a draped coffin and bearing aloft triangular banners of lights. Many wept and groaned, and such as had their hands free were tearing their clothes and beating themselves, as Shir Ahmad had described. We are staying with an old Turk, who used to be British vice-consul here, and offers to arrange a tiger-shoot for us.

Gumbad-i-Kabus (200 ft.), April 24th.—After following the Bandar Shah road a little way back, we turned to the right down a track between wattle fences. High reeds obscured the view. Suddenly, as a ship leaves an estuary, we came out on to the steppe: a dazzling open sea of green. I never saw that colour before. In other greens, of emerald, jade, or malachite, the harsh deep green of the Bengal jungle, the sad cool green of Ireland, the salad green of Mediterranean vineyards, the heavy full-blown green of English summer beeches, some element of blue or yellow predominates over the others. This was the pure essence of green, indissoluble, the colour of life itself. The sun was warm, the larks were singing up above. Behind us rose the misty Alpine blue of the wooded Elburz. In front, the glowing verdure stretched out to the rim of the earth.

Bearings, landmarks, disappeared, as they would from a skiff in mid-Atlantic. We seemed to be always below the surrounding level, caught in the trough of a green swell. Sitting down, we might see for twenty feet: standing up, for twenty miles—and even then, twenty miles away, the curve of the earth was as green as the bank that touched the wheels, so that it was hard to tell which was which. Our only chart was by things whose scale we knew: groups of white-topped kibitkas, dotted like mushrooms on a lawn—though even in their case it needed an effort of reason to believe they were not mushrooms; and droves of cattle, mares with their foals, black and brown sheep, kine and camels—though the camels were deceptive in the opposite sense, seeming so tall that it needed another effort to believe they were not antediluvian monsters. As the huts and animals varied in size, we could plot their distances: half a mile, a mile, five miles. But it was not this that conveyed the size of the steppe so much as the multiplicity of these nomadic encampments, cropping up wherever the eye rested, yet invariably separate by a mile or two from their neighbours. There were hundreds of them, and the sight, therefore, seemed to embrace hundreds of miles.

As plans of cities are inset on maps of countries, another chart on a larger scale lay right beneath our wheels. Here the green resolved, not into ordinary grass, but into wild corn, barley, and oats, which accounted for that vivid fire, as of a life within the green. And among these myriad bearded alleys lived a population of flowers, buttercups and poppies, pale purple irises and dark purple campanulas, and countless others, exhibiting all the colours, forms, and wonders that a child finds in its first garden. Then a puff of air would come, bending the corn to a silver ripple, while the flowers leaned with it; or a cloud-shadow, and all grow dark, as if for a moment's sleep; though a few feet off there would be no ripple and no darkness; so that this whole inner world of the steppe was mapped on a system of infinite minute recessions, having just those gradations of distance that the outer lacked.

Our spirits had risen when we left the plateau. Now they effervesced. We shouted for joy, stopping the car lest the minutes that were robbing us of the unrepeatable first vision should go faster. Even the larks in this paradise had lost their ordinary aloofness. One almost hit my hat in its inquisitiveness.

We found the Gurgan river in a cutting thirty feet deep, whose bare earth cliffs traced a gash of desolation through the green. It was as wide as the Severn in its upper reaches, and we crossed it by an old brick bridge on tall pointed arches. This was defended, on the north bank, by a gate-house, whose overhanging upper storey had a broad-caved tiled roof such as one sees in the Apennines. From here smooth green tracks began to radiate over the steppe in all directions, and we could hardly have found the way but for the occasional traffic of riders on horses and camels and high-wheeled gigs who pointed it out to us. They were all Turcomans, the ladies in red chintz covered with flowers, the men in plain red or more rarely in gorgeous multi-coloured silks woven with lightning zigzags. But there were not many fleece hats. Most of the men wore Marjoribanks's substitute, or at least a cardboard peak attached to a fleece cap.

The Elburz now began to curve round in front of us, enclosing a green bay. In the middle of this, twenty miles away, a small cream needle stood up against the blue of the mountains, which we knew for the tower of Kabus. An hour later, steering by this point, we reached a small market town, whose broad straight streets recall the Russian occupation of the district before the War. The tower stands on the north of the town, helped into the sky by a green hillock of irregular shape, but artificial, and of great age.

A tapering cylinder of café-au-lait brick springs from a round plinth to a pointed grey-green roof, which swallows it up like a candle extinguisher. The diameter at the plinth is fifty feet; the total height about a hundred and fifty. Up the cylinder, between plinth and roof, rush ten triangular buttresses, which cut across two narrow garters of Kufic text, one at the top underneath the cornice, one at the bottom over the slender back entrance.

The bricks are long and thin, and as sharp as when they left the kiln, thus dividing the shadow from the sunshine of each buttress with knife-like precision. As the buttresses recede from the direction of the sun, the shadows extend on to the curving wall of the cylinder between them, so that the stripes of light and shade, varying in width, attain an extraordinary momentum. It is the opposition of this vertical momentum to the lateral embrace of the Kufic rings that gives the building its character, a character unlike anything else in architecture.

There is nothing inside. The body of Kabus used to hang there, suspended from the roof in a glass coffin. He died in 1007. For more than a thousand years this lighthouse has announced his memory, and the genius of Persia, to the nomads of the Central Asian sea. Today it has a larger audience, which must wonder how the use of brick, at the beginning of the second millennium after Christ, came to produce a more heroic monument, and a happier play of surfaces and ornament, than has ever been seen in that material since.[20]

Eventually, Byron returned safely to England, "drab and ugly from the train, owing to the drought." He felt dazed by impending domesticity at home. Nineteen and a half days after he left Kabul in Afghanistan, Byron was greeted by the family dogs and his long-suffering mother: "What I have seen she taught me to see, and will tell me if I have honoured it."[21]

Robert Byron was far from unique, for there were many others who ventured far from the well-worn paths of archaeological travel before the days of jumbo jets and helicopters. All of them were adaptable, hardy travelers, who treated the untoward as just part of the daily routine of exploring the past in remote lands. They visited unsanitized, unfenced sites, some gradually crumbling into dust, others decimated by earthquakes, some still revered by ancestors of their creators. To them we owe tantalizing accounts of what survived before the days of mass tourism, and before what Byron called the "rush of professors" to even hard-to-find places. Many of these locations would still be virtually unknown except as fanciful rumors were it not for Byron and his generation of compulsive travelers.

Chapter Thirteen
Travel as Commodity

For there to be any point in traveling, you have always to be looking for things as they were and dodging things as they are.

Philip Glazebrook
Journey to Kars (1984)

CHAPTER THIRTEEN

Travel as Commodity

Thomas Cook started it all with his meticulously organized archaeological tours up the Nile. He harnessed the revolutionary technologies of Victorian travel to a growing desire on the part of the middle class to explore the world and its ancient history. Cook was the first to realize the potential of the railroad for group tours. A devout Baptist and an advocate for temperance, he began his business by organizing rail excursions to temperance meetings in nearby towns in central England. The enterprise was so successful that he took advantage of steamships and continental railroads to organize what we now call package tours to France and Germany. From that, it was not much more difficult to organize tours to Egypt and the Holy Land, now readily accessible thanks to the new technology for Victorian travel: the railroad, the steamship, and the telegraph.

Then, in the twentieth century, came ocean liners, massive cruise ships, and the Boeing 707, followed by the jumbo jet, all of which together made archaeological travel part of popular culture. We live in a completely accessible world of intricate airline schedules and instant communication, where you can visit the great *moiae* of Easter Island as easily as you can take a journey to Stonehenge or the Parthenon, the difference being a longer flight and the need for the correct visas and a foreign rental car at the other end. And if you become sick or injured, you can be evacuated from most places within hours: Peter Fleming or Ella Maillart would have been in real trouble had they become sick or injured in the vast expanses of central Asia. We forget that to travel east of the Holy Land was considered highly adventurous until after World War II, and that central Asia was virtually inaccessible to outsiders until the late twentieth century. Much of the adventure of archaeological travel has vanished since the 1960s in a tidal wave of mass tourism and its attendant businesses. Leisure travel is now the world's largest industry, and the mainstay of many national economies, including that of Egypt, where at last count six million tourists visit each year. According to Statistics Canada, global cultural tourism will grow at a rate of about 15 percent annually through the year 2010. The demand is apparently insatiable. Ninety-three percent of American travelers included a "cultural" trip in their itineraries in 2000, and the percentage has risen since then.

Paul Theroux Along the Nile

Paul Theroux is a travel writer who writes with a cynical, sometimes satirical eye. He often captures the casual way in which tourists view the past. In a memorable book about railroad journeys in China, he described a stop at Leshan, a riverside town on the main line to Kunming in the south. A huge statue of Buddha and its surrounding temples make Leshan a place of pilgrimage at a confluence of three rivers, the Dadu, the Minjiang, and the Qingyi. Theroux tells us that the statue was erected some 1,200 years ago to protect boatmen navigating the turbulent waters below.

But this Buddha was less an object of veneration than an example of the Chinese fascination with freakishness—the very big, the very weird, the highly unusual.

13-1 A perennial favorite with tourists, the striking *moiae* of Easter Island are more accessible at present than ever before.

13-2 The Great Buddha of Leshan in China, carved from the rock face sometime between A.D. 713 and 803, grows ever more camouflaged as plants spread across the enormous figure.

This Buddha's ears were twelve feet long. Chinese tourists frolicked on his feet. You could park a car on the nail of his big toe. Close up he was Brobdingnagian—big, plain, disproportionate—with weeds growing from his cracks. I imagined he did not look so grotesque from the river.[1]

On another trek, Theroux started the first leg of a journey from Cairo to Cape Town with a boat trip on the Nile. He traveled in the company of affluent tourists on an excursion quite unlike his later adventures south of the Sahara, and he gives us a perceptive glimpse of the life of a twentieth-century archaeological traveler:

In a corner of the rescued and reconstructed Temple of Isis at Philae, in the river south of Aswan, was a bull in stone, the image of the god Hapi, or Apis, surrounded by protective snakes. Apis was the sacred bull of Memphis, associated with the river and so with fertility, and worshiped as the god of the Nile. Nearby was the image of Osiris, god of the earth, in his candlepin headgear, personification of the Nile, the flooding of the river symbolizing his rebirth. Osiris's features were smashed, and so were those of Horus, its falcon face obliterated by fanatic early Christians. There were lots of Napoleonic graffiti on the walls. The Nile cruise past Egyptian ruins is an experience of obliterations and graffiti. More than one hundred and fifty years ago, the young Gustave Flaubert lamented these very things in a letter to his mother: "In the temples we read travelers' names; they strike us as petty and futile. We never write ours; there are some that must have taken three days to carve, so deeply are they cut in the stone. There are some that you keep meeting everywhere—sublime persistence of stupidity."

The human faces were scratched away, the gods' images were chipped off, the walls have been stripped and chiseled into. Though the experience of the ruins is the experience of millennia of vandalism, the proof of the strength and glory of the ruins is that they are still beautiful, even cracked and defaced and scribbled on.

The tall pink granite obelisks that you see in London and Paris and Central Park originated at the ancient quarry outside Aswan, where work in stoppage shows the famous Unfinished Obelisk. This stone pillar, eighty feet long, distinctly geometric and symmetrical, partly chopped from the granite ledge, lies half hewn and is gaped at and trodden upon by bewildered admirers.

"It was all by hand!"

"Maybe they just got sick of working on it."

"How in heck did they manage to lift these things?"

An Egyptologist was saying, "So Osiris was killed by his evil brother Seth and cut into fourteen pieces. One of them was eaten by a fish, and Isis used it to revive Osiris and give birth to Horus. Which one, do you think?"

His leer suggested the obvious answer, but speaking for the group, one passenger asked, "Any crocs in the river here?"

The answer was no, none here, none even downstream at Crocodilopolis—though one had been kept and worshiped at the temple there, as the cat—image of the goddess of joy and love—had been worshiped in the temple at Bast. The big crocs these days lazed on the banks of the White Nile, in the swampy Sudd in southern Sudan and farther upriver at the source of the Nile, Lake Albert and Lake Victoria. The crocs here had long since been made into handbags and belts.

We visited the high dam and Lake Nasser, then waited until our flight to Abu Simbel, two hundred miles south at the border of Sudan and the head of the lake, was canceled.

The pleasantest aspect of the river cruise was the combination of gourmandizing and sightseeing, gliding with the current and stopping every now and then at a resurrected ruin. I liked the ruins most for the way they were overrun by the rackety bazaar, not just curio sellers but browsing donkeys among the pillars, goats in the roadway, hawkers' stalls in the foreground and Ptolemaic colors on the sheltered upper parts of the temples, still bright after thousands of years. Kom Ombo, where the *Philae* stopped the first day, was an example of these features: the bazaar, the ruins, the chewing animals, the loud music, the double shrine to Horus and the croc god represented by mummified crocs inside the temple. Kom Ombo was not just a temple but a small town, and its name, meaning "Pile of Gold," was both flattery and mockery. The temple looked more appropriate as part of the life of the town rather than as a fenced-off museum piece. It did not gain dignity in being reconstructed; it looked false and approximated. The town itself, with its Nubian name, was ancient.

"Who lived here way back?"

"Many bibble."

The walls of the temple at Kom Ombo were Egyptology in pictures, history and culture. As a reminder of the wisdom and skill of the Egyptians, one wall depicted medical instruments: pliers, forceps, knives, hooks, suction devices, all the paraphernalia for carrying out serious surgery, possibly more surgery than was being carried out in the present-day Kom Ombo General Hospital. Childbirth was illustrated in one hieroglyph. I sketched a picture of the Eye of Horus, which in a simplified form became the symbol (℞) for a prescription. Elsewhere on the temple walls were representations of the natural world—vultures, ducks, bulls, and hawks, and farther on, warriors and a pantheon of the Egyptians' enemies, including an unmistakable Negroid head and torso, a fierce soldier with the heavy-lidded gaze of the Nubian. It was wonderful to see such assertive black faces glaring from the walls of these ancient temples, like DNA in bas-relief, proof of the power and persistence of the African.

We floated onward in the *Philae*, nibbling delicacies, sipping fine wines, leering at the honeymooners on board, dodging the boisterous little Indian boy. We came to Edfu. "The Temple of Edfu serves as a latrine for the entire village," Flaubert noted in his diary in 1850. But it was disinterred and tidied up and is said to be the best-preserved temple in Egypt.

Until the late-nineteenth century, all these temples were torsos, broken and fallen, just smashed-up carvings and fat pointless pillars scattered in the Upper Nile Valley. "There is always some temple buried to its shoulders in the sand, partially visible, like an old dug-up skeleton," Flaubert wrote. The great delineator of wrecked Egyptian sites, David Roberts, loved the ruination, and in 1840 he said the structures seemed to him more beautiful half buried and bruised. They reminded him of Piranesi etchings of the Forum in Rome.

I saw what he meant when I came across a ruin in the middle of nowhere—a brilliant image, the lovely carving fallen and forgotten in the desert, a much more dramatic subject than a rebuilt temple teeming with hot-faced and complaining tourists. Flaubert took delight in reporting how dilapidated the temples were, and because he was not in search of ruins, he preferred the oddities of the Nile journey and dallying with dancing girls and prostitutes. Twenty-seven years after Flaubert visited, another traveler reported that the two-thousand-year-old Temple of Edfu was being dug out and had begun to look like its old self, as in the festival days of Edfu's greatness, celebrating the enactment of Horus avenging his father, Osiris, by stabbing hippo-bodied Seth.

But he admitted that no one knew. What drew me was the fact the the defacers had not wrecked the temple or gone at the wall with sledgehammers. They had poked away at the carvings with a care bordering on respect, and you had to conclude that they could not have done it in this way, removing little, leaving so much, if they had not felt a certain terror.

Whatever the reason, and as with the Napoleonic graffiti, which has acquired significance over the years, the defacings are as fascinating as the finished sculptures, giving the figures the eeriness and mystery of a mutilated corpse at a crime scene.

Syrians, Asians, and Nubians were pointed out on the temple walls, and while the Egyptologist was explaining their features and their characteristic clothes, some of the cruise passengers were becoming impatient, jostling in the little cluster of concentrating and querulous tourists to ask a supplementary question. "Which Ptolemy was that?"

At last when Fawzi was done, the question came: "What about the Jews?"

It so happened, Fawzi said, that for the length and breadth of the Nile Valley, from the Delta south to Upper Egypt and to the dark pyramids and temples of Nubia, there was no mention of the Jews, nothing of Israelites, and even when captives were shown, their religion was not indicated; they were merely a mass of undifferentiated pagan prisoners. There are potbellied hippos and bat-eared jackals, plump-lipped Nubians and Asiatics squinting across the millennia, but there are no Jews. There are whole dynasties of pharaohs depicted, but not the faintest trace of Moses on an Egyptian wall.

So he said. Yet there was a people whose generic name, "Other-siders" or "Crossers-over," occurred now and then on Egyptian tombs and temples and in papyrus scrolls. The pharaonic word for these people was *Apiru* or *Habiru*, and was derived from an Aramaic word, *ibri*, which meant "one from the other side." It is not a great phonetic leap from *Habiru* or *ibri* to "Hebrew," a crudely descriptive name (like "wetback," for Mexican) for people who had crossed the water, in this case the Red Sea. And the word for "Hebrew," in Hebrew, is *Ivri*.

Some of these migrants ("*Habiru*, in cuneiform sources") found employment doing the heavy lifting on building projects in the eastern Delta. The Egyptologist K. A. Kitchen described them, in his life of Rameses II, as "displaced, rootless people who drifted or were drafted into various callings . . . Lumped in with the Apiru generally were doubtless those who in the Bible appear as the Hebrews, and specifically the clan-groups of Israel." Those people had been resident in the eastern Delta since the time of Jacob and Joseph, when their forefathers fled to Egypt to escape famine.

That I found out later. While I listened to Fawzi's explanation, and someone saying "I guess it's all a riddle," a woman approached me and hit me on the arm.

"Hey, that's a dandy idea!" She was from Texas. I had seen her on the boat, looking unsteady. She had a new hip. New hips are common on cruise ships, and among cruise passengers chitchat about hip surgery is frequently audible.

"What is?" I said.

"Little old notebook to write stuff on."

I shut my notebook and held it like a sandwich.

"Little old pen."

I had been doodling a hieroglyph, a squatting man in a stool-shaped hat, one knee up, both arms crooked and raised above his head in a gesture of amazement, as though saying, "This is incredible!" This lovely, compact, and comic image was the hieroglyph for "one million."

The woman punched my arm again as a sort of compliment, and when she moved off, favoring one leg, I wrote, *Hey, that's a dandy idea.*

Some aspects of the touristy Nile cannot have changed much in a hundred years. Edfu had no taxis, only pony carts, and they clashed and competed for customers, the drivers yelling, flailing their whips, maneuvering their carts, scraping their wheels. There was something ancient, perhaps timeless, in the way a driver—my Mustafa, say—turned, as the pony trotted toward the temple, and demanded more money, double the price in fact, whining, "Food for my babies! Food for my horse! Give me, bleeeez!"

. . .

In a new interpretation of these images, Horus is seen by some astronomers as the representation of a failed star in our solar system. The Egyptians had seen this so-called brown dwarf in the skies at its perihelion, spinning around the sun beyond the known planets. That this massive phantom star, out there unseen in the wilderness of space, crucially controls our own planet is only one aspect of the dark star theory.

The Greeks learned how to make columns by studying the symmetry of Egyptian pillars like those at Edfu. If a temple is buried deeply enough and the soil is dry and no archeologist or treasure hunter disturbs it, there is a sort of preservation in that very neglect. The Temple of Horus looks whole, cathedral-like in the way the pillars soar, some friezes retaining the reddish flesh tones on human figures and bluebirds and green snakes coiled on the upper walls. At the main gateway the upright falcon Horus, its eyes the sun and moon, stands sentinel, its halo the disk of the sun god.

Some images were defaced. In the past, tourists broke off pieces of Egyptian sculpture to keep as souvenirs—Twain describes an American chipping off a chunk of the Sphinx. But in Edfu, defaced was an exact word: it told precisely what had happened to the depictions of these soldiers, workers, and striding women on the walls. It was so consistent and stylistically similar as to seem a kind of negative sculpture, the art of obliteration. As striking as the images of gods and humans and animals on this temple—and it was a theme throughout—was the vandalism: defaced human heads, scratched-out hands and feet, chopped-off legs, hacked bodies, everything representing flesh was chipped away, even the heads and hooves of animals. Headdresses, hats, and cloaks were left, so that in a particularly pretty sculpture of an elaborately dressed prince, all the finery would be intact, but the face would be scooped out and the hands scraped off.

"Done by early Christians" was the usual explanation. But it might have been done by fanatical Muslims, who abhor human images. Muslim Egyptologists denied it, and insisted that Christians—especially Christians from Ethiopia—were to blame for these amazingly methodical defacings.

"Maybe not out of anger," Fawzi, one Egyptologist, said. "Maybe because the Christians had been persecuted. Maybe to obliterate pre-Christian history."

Although I was alone at my table, I was one of a hundred passengers—mainly those plump, rich, amphibious-looking people for whom travel is an expensive kind of laziness, spent in the company of other idle people to whom they relate details of their previous trips. "This reminds me of parts of Brazil," and "Now that, that could be Malta." They were American, British, German, with a scattering of South Americans, and of course the gloomy Indians with the boisterous child. The Americans on board could be divided into young friends traveling happily together, contentious aged couples traveling alone, and honeymooners, three pairs, everyone's favorites.

I resisted mocking them because they were harmless and most were committed to geniality, but except for one friendly pair of honeymooners who insisted that I dine with them from time to time, I ate alone. As for the others, trying to recall them, I only see them eating—feeding time was always closely observed on shipboard, and they were at their most animated then. The table of older blond German women, exquisitely dressed; the four German men who were often curt with the waiter, and one was actually named Kurt; the young American couples, distressed by the news of the failing stock market; the hard-faced woman and her bosomy husband, each seemingly midway through a sex change; the Indian couple and their bored bratty child.

Of the Germans, the sextet of aging, occasionally exuberant blondes, like the reunion of a chorus line, interested me most, because they were traveling with a Levantine doctor. We were on the upper deck one day, having a drink, and he said to me, "My field is reconstructive surgery." I turned to the women who were talking and sunning themselves, in that odd heliotropic posture of sunbathers, canted toward the sun, grimacing and just perceptibly turning.

I was struck by their similarity—the sharp noses, the smooth cheeks, the tight eyes, the bright brittle hair—and I realized that he was traveling with his patients, all of whom were so pretty that he, not they, deserved the compliment. This peculiar revelation seemed to me a great subject for a story—say, a young man's involvement with a much older woman who looks thirty, traveling with her plastic surgeon. To calm myself with the illusion that I was working, I began writing this story. *This is my only story. Now that I am sixty I can tell it . . .* As the days and weeks passed, the story became by turns melancholy, comic, reminiscing, and consolingly erotic.

Inevitably, on the *Philae* there was one of those helpfully nosy couples who asked all the questions the rest of us did not dare to ask for fear of revealing our ignorance. "How in heck did they manage to move those things?" and "Is that fronic?" were two of their questions. The wife interrogated the women, her husband badgered the men for information.

"Do you work?" the bullying wife asked the shyest-seeming woman, one of the petite and pretty honeymooners.

"I'm a prison officer," the new bride said.

"That must be so difficult!" was the predictable rejoinder.

When the honeymooner said "Oh, no. We have some wonderful inmates," all conversation ceased.

The nosy woman's husband, an irritating old philistine who looked like Piltdown man in a golf cap, kept saying to me, "I guess I'll have to read one of your books now."

I begged him not to, in a friendly way. One thing I had learned about traveling with lots of other people was that it was usually a good idea to hold my tongue. The talkers were self-advertisers, people to avoid, along with the networkers, the salesmen, and the evangelists. The quieter ones were often worth knowing, but in any case I regarded the whole boatload as one of the sights of Egypt, like the fat stone hippos and the mummified cats and the pesky curio sellers. I guessed that after Egypt I would not see many more tourists.

None of us knew much about Egyptology, we were hazy on dates, and "My history's real shaky" was as common a remark as "How in heck did they manage to move those things?"

For me this cruise was a picnic, and I suspected my last picnic before plunging deeper in Africa. It was comfortable, undemanding travel among mostly companionable people, and if it was true that we didn't know much about Egyptian history, neither did the Egyptians. It would have been very tedious if some pedantic historian had been on board, correcting impressions and setting us straight. I preferred listening to the improvisations:

"They must have used those for climbing up the wall."

"I imagine they took baths in that thing."

"Those ruts were probably made by chariots, or wagon wheels of some kind."

"Looks like a kind of duck."

"That's definitely fronic."

Some countries are perfect for tourists. Italy is. So are Mexico and Spain. Turkey, too. Egypt, of course. Pretty big. Not too dirty. Nice food. Courteous people. Sunshine. Lots of masterpieces. Ruins all over the place. Names that ring a bell. Long, vague history. The guide says "papyrus" or "hieroglyphic" or "Tutankhamen" or "one of the Ptolemys," and you say "Yup."

What you remember most is the friendly waiter, the goofball with the cell phone on the camel, the old man pissing against the ancient wall, the look of a tray of glossy pomegranates in the market, the sacks of spices, the yellow cow ruminating in the temple, or just the colors, for the colors of Egypt are gorgeous. Edward Lear wrote in his diary on the Nile, "Egypt is at least a land to learn color in."[2]

Crowds, Crowds . . .

Surprisingly little has changed since the heyday of Thomas Cook's tours on the Nile a century ago, except for an explosion in the number of riverboats and in the number of people flocking to the same Egyptian monuments. The relics of every major civilization are now bombarded with international tourists, among them the relics of the Maya, who exercise a profound fascination on many North Americans. Thousands of people follow what has become known as the "Ruta Maya," a quick tour of the major Maya centers. Many of these people are faithful readers of *National Geographic*, which has made Maya civilization one of its major emphases.

Most come to admire the unique architecture, the great cities shrouded in clinging rain forest foliage. But you find other visitors, too—people in search of spiritual enlightenment, many of them under the influence of Carlos Castañeda, writer, anthropologist, and self-proclaimed shaman of controversial repute. I have seen such people sitting in Tikal's temples, sometimes accompanied by a shaman, seeking their authentic selves, trying to acquire the wisdom of the ancients. Others may laugh, perhaps, but many people find solace in such musings.

Today's archaeological traveler is usually a cruise ship passenger or a member of a well-structured package tour, a participant in a cultural experience marketed in the same way that hotel rooms, airline tickets, or seats at football games are marketed. Last year, I watched a large cruise ship disembark its 1,100 passengers on the quayside at Mykonos in the Cyclades Islands at the heart of the Aegean. Crewmembers with signs directed the passengers to different excursions—shopping tours, a beach experience, and, one of the most popular of all, an excursion to the shrines of Apollo on the island of Delos a short distance across the water. At a conservative estimate, I counted over 400 people, young, middle-aged, old, and a few infirm, boarding the ferries. I knew that they would have trained guides who would take them around the ruins in groups of thirty or more, on a carefully planned itinerary designed to last no more than just over an hour before they were allowed to wander by themselves for another thirty minutes or so. I remembered my own visit to Delos in September 1979: I and three friends visited the island in our own boat, in order to manage our time of arrival, but even then there were only a few dozen people among the ruins, all taking their time, admiring the view, and using a guidebook to find their way around. Delos was a truly memorable experience, for you could have a corner of the ruins to yourself and let your imagination run wild. I am sure there were a few independent travelers on Delos that day last summer, taking their time and consulting guidebooks for telling detail. But for most of the time they would be crowded among regiments of cruise ship passengers getting the quick once-over. Most of the people on the ship cannot have been serious archaeological travelers, and it was good that they had a chance to see one of the great sites of antiquity. But it cannot have been a particularly memorable experience or an especially evocative one.

There are people who continue to design modern-day versions of the grand tour, traveling by bicycle, although the preferred means of transport is a camper van. As recently as the 1970s, you could still take your time at many Mediterranean sites, park in the shadow of marble temple columns, or stay in a cave at Ephesus. Today, the sites are fenced and policed, partly out of a laudable concern to protect them from looters and generally to conserve them, but also to ensure that the tidal waves of visitors are effectively managed and produce revenue to offset preservation costs. The shadow of the past is diminished when the great sites of antiquity—and many minor sites as well—become mere commodities rather than places for an experience to be savored and lingered over.

Crowds have broken the spell. One of the great experiences of archaeological travel is to enjoy a sunset at a site like the temple of Poseidon at Sounion at the tip of Attica, or at the temple of Athena at Aphaia on the island of Aegina. Charles Cockerell nearly had Aphaia to himself in 1811. On two occasions in the 1960s and 1970s, I was myself lucky enough to see sunsets at both sites. At Sounion, I anchored my boat in the cove in the lee of the point and climbed up to the temple in the late afternoon. I searched for, and found, Lord Byron's name inscribed on the salt-white marble, for I was able to walk among the columns. Then I watched the sun set in the west in a spectacular blaze of red and pink. I was the only person there, and I lingered long after dark, captivated by the silence and solitude. Five years ago, I was at Sounion for the sunset once again. This time there were at least a dozen buses in the parking lot, the temple was fenced off, and Lord Byron was inaccessible. There were hundreds of people clustered on the hilltop, chattering, taking photographs, getting in each other's way. I stepped away from the crowds to the cliff top, but the spell was bro-

13-3 A photograph of a sunset as seen from the temple of Poseidon at Cape Sounion, Greece, is perhaps the only way to experience now the quiet tranquility that archaeologists were able to find there before the advent of packaged tours spoiled much of the magic.

ken and I realized that sunsets at Sounion would never be the same again.

Aphaia was quiet on my first visit, too. I watched the sunset with only a few others for company. Again I lingered, remembering how Cockerell and his young companions feasted on lamb and partridges in the shade of the crumbling masonry. When I went back a few years ago, the scene was very different, as I lamented in a column for *Archaeology Magazine*:

We anchored off Agia Marina at the northeastern corner of the island of Aegina on a calm September afternoon. High above us, on the crest of a hill, the Temple of Aphaia stood beckoning in the brilliant sunshine. We followed a narrow, winding path through hillside olive groves and savored the smell of pine needles that I will always associate with classical sites in Greece. There was no sound except the occasional birdcall or the gentle rustling of the sea breeze in the trees. The temple was deserted that lazy September day eleven years ago, its caretakers yawning in their small kiosk. We lingered for several hours, wandering through the temple, watching the lengthening shadows of its columns on the worn stone floor. Around us, the panorama of Salamis, the Peloponnese, Attica, and the blue ocean became softer, the folds of distant hills lying in ever deeper evening shadows. The air was warm and still, and the setting sun cast a magnificent rosy light on the ancient temple.

A few days later, we anchored in the shelter of the Temple of Poseidon at Sounion, as countless small ships had done before us. An hour before sunset, we stood beside its brilliant white, salt-encrusted columns. We had the place to ourselves except for an English couple in sensible tweeds and walking shoes. They sat to one side and read from the guidebook while we searched for Lord Byron's name on the columns. The setting sun bathed Sounion in pink, mystical hues. We asked the English couple back to the boat to drink wine, and read aloud from the *Odyssey* until the moon rose over the hills.

We visited the amphitheater at Epidauros, which also cast its magic spell. I sat on the highest tier of seats in the hot sun and listened to a German professor recite Euripides to his students. They were well schooled in the poet, joining in with the chorus to the professor's evident delight. I listened with closed eyes.

A few months ago an opportunity arose to revisit those magical sites. I jumped at the chance, tantalizing my companions with accounts of the magic of Aphaia, Sounion, and Epidauros. When we reached Aegina, I could hardly wait to rent a motor scooter and return to Aphaia's shrine. But this time the magic was gone. For one thing, the parking lot was jammed with tour buses. We choked on diesel fumes. The temple itself was cordoned off; one could not wander among the columns. At one point we had the temple more-or-less to ourselves when a crescendo of laboring motors brought another busload of tourists, and the chance for solitude was gone.

I left depressed. The visit had hardly been an elevating experience. Even when the tour buses were gone and the site was quiet, the sense of communion with the past eluded me. Back aboard ship, I took out my well thumbed copy of Rose

Macaulay's *The Pleasure of Ruins*, which I consider, together with Homer, to be an essential traveler's companion in Greece. It was comforting to find her lamenting the "excavated, tidied up monuments of the world." Like her, I envied one Colonel P.M. Skyes, who in 1914 rode his horse up the great staircase at Persepolis, so overwhelmed had he been by the view. An Englishman named Robert Byron (no relation to the poet) subsequently rode up the stairs and camped there, "while the columns and winged beasts kept their solitude beneath the stars, and not a sound or movement disturbed the empty moonlit plain." Byron returned some years later by car and was bitterly disappointed by the clouds of dust from passing trucks, and by the excavations that had cleaned up the site.

Epidauros was equally disappointing. No Euripides this time. The theater was crowded with a polyglot crowd of tourists, including a group of French high school girls sunbathing topless. I fled to a deserted field and found a measure of peace.

Perhaps my generation was one of the last to be able to enjoy the world's great archaeological sites in solitude—Stonehenge in the evening, the seried ramparts of Maiden Castle at full moon, the Great Enclosure at Zimbabwe at dawn. I suspect that today's generation has little opportunity to absorb the full impact of these ruins. Ten years ago, just the smell of pine trees at Aphaia was enough to recall what it must have been like back in 1810 when antiquarian Charles Cockerell and his young friends camped among the ruins, dug up and removed the fallen carvings from its pediments, and dined off wild partridges, roast lamb, strong retsina and raki. The local villagers "lightened our toil with the rustic lyre, the song and the dance." Today, the site is sanitized, sterile, and overwhelmed by multitudes of visitors.

Do not misunderstand me. I am all for international tourism that promotes an understanding of archaeology and a heightened appreciation of our common cultural heritage, especially when it contributes to developing national economies. But, increasingly, both casual tourists and more serious visitors are enjoying places like Epidauros and Sounion less and less, simply because these sites have absorbed about as many people as they can. So I can hardly blame one member of our party for remarking that she did not want to go to Delphi because it would be "just another pile of rocks." The archaeologist in me shuddered, but the tourist in me sympathized.

I confess that I too would like to ride a horse up the staircase at Persepolis and to explore the American Southwest on a mule. But I'll probably have to settle for a quick visit to Aphaia when it first opens in the morning, before the crowds gather and before the site is engulfed by diesel fumes. Even then, I fear that once savored aura of this special place will continue to elude me.[3]

Solitude on the Great Wall

As the lure of "adventure travel" attracts more and more people not only to the famous sites, but to extremely remote and lesser-known places, so it becomes harder to experience the kind of feelings that Robert Ker Porter experienced at Birs Nimrud or that John Lloyd Stephens experienced at Copán. There are just too many of us in pursuit of some relics of the past. The crowds, even during off-peak hours and in the off-season, can defeat any search for a poignant moment, or even for a sense of the past. Only occasionally can you wander off the intended path and enjoy solitary communion with a monument, and to do so often requires a knowledge of the tour guides' itineraries and of the length of time they spend in each place. Your best strategy is to walk away from the crowds, to select places where you can enjoy at least a measure of solitude, like, for example, parts of Hadrian's Wall in northern England, which can be almost deserted in late autumn or early spring.

A modern-day traveler, David Atherton, who was teaching English in rural Japan, was determined to experience China's Great Wall to the full and in solitude, far from the throngs of tourists who visit a reconstructed and manicured section near Beijing. The Great Wall of China was the longest structure ever built, stretching 3,700 miles (6,000 kilometers) from Shanhaiguan on Bohai Bay in the east to Jiayuguan on the edge of the desert in Gansu province in the west. In A.D. 500, no caravan from the

13-4 Unlike so many archaeological sites popular with tourists, the Great Wall of China is so vast that it is still possible to find places along its length untainted by incessant traffic.

west could enter China without passing through one of the wall's gates. Vibrant market towns developed at strategic entrances as China enjoyed an era of great prosperity, in part thanks to the wall. Today's fortification was reorganized and refurbished by the Ming dynasty emperors (1368–1644), after which it fell into disuse.

Over the centuries, the wall has become far more than a fortification; it is a symbol of Chinese history. The section of the wall near Beijing—the section that most tourists visit in carefully choreographed package tours—has been heavily restored by the government since 1984. It stands 24 feet (7 meters) high and 18 feet (5.4 meters) wide, snaking over hillsides near Beijing. Few visitors pause at the wall to reflect at leisure, to enjoy its deep sense of history. They have just enough time to take some digital pictures and shuffle along the designated route. Atherton was by himself and determined to get away from the throngs so that he could experience the true historic aura of the world's greatest fortification. His evocative description of a night spent atop the wall, which appeared in the *Los Angeles Times* in March 2002, makes the reader pause and wonder what the ancients would have made of the swarms of camera-toting tourists who now crowd the wall's walkways.

Beijing at first glance looks like a modern city, full of tall glass buildings, bright lights and broad highways. Even its nearby well-preserved ancient sights, like the Great Wall, are so inundated with tourists and trinket sellers that the essence of the past evaporates in the cacophony of the present.

But if you know where to look, just beyond the glare and bustle of new Beijing, the aura of the past is still so vibrant and close that it is almost tangible. I found it in spring two years ago while hiking and sleeping atop an unrestored and deserted stretch of the Great Wall.

The wall's reputation as a world wonder is no exaggeration. When I saw it for the first time—a 24-foot-high, 18-foot-wide mammoth snaking up the sides of ravines and along jagged mountain ridges almost as though it had grown there naturally—I found it hard to grasp its enormousness.

The idea of massive defensive walls is as old as China itself. In the Qin Dynasty of the 3rd century B.C., the connection of these series of rammed-earth walls was ordered for protection against invasions from northern nomads. Subsequent dynasties continued the Great Wall project, repairing and reconstructing the wall over centuries.

The wall we know was built in the 15th and 16th centuries, during the Ming Dynasty. Laborers enclosed its rubble core within stone siding, then topped it with brick to form its familiar towers, turrets and crenelations.

Although the 4,000-mile wall has two distinct endpoints—at Shanhaiguan, on the Pacific Ocean near Beijing, and Jiayuguan more than halfway across China in the west—it is not a single connected line but actually a series of walls, often built in strategic, inaccessible places, from mountain ridges to desolate swaths of desert. Because Beijing was the Ming Dynasty's capital, there are several sections of wall close to the capital, and since 1984 a few sections have been restored, bringing throngs of tourists.

The trick to spending the night, or doing some out-of-the-way hiking, is finding a well-preserved but unrestored part of the wall. The Huang Hua section was perfect for my overnight stay. Two hours north of Beijing by bus, it has no souvenir stands, no crowds, no pay telephones or lighting systems. There's only a dramatic slice of countryside that happens to have a 500-year-old wall draped spectacularly over its mountains. And although Huang Hua has not been restored since the 1500s, it is in remarkably good shape.

A section of the wall at Huang Hua was removed to make room for a road and a reservoir. The bus drops passengers here amid a small collection of restaurants, and a trail across the dam takes hikers to the more-trafficked and less-steep eastern section of the wall.

But a jolly woman working at a tiny shop next to the path to the reservoir urged me to take the western route instead. "Plenty of people have already headed up the east side for the night. It'll be crowded," she said.

"What's your idea of crowded?" I asked.

"Six, maybe seven people. But nobody's headed up the west side today. And you know, the people who come back here again and again say the west side is better."

She pointed out a small dirt path through some orchards. I followed it up a slope and along the base of the wall to an ancient stone staircase, which I climbed.

THE BIRDS AND THE BREEZE

A crisp breeze welcomed me at the top of the wall, and a panorama of my challenging route stretched before me. The wall climbed steeply to the top of a high hill, then ran along the ridge before descending sharply.

Two hours later, as I stood at the point where the wall cut sharply down, I could see that an even steeper climb up another hill lay ahead of me. Whenever the path cut through brambles, the rubble beneath my feet grew treacherous, and I almost lost my balance several times. The wall's designers, unfortunately, had a tendency to leave out stairs at some of its steepest places. In other areas it had crumbled away, and the path snaked across a large pile of stone.

But my slow, careful pace allowed me to take in the wall's subtle beauty. Though impressive from afar, the Great Wall is even more rewarding up close. Ancient stones mottled with lichens quietly grew warm in the sunshine. Next to an old staircase, a buzzing bee drew my attention to a vine-covered inscription left by the laborers who laid those stones.

On this late-spring afternoon, blossoms shaded the hillsides pink, and petals hovered in the air about me. In more than one place I discovered a flowering tree growing from a crack between two stones in the wall's side. A cuckoo called lazily from the brush, and I found myself falling into a quiet rhythm. My soul felt at peace as I walked this ancient structure with only birds and breeze for companions.

The sun began to lower in the sky, and as the slanting light lent the stones a golden hue, scenes from the past rose before my eyes. As I climbed, I thought about the wall's history with a growing sense of unease.

Conscripted laborers built the wall, quarrying stones, hauling rubble, spreading mortar, laying bricks. Many had been forcibly taken from their families to work on a frozen frontier. Many died of exhaustion. An ancient Chinese ballad says the wall is stacked with the bones of fallen laborers. Those skeletons might rest beneath my feet.

Later, when the wall was complete, it crawled with soldiers watching for signs of a raid. For them, the wall marked the edge of civilization. Behind lay their mighty empire; before them stretched a perilous and unforgiving world. I could not see any sign of other people, but once lives had ended all around me here, part of a huge effort to keep out the rest of the world.

I reached the top of the last rise just as the sun dangled above the jagged hills. Beyond the watchtower where I stood, the wall made a sharp left turn downward, then continued over mountain after mountain until it disappeared into the mottled mists and shadows of sunset. The air had turned pleasantly cool, but the stones held on to the heat of the day.

The weather was warm enough that I decided to sleep under the stars rather than inside the tower. I found a relatively flat spot, rolled out my mat and bunched up a shirt into a pillow. As I contentedly munched my dinner—a banana, bread and some ramen noodles—insects took up buzzing in the brush below the wall, and a cuckoo let out a few plaintive notes. I stretched out under the single sheet of my makeshift bed, and before I knew it, I was asleep.

A DIVIDE THAT UNIFIES

I woke in the middle of the night. The nearly full moon bathed everything in milky white, and stars twinkled through the windows of the watchtower above me. I felt alone in this ethereal scene, but it was a loneliness I relished. In the darkness, I could almost believe that the wall beneath me was new. That soldiers were asleep in the tower next to me. That fires were roaring in the beacon towers. That lonesome watchmen stared tiredly into the chilly night air. In a way, wrapped in the silence of the wall, I was closer to those long-vanished ghosts than to any living person.

I thought of the bustle and fanfare of the restored sections of the wall, where international crowds snap photos and talk into cell phones in a variety of tongues. What would these ancient ghosts make of that rambunctious scene?

Far from keeping out the rest of the world, the Great Wall brings together people from its farthest corners. In the eyes of those who gave their lives here, was this unintended result a success or failure?

Wondering, I soon fell asleep again. When I woke, one edge of the horizon had begun to grow bright. The idea of hiking the wall in the emerging light of a new day got me on my feet and walking. The brush on the wall waved in the cool morning wind. The cuckoo stirred drowsily, and the sparse clouds above the mountains began to glow.

Sunrise would light the way back to my century.[4]

Tom Bissell in Central Asia

Despite all the crowds, even at remoter sites like Palmyra, Petra, and Tiwanaku on the shores of Lake Titicaca, Bolivia, the lure of far-away places still attracts the travel writer. Tom Bissell served in the Peace Corps in Uzbekistan in 1996. He witnessed the disastrous shrinking of the Aral Sea to a third its original size—the result of short-sighted Soviet irrigation policies. After seven months, he returned home with a compelling fascination with the country and its people. Five years later, he returned to Uzbekistan on a magazine assignment to document the environmental catastrophe and traveled through the country with a high-spirited young Uzbek named Rustam, who sometimes seemed only one step ahead of the police. Bissell's eventful journey took him through the land of a people oppressed by Genghis Khan and Joseph Stalin, and took him to the land's ancient cities—Tashkent, Samarkand, and Bukhara. Sometimes hilarious, often sobering, *Chasing the Sea* is a memorable chronicle of ecological disaster and of great monuments caught in the crosscurrents of the turbulent world of central Asian politics.

Bissell found Samarkand to be a curious mixture of the ancient and the modern, crowded with homogeneous tour groups, and the victim of heavy-handed restoration and more often neglect.

We walked through the lobby, passing a Salon of Beauty and a pair of gold lions, into the side streets of Samarkand. A pattern soon emerged. For blocks the streets were clean. Then, a mastodonic pile of rotting communal trash clouded with wasps. Spiky weeds grew knee-high seemingly from every crack. Every fifty feet along the mud walls shared by the streets' homes stood a metal gate with a number and mail slot. From behind the walls floated household chatter and an occasional low radio. All around us children played kickball. They scattered whenever a beeping Lada or taxi came barreling through, splattering the walls with muddy water from the puddles collected within Samarkand's countless backstreet potholes. The city was all charmed antiquity until I looked up at a netting of telephone wires and noted along the walls dozens of gutters rusting off their moors. Dusk had just begun to fall, the sky as colorless as snow.

Like spies, we approached Tamerlane's tomb, properly known as the Guri Amir (Tajik for "Tomb of the King"), from the rear. Nearby, police officers were investigating a disturbance of some kind, a trio of what I assumed were witnesses sitting dolefully on the curb while the officers conferred. My desultory attempt to probe further was discouraged by the lead investigator's sudden black glare. As I walked back to join Rustam, a three-legged dog ran between us, chased higgledy-piggledy by two cackling children on bicycles. The Guri Amir was six hundred years old and yet all around it, with a sad sense of having somehow been widowed, huddled bulwarks of modern life. Adjacent homes' windows were open, close enough to the tomb's grounds to allow their occupants to lean outside and pluck a leaf from the outlying hedges or fruit from its mulberry trees.

Tamerlane, or, as Uzbeks know him, Amir Timur, built the Guri Amir in the early 1400s. Timur's architects botched their first attempt at the tomb, intended for Timur's sons, and upon pain of death were given ten days to raze the miscarriage and get it right. Timur wound up being buried here because the road to his nearby hometown, the site of his intended mausoleum, was, when he died, blocked off by snow. The Guri Amir was once a much larger complex. All that was left of the original founding religious college was a huge stone arch that opened onto the empty courtyard before the tomb itself. Its four surrounding minarets were survived only by their foundations, its hospice by nothing at all. What remained was still magnificent, even allowing for Soviet efforts to "restore" Guri Amir. Soviet restoration lasted for thirty years and continued with the Uzbeks today. "Unfortunately," in the words of one authority on Islamic architecture, "the authentic, majestic ruins of this mighty building have consequently been immured within a sham brick and concrete case and therefore to all intents and purposes destroyed."

The tomb's most striking feature was its bulbous cupola, a ribbed cylindrical drum unique to Central Asia. Atop the cupola was a small onion-shaped gold tip that, like much Central Asian architecture, lacked an Islamic crescent. The cupola's sixty-four ribs, which gave the structure much of its visual audacity, were as fat as goalposts. Covering the cupola was a skin of glittering turquoise tilework common to the Timurid period, regarded by scholars as lighter and more playful than most Islamic architecture. The word "turquoise" has (rather obviously, when one thinks about it) a Turkic etymology. Indeed, turquoise is the color of Turks. Samarkand was famous for this mystically bright blue, engineered by wizardly medieval alchemists for the precise purpose of sparkling in the region's harsh desert sunshine. In bright white Arabic calligraphy ten feet high, the tautology GOD IS IMMORTAL encircled the cupola's lower reaches.

We walked through the first gate's tall bullet-shaped portal (called a *pishtaq*) and lingered in the courtyard. Suddenly, our fellow Afrosiabians descended, the French and the Germans, and began to photograph the hell out of the place. Rustam sat down to smoke, laughing with the peculiar sadness of the tourist made native by other tourists, and I crept around the building's perimeter to find Guri Amir's keeper feeding some birds. Behind him one of the tomb's low munchkin-sized iron doors stood open. The door's padlock hung from the man's cloth belt.

After mutual salaams I asked him why these doors were so small. "For Allah," he said. "One must bow to Allah to enter such a place." He smiled at me. His strangely tiny face was old but smooth, worn down to its veins. He sported a large gray beard but no mustache and looked rather Amish. A bundle of folded and tucked white cloth sat smartly upon his head. "Where are you from?"

"America."

"Samarkand is a great city," he said, then clucked his tongue at the birds stepping trustingly about his robe's hem.

"Yes," I agreed.

His courtly, unimpressed air suggested that he had been working here for some time. He would have been a boy when Stalin died and would have experienced vividly the decades of wild Soviet fluctuation on Islam and Central Asia. The great travel writer Robert Byron, while decamped in Herat, Afghanistan, in the 1930s, wrote of Samarkand as desirously as a lover: "Afghanistan, till literally the other day, has been inaccessible. Samarcand, for the last fifty years, has attracted scholars, painters, and photographers. . . . Now the position is reversed. The Russians have closed Turkestan. The Afghans have opened their country." And now the grim about-face had happened again. . . .

He smiled again, as though in recognition that Amir Timur was not a great man; as though admitting, privately, between new friends, that Amir Timur ranked among the worst mass murderers in world history. Timur may have been the greatest: no single human being, not even Jenghiz Khan, managed to amass as large an empire, which spanned from Turkey to India, allowing Timur the chance to kill an unprecedented variety and number of people.

He was born around 1336 fifty miles southeast of Samarkand in the hamlet of Shakhrisabz, then called Kesh. (It is said the infant Timur's tiny fists were prophetically filled with blood.) Timur's birth, Gibbon wrote, with uncharacteristic stupidity, "was cast on one of those periods of anarchy which . . . open a new field to adventurous ambition." Shakhrisabz, today regarded as one of Uzbekistan's nicest cities, was by most accounts a place of mild, sun-washed loveliness even in Timur's time. Slavery had always been outlawed there, and the city's traditional method of execution was hanging—as opposed to Khiva, which preferred unzipping throats, and Bukhara, which preferred decapitation. A small pile of bricks in a village outside of Shakhrisabz marks Timur's proper place of birth—perhaps an admission, however demure, of the incarnate terror gentle Shakhrisabz unwittingly unleashed upon the world. . . .

Timur's capital was "the threshold of paradise," Samarkand, which he pampered as thoroughly as he did his eight wives. Under his tutelage Samarkand became the site of one of the most determined public-works efforts in human history, and the city was rewarded with ambassadors from China, Constantinople, Baghdad, and Cairo. A single public garden in Samarkand was so large that, when a diplomat's horse went lost upon its grounds, the creature was not found for six weeks. Structures both holy and secular were spared no expense, and Timur, who often threw coins and lumps of meat to his toilers, never saw his orders, however unreasonable, go neglected. Timur (yet again, like Jenghiz) usually spared the artisans of the regions he conquered so they could be put to beautifying use back home. Thus thousands of architects and painters from around the world were shuttled to Samarkand to contribute to its grandeur. In this way Samarkand's remaining Timurid architecture combines Indian motifs with Azerbaijani motifs, Persian with Caucasian, a fusion of utterly different schools of artistry to the result of a gorgeously peculiar magnificence. Timurid tilework was among the most easily appreciable of these innovations, but shield-shaped spandrels in-filled with tile and the ribbed, bulbous dome of the Guri Amir and elsewhere became equally characteristic of Timur's grandiosity.

But a few peerless buildings do not excuse barbarity, and Timur was a barbarian in the most literal sense of that discredited word. While Samarkandis exulted in the desert paradise Timur created, no other land upon which he had designs was spared. . . .

We fell in line behind some Germans excitedly gesticulating at the tomb's—yes, I admitted it, even then—exquisitely brilliant tile.

A rough stone passageway led to the actual mausoleum. I could hear the Germans and French busily clicking away with their cameras, the occasional flashbulb filling the dim passageway with compressed bursts of light. Old Uzbek and Tajik women, silent and mendicant, wearing bright pajama-patterned housedresses, sat cross-legged along the passageway selling Timur posters, maps, and calendars. Uzbek mythologists had divined for Timur a consistent look—one of bald, scowling, black-goateed nastiness. Spandrel-shed pieces of tile could be purchased here for $3, an outrageous sum considering that very few of these tiles, however painstakingly approximated, were more than a few decades old. A French woman bought $12 worth of reputedly ancient tile, then darted off toward the inner sanctum.

Rustam and I followed her into a surprisingly small, squarish chamber lit with a blaze of perpetual sunset. My arms changed color, their faint tan suddenly butterscotch, while Rustam shone as brownly as kiln-fresh clay. Our dermal luster was due not to any outside light—the tomb's four fretted windows allowed in only the whitish nebula of a fading afternoon—but to the massive glass chandelier suspended in the middle of the cupola's recessed inner dome, every square inch of which was covered with gold reliefwork. The refurbishment of this inner dome—the Soviets spackled it with something like twenty pounds of melted-down gold in a 1970 restoration—was thought to have been much more successful than that of Guri Amir's exteriors, probably because the restorers were able to base their work upon more surviving elements.

From this enchanted belfry my overpowered eyes eventually dropped. The chamber's greenish gypsum walls were paneled with onyx hexagonal tile and Arabic inscription of Timur's deeds and genealogy. Two separately employed Uzbek guides related this information for the German and French tourists. The Germans' guide spoke German while the French guide spoke English. I walked amid this odd Babel to the marble railing that blocked off the seven cenotaphs of Timur, his sons and grandsons, and his favorite Islamic sage. As with most Muslim tombs, these were mere markers; the real tombs, which Guri Amir's keeper had offered to show me, were found in a not-so-secret secret cruciform burial chamber beneath us.

Six of the seven cenotaphs were rectangular, lightly inscribed blocks of rather plain marble. The large central cenotaph belonged to Timur, next to which some maudlin soul had placed a fresh batch of roses. Upon his cenotaph was a massive slab of cloudy, blackish jade once thought to be the largest piece of jade in the world. As Timur lay dying, he had supposedly muttered that all he desired for a grave marker was "a stone, and my name upon it." It was probably the only order he ever gave that went unheeded. Even now the cemented fracture running down the middle of Timur's jade block was visible. For this severance various explanations are given. One holds that, in 1740, three hundred years after Timur's death, a Persian invader named Nadir Shah, fresh from demolishing Khiva and still incensed by Timur's butchery of his people, split the block in two with one Herculean blow of his sword. (This is, obviously, the Persian version.) Another story claims that Nadir Shah cracked the block while in the process of stealing it away to Persia. After the slab's breakage Nadir Shah is said to have been plagued with bad luck that ended only when the chagrined plunderer respectfully returned the marker to its rightful place. For years this jade block had collected dust in a Moscow museum. The Soviets also stole from Samarkand the oldest Qur'an in existence, that of Uthman, the Third Caliph, whose blood speckled a number of its pages. But the jade marker was returned, and Uthman's Qur'an was stored safely in Tashkent.[5]

He stopped at the ancient city of Bukhara, where, he was told, the ubiquitous state police had less power and instead the moderate clergy held sway. Bissell was lucky, for he had accreditation from the Ministry of Foreign Affairs that gave him ready access to almost everything. He described Bukhara as a city where superstition and cruelty once ruled, a city once celebrated for its well-trained falcons—which were described by a nineteenth-century Russian diplomat as better educated than any of the inhabitants. Only a little of the ancient settlement remained.

And so it was. All around us shadows lengthened and faded and disappeared on Bukhara's distinctive buildings, none higher than two or three stories and all made of swiss-colored baked mud or stone. The alleys between them were often no wider than an arm span, the rooftops so close, it had been said, that one could sprint across the city without once dirtying one's soles on its streets. On its sunward side the Old City glowed an impossibly vivid orange, while its lee side seemed dipped in plum-colored darkness. The mulberry trees glowed so brightly their leaves seemed gilded in fresh magma. Bukhara's Old City was no less than a living, functioning sanctuary of preserved medieval architecture. Rick lived near its center, and thousands more lived all around us. Many of these buildings had been wired for electricity only since the 1960s and upwards of two hundred were protected by surprisingly tough laws. But for a few Kodak signs and parked cars,

Bukhara was blessed with one of the least noticeably altered city centers of all the surviving urban pillars of the medieval Muslim world. Neither Baghdad nor Herat nor Samarkand nor Mecca itself could claim as little intrusion. Especially Mecca, so much of it ruined and kitschified, non-Arab Muslims often complained, by a tasteless well-known Saudi construction family known as bin Laden.

Bukhara played a significant role not merely in Uzbekistan but within all Central Asia. It was, perhaps, the region's finest city. Tashkent belonged to the world, Samarkand lived too complacently off its past, Khiva went to sleep at eight, Almaty was run by gangsters, Bishkek was a glorified village, Ashkabat was a political Jonestown, Dushanbe was a series of checkpoints, Kabul was a shooting gallery, and Mazar-i-Sharif was sealed. But Bukhara was a great city. It had not always been an especially kind city, and its name (alternately said to come from *vihara*, a Sanskrit word that means "monastery," or *bukhar*, a Farsi word that means "source of knowledge") was for centuries enough to cause nervous Western travelers to mess their saddles. Bukhara, along with Khiva, was the boomtown of the region's slave trade. The city was also—though not always—famous for its fanaticism. Isolation is the nursery of fanaticism, and in few places had fanaticism been suckled on such poisonous milk. There were several explanations for this. Except for the Samanid period in the tenth century (a time when Bukhara was actually more populous than today) the city had not served as capital to any significant kingdom until the sixteenth century. Until that point Bukhara had in most territorial hierarchies played the role of a remote and exotic desert mistress: admired, even loved, but grudgingly subsidized and easily ignored.

13-5 Standing in front of a madrassa (or Qur'an school) on Registan Square in Samarkand, Uzbekistan, it is possible to observe aspects of the past mingled with modernity.

Bukhara was thought to be between two thousand and three thousand years old. When the hurricane of Islam first moved east, prompt and attentive tributes paid in Bukharan gold managed for decades to hold Arab jihadists at bay. In the early 700s the sons of Mohammed finally took the city. Bukhara's wealthiest families escaped to Afghanistan rather than stomach Arab rule, which turned out to have been a wise decision. Neighborhoods were emptied and Zoroastrian temples mercilessly Islamicized. An Arab soldier was stationed within every Bukharan household to make sure the fire-worshiping pagans were obeying proper Islamic ritual—a useful reminder of the cyclical nature of oppression. These Gestapo tactics successfully wore down the fierce mental nubs of Bukharans' resistance, and the city quickly gained a reputation as one of the Arab-ruled world's holiest cities—the Cupola of Islam itself, where, according to the angel Gibreel, the light did not shine down but up. Two hundred years later the Samanids cunningly slipped Bukhara out from under Arabia's thumb and steered the city toward its cultural and historical apogee, of which the medical texts of ibn Sina and the encyclopedia of al-Beruni are immodest relics. . . .

Here loomed three structures easily as commanding as Samarkand's Registan. The first was the 150-foot high Kalon Minaret, which towered slightly off center between the Poi Kalon's two other major buildings, the Kalon Mosque and the Mir-i-Arab Madrasa. The Kalon Minaret's colorful history was best captured by its other name: the Tower of Death. The thousand-year-old minaret was one of Bukhara's oldest surviving structures. From 1127—its year of construction—until the 1300s, the Kalon Minaret is thought to have been the world's tallest building. Round and made of fourteen sections of diversely reticular gold-tinted brick—each section divided by a thin belt embroidered with "God Is Immortal"–type Arabic script—the Kalon Minaret thinned and tapered as it rose to meet its beautiful and many-windowed crown-shaped summit, called a "lantern" likely due to the minaret's peacetime function as a lighthouse for desert caravans. Beneath the lantern the minaret's one burst of color, a slender girdle of bright turquoise, burst out at the eye. Part of the minaret was destroyed in 1920 when General Mikhail Frunze, the Soviet vanquisher of much of Central Asia, rudely introduced it to modern artillery.

This was the third minaret to bless Bukhara with its majesty. The first was erected here in the early 900s and burned to the ground a century later. The second, built around 1070 during the Karakhanid era, was made of either wood or brick. It also collapsed, unfortunately onto an adjacent mosque, to a massive loss of life. (Official cause of the collapse: the Evil Eye.) Frunze's shelling was not the first time the surviving Kalon Minaret very nearly met the fate of its predecessors. When Jenghiz Khan arrived in Bukhara, he galloped right up to its octagonal base and dismounted. He is said to have stared up in wonderment at the lantern for some time, leaning back so far that his hat fell off. As Jenghiz knelt to retrieve his hat—an unfamiliar position for him—he ordered that the minaret be spared, virtually the only part of Bukhara that was. One can imagine Jenghiz's delight when he learned of one of the minaret's time-honored sideline uses. This was jaculation, or, more bluntly, sewing people in sacks and pitching them from one of the lantern's windows. This mode of punishment achieved its greatest popularity under debauched Mangit rule. Typically, jaculation was carried out on bazaar days on the order of the amir himself. The victims were most often petty criminals, religious apostates, and wives accused of adultery. A nineteenth-century French traveler reports that the bodies fell from the tower as though they were "large parcels," twisting and turning as they plummeted. The Frenchman witnessed so many jaculations during his brief visit that it became to him a "distraction." Fitzroy Maclean claims that "the repeated impact of these terrible packages produced a little hollow in the hard ground at the foot of the minaret," which I attempted and failed to confirm. Rick told us that most Bukharans, embarrassed by the stories, insist no one was ever thrown off the minaret; it was all a legend. The Soviets maintained the practice ended in the 1880s, but at least one visitor mentions seeing jaculations in the 1920s. Another use of the Kalon Minaret, according to Alexander Burnes's *Travels into Bokhara*, was as Bukhara's prime spot for peeping Mohammeds to spy on the city's women, no doubt allowing for a different sort of jaculation.

We walked thirty feet to the entrance of the Kalon Mosque, built upon the foundation of the earlier minaret-crushed mosque, and stepped through its primary pishtaq. The portal tympanum was decorated with pinwheelish designs set against a dark blue. Stairs led down into the mosque's spacious open courtyard, its paving glowing salt-white in the sun. Planted in the middle of the courtyard was a large, squat mulberry tree, its trunk coated in a whitish paint-based insecticide to keep off burrowing insects. Mulberry trees were often found around holy sites in Central Asia, an ancient pagan tradition absorbed into the nucleus of monotheism: the Islamic equivalent of Christmas trees. We had the courtyard to ourselves, and each of us walked off to a different corner. *Kalon* means "great," and this was the second-largest mosque in Central Asia, able to contain 10,000 faithful, a number said to parallel the number of Bukhara's of-age male population at the time of its reconstruction in the 1100s. Tradition holds that Bukhara's amirs all came to the Kalon Mosque to pray. From 1920 to 1989, however, worship was forbidden here. (Under Stalin alone, an astonishing 26,000 mosques were closed in Central Asia. To wrap one's mind around that number, imagine every hospital in America being closed, virtually overnight. Now multiply that by a factor of four.) Jenghiz cottoned equally little to the great mosque, mostly demolishing it after sparing the Kalon Minaret. Where the four of us now strolled idly, the Mongols had executed thousands. It is said that, when Jenghiz ascended the steps back to the Poi Kalon's foundation, the slosh of blood in this courtyard came up to one's shins. The mosque was not fully rebuilt until three hundred years later, when the Shaybanids began their revitalization of Holy Bukhara.

Rustam drifted over to me, his face awash with perspiration, looked at his watch, and sighed.

"Pretty amazing place, huh?"

He shrugged irritably and glanced about the courtyard. "I don't know, bro. It takes more than this to impress me. To be truthful, I'm getting a little sick of all these sacred spaces."

I watched a bird fly overhead, its shadow gliding across the courtyard's paving, shooting up onto a wall, and disappearing. "We're almost done, I guess. I just want to see the madrasa."

Rick joined us, sweating equally. "What's up?"

"Madrasa," I said.

"You can't go in, you know. As an unbeliever you can only go as far as ten feet inside."

"We'll see about that, Reek." I held up my accreditation card. "Just wait until the mullahs have a gander at this little baby. They're liable to kill something in our honor."

The Mir-i-Arab Madrasa faced the Kalon Mosque directly across the plaza, a placement system known as *kosh* (pair) that achieved wide use in Central Asia during the sixteenth and seventeenth centuries. A game of soccer had migrated over from the Poi Kalon's far reaches, and the children were now using a portion of Mir-i-Arab as a goal. They were quickly chased away by an old man with a stick. Once the children were gone, we walked over. This madrasa was built in 1535 by one Sheik Abdullah Mir-i-Arab (Prince of the Arabs), a Yemeni who tried to help along the Uzbek Shaybanids' not always facile interpretation of Islam. It was a massive building, reminiscent of the Tilla Kari Madrasa in Samarkand, which was likely modeled upon it. Much of the decorative mosaic found upon the large central pishtaq's tympanum and facing had been faded by time, making its gigantic stone plainness more akin to a rough, carved mountainside than to an Islamic seminary. The mosaics and stucco stalactites respectively found upon the madrasa's inner portals and domes—everything we were not allowed to see, in other words—was according to one scholar "extremely refined."

The Mir-i-Arab functioned for centuries as the Harvard of Central Asian Islam. History tells us that it was closed from the mid-1920s until the mid-1940s, and upon reopening became one of only two madrasas allowed to operate by the Soviets, the other being the Imam Bukhari Madrasa, the resting place of Uthman's Qur'an, which despite its name is found in Tashkent. Bukharans themselves claimed it had never closed. It was a working religious seminary today, many of its 250 students living in quiet balconied quarters within the Mir-i-Arab, an overcrowded few consigned to cells in the next-door Kalon Mosque. Study was in Arabic, the holy language, and most students weathered a seven-year-long course devoted to a curriculum of the Qur'an, theology, the Qur'an, theology, theology, and the Qur'an.

As Rick predicted, ten feet into the madrasa a plaque explained that infidels were not allowed. Rick and Rustam lingered inside its dark stone-cooled foyer, watching the pitiless sun beat down on the plaza outside, the light as thick as a waterfall. I stepped a little farther than advisable into Mir-i-Arab to find myself mere inches from a lattice gate. I approached it gingerly, steeling myself for a glimpse into the secret gears of Islam. I fit my eye against one of the lattice's diamondine openings. In the courtyard of the Harvard of Central Asian Islam, a half-dozen bearded young men were playing Ping-Pong.[6]

Obsessed with the Never-lost Inca

On the other side of the planet, the Andes is a place where you can still search for lost cities, cities not necessarily unknown to, but rather mislaid by, archaeologists. The filmmaker and explorer Hugh Thomson became obsessed with the last settlements of the Inca in remote mountain valleys and followed in the footsteps of Hiram Bingham to Machu Picchu and to isolated Llactapata, a satellite of the city, a road terminal and shrine. Visited by Hiram Bingham for a few hours in 1911, it was largely forgotten until 2003, when a survey showed that Llactapata was much larger than originally reported. Thomson found it "hallucinatory," for it lay "close to the world which was known. From the ruins we had been able to hear the sound of the train echoing up to us from the other side of the valley. It was a reminder that one could be yards from a site and never realize it, so thick was the jungle vegetation that creeps up the Andes from the Amazon."[7]

The same aura of mystery surrounded the ruins of the high Andes that had permeated them in Bingham's time. The ruins were difficult of access, often hidden by rain and swirling mists. In 1982, Thomson and his party penetrated deep into the Vilcabamba Range, where the surviving Inca royalty had fled after the Spanish conquest and survived for several decades, maintaining roads and shrines throughout the region until 1572. Thomson and his party braved police checkpoints and arrived at the village near the Choquequirao site in the back of a beer truck. Three-quarters of a century after Bingham, these most remote of Andean sites were still a unique adventure, despite the thousands of visitors flocking to Machu Picchu and hiking the Inca trail that leads to those ruins.

The village had an idyllic setting—groves of eucalyptus, trout pools and a wide street that curved over a hill. It was market day and we passed many clear-faced, smiling women, with an independent air about them. This was also a village of horses—they were everywhere, tied up to the posts outside houses and grazing in the nearby meadows, while horsemen down from the hills drank outside the shacks that passed for bars.

We asked a couple of boys to take us up first to the old palace of Vitcos and then on to the White Rock. Alfredo and Wilfredo can't have been more than about seven or eight. We stopped by the river to wash—the boys were fascinated by my electric razor. Then they led us up a winding path above the valley, spinning tops as they went, and after an hour or so we came round a corner to see the old palace of Vitcos ahead.

The ruins of the palace lay on a ridge which rose like a throne in the very middle of the Vilcabamba valley. From the rounded summit, Manco and later his sons could survey not only the valley, but the many passes that led into it from almost every point of the compass: this was the Incas' centre of operations while in exile.

A narrow spit of land led us out onto the summit and the main buildings—and we could see at once that these had been Inca buildings of the first order, although now dilapidated and covered with tangled weed and some plants that looked like overgrown cabbages. The plaza was surrounded by fine gateways and ashlars worked with the almost casual ingenuity the masons liked to display, as if to show how many sides a stone could have and still be made to fit with another. Large lintels were still in place over the doors, although treasure-hunters seemed to have repeatedly excavated beneath the doorways themselves. The building that fronted onto the plaza was a full 250 feet long. There was no doubt that this had been a palace.

It is probable that much of it had already been built by Pachacuti and earlier Incas when Manco arrived here with some relief, thinking that he had outrun his pursuers. He ordered that a new house be built for himself and organised a festival at which to parade the mummies of his ancestors before the locals and his jungle allies.

If Manco thought that he had reached sanctuary, he was to be rudely disabused. His pursuer Orgóñez, once he had crossed the bridge at Chuquichaca, made good time and caught the Inca unawares. It was a rout. The Incas, according to Manco's son Titu Cusi, were as drunk as they were accustomed to be at such festivals and were completely taken by surprise. Manco himself was only saved by the Spaniards' greed. They were so excited by the amount of gold and loot they found (much of it on public display for the festival) that he was able to get away over one of the passes that led from Vitcos. Before Orgóñez could mount a further chase, he was recalled to Cuzco to take part in the interminable civil war that was rumbling on between two factions of the conquistadors (a civil war in which Orgóñez later lost his life) and Manco could return to Vitcos, although he had lost many of his treasures and troops.

He was not able to relax for long—a second punitive expedition was launched against him a few years later by Gonzalo Pizarro, the same Pizarro brother who was later to try to sail down the Amazon. Gonzalo was the youngest brother of the four who had come to Peru: Francisco led the expedition, Juan died at Sacsahuaman, while Hernando, the only legitimate son and Prescott's 'evil genius', was eventually imprisoned in Spain for his crimes, although for those against his fellow conquistadors rather than against the Indians. Gonzalo was as tough as his older brothers, if not always as intelligent. In 1539, he chased Manco even further than Orgóñez had—over the mountains beyond Vitcos and right down into the Amazon. Again Manco managed to escape and was reported to have shouted defiance at his persecutors as he was borne off into the depths of the jungle.

So once more Manco lived to return and rebuild his kingdom. He was nothing if not a survivor. So confident did he become in his Vilcabamba stronghold that he launched punitive raids against the Spanish on the old Royal Road from Cuzco down to Lima and mounted an effective guerrilla campaign. He was helped by the continuing civil war between the conquistadors, in which Gonzalo Pizarro was eventually executed and his brother Francisco assassinated. Manco, always a cunning politician, welcomed the assassins of Francisco Pizarro to his palace at Vitcos on the grounds that any enemy of the Pizarros was a friend of his (understandable given that Francisco had tortured and killed Manco's wife, then floated her mutilated corpse down the Urubamba river so that Manco could see it).

But Manco's kindness to the Spanish refugees was to be his undoing. Standing in the plaza, with a gentle wind blowing up from the valley below, it was impossible not to remember how Manco had finally died on that same spot.

Manco sheltered Pizarro's assassins for a few years. After a while, they decided to curry favour with the Spanish authorities and obtain a pardon by killing Manco. Although kept unarmed while they were at the Vitcos palace, they somehow managed to obtain a dagger. While playing a game of quoits with Manco, one of them produced it and stabbed the Inca to death.

Manco was only twenty-nine when he died in this final act of Spanish treachery. He had been a great leader. Prescott put it well in the nineteenth century when he wrote (perhaps surprisingly for a North American at the time): 'Manco did not trust the promises of the white man and he chose rather to maintain his savage independence in the mountains, with the few brave spirits around him, than to live a slave in the land which had once owned the sway of his ancestors.'

Vitcos was a theatrical setting for a death—a stage playing to the amphitheatre of the valley. How Manco's unarmed assassins thought they would get away with it when they were so exposed, virtually unarmed, and a hundred miles inside enemy territory, is unclear: they were promptly chased down and burnt to death. It was a strange result of the twists and turns of politics in the tumultuous years after the Conquest that the same assassins should have killed both the Spanish and Inca leaders.

Vitcos had never been reconstructed (spared the fate of Machu Picchu, the purists would argue) and had been only partially excavated. There was a sadness to the few items which had been found there by Bingham: 'a mass of rough potsherds, a few Inca whirl-bobs and bronze shawl-pins, and also a number of iron articles of European origin, heavily rusted horseshoe nails, a buckle, a pair of scissors, several bridles or saddle ornaments, and three Jew's harps'—a sense that the refugees had been forced to use the scrapings of the culture that had displaced them.

"Here before us was a great white rock. Our guides had not misled us. Beneath the trees were the ruins of an Inca temple, flanking and partly enclosing the gigantic granite boulder, one end of which overhung a small pool of running water. Since the surface of the little pool, as one gazes at it, does not reflect the sky, but only the overhanging rock, the water looks black and forbidding, even to unsuperstitious Yankees.

It was late on the afternoon of August 9, 1911, when I first saw this remarkable shrine. Densely wooded hills rose on every side. The remarkable aspect of this great boulder and the dark pool beneath its shadow had caused this to become a place of worship. Here, without doubt, was 'the principal *mochadero* of these forested mountains'. It is still venerated by the Indians of the vicinity. At last we had found the place where, in the days of Titu Cusi, the Inca priests faced the east, greeted the rising sun, 'extended their hands towards it and threw kisses to it, a ceremony of the most profound resignation and reverence.'"

Little visited, this was still a strange and melancholy place. It lay in a side-valley, in the shadow of the ridge on which the palace of Vitcos stood. The smallness of the valley helped to emphasise the presence of the rock, the shape of which seemed consciously to have been sculpted to reflect the skyline of the mountains directly behind it (there are numerous examples of this style of reflective sculpture in Inca work, at Machu Picchu and elsewhere). We came to it from above, so we could see the layers of terraces stretching away beneath it, many filled with arum lilies and grazing horses.

The White Rock itself was perfectly formed, rather than monumental: the length was about fifty feet. As a sculpture it was magnificent. Because it was carved from the natural rock, it was asymmetric and almost impossible to photograph from any angle without reducing it. Not all the rock had been carved, but there were sweeping planes that had been smoothed on some sides, including the top, planes emphasised by the steps that had been cut to meet them.

Under the rock was a spring and the water was carefully channelled away from this and through a small *baño*, a ceremonial bath, before flowing off down the meadows and past many other smaller rocks, also partially sculpted.

Because we stayed for a full twenty-four hours, we were able to observe the way the light played off every facet as the sun moved around the rock, including a high wall that featured some ostentatious stone bosses studded across it, on the eastern side (first light brought out the bosses in strong relief, just as it did for similar stonework at Ollantaytambo). Around the rock were scattered elaborately carved boulders and the remaining foundation walls of the temples that had been built here, although none were high enough to show the ornamental niches they probably once had.

The rock had been called many things by many different people: 'The White Rock', 'Chuquipalta', 'Yurak Rumi', 'Ñusta España'—the very confusion of different names for the place gave a sense of the talismanic qualities it held.

We are used to the idea that the Incas quite literally worshipped stone, but few question why. There is an idea in the West that stone must imply some notion of permanence, but this is not necessarily true in the Andes, which is not a static landscape. An area of incipient volcanic activity and landslides, with recurring and violent El Niño activity over the millennia, the landscape has always been changing. For the Incas, stone was a much more volatile, organic medium. . . .

What one saw now at Chuquipalta was the aftermath of that destruction. A few blocks lay toppled to the ground and the nearby temple buildings had been razed to just a few feet in height, but the priests were unable to destroy the rock itself. Like a bombed church, the spirituality of the place remained. The White Rock was part of what had survived the Spanish Conquest—the heart of old Peru.

Cooking by candle-light with our shadows thrown back against the rock, we had an eerie meal crouched under the giant Inca stone, the petrol-flame of the cooker guttering in all directions. The frogs started croaking from the water under the rock, their noises amplified into an echo. We used our torch to pick out their coal-black eyes in the water. Outside in the night, the fire-flies hung over the banks of the water-channel, twitching with static.

In the morning I woke early and sat on one of the large carved seats that surrounded the rock itself. The sun rose at full strength from behind a hill, as it does in the mountains (there are no soft sunrises). I felt suddenly an intimation of mortality. Like most twenty-one-year-olds, death had always seemed at most a remote possibility and something that happened to other people. But in the cold of the morning and surrounded by the stone *disjecta membra* of the monument, with the white arum lilies against the green of the meadows, I felt a chill.[8]

The Inca trail has become a familiar adventure for hundreds of people every year, so much so that access to the trail is now tightly controlled to prevent further erosion. Karin Muller traversed it in 2000 while writing a book for the National Geographic Society, surviving such experiences as a traditional guinea-pig healing session and a trip deep into a primitive gold mine. Muller weaves a lively history of the Inca Empire as she traces the remarkable legacy of shamanism, vicuña round-ups, and the farming of coca leaves. Coca was, and still is, the ultimate marker of indigenous identity, and she describes their using it as akin to our sharing a cup of coffee. Near the end of her sojourn, she visited the Island of the Sun on Lake Titicaca, one of the most sacred places in the Inca Empire, where once again she found a sacred place.

I knew where Manco Capac had sunk his golden staff into the ground to found the Inca Empire. I even had some idea of the route he might have taken to get there. It was time to retrace his footsteps to where it all began—the place the Inca called their Eden: the Island of the Sun.

Some say it was the birthplace of the sun itself. The Spaniards believed it held the legendary Fountain of Youth. Today the Island of the Sun has some 5,000 inhabitants who live and work the land much as their ancestors did. They speak Aymara, a dialect that existed long before the Inca first arrived. It sits smack in the center of Lake Titicaca, and beside it lies the Island of the Moon, where the Inca's sun virgins once dwelled. Modern politics have split the "greatest lake in the Indies" in half. The sacred cave where Manco Capac once emerged now lies on Bolivian soil.

We caught a boat to the village of Cha'llapampa near the island's northern end and found the cave after two hours of hard hiking. It was a couple of stories high and not quite deep enough to keep out the rain. Our guide pointed out two jaguars that proved the presence of a supreme deity.

"Where?" I asked.

"There," he said, "an eye, the mouth, an ear."

I stood right next to the cave. I backed up 10 feet. I tried from 50 feet away. I couldn't see it. The place looked like an ordinary hole in an unimpressive stone wall.

We decided to try our luck at the Palace of the Inca on the other side of island. It wasn't really a palace at all, but rather an administrative center built in an elaborate maze of walls and doorways. The masonic masterpieces of Machu Picchu and Cuzco had spoiled me. I was disappointed. I headed out to sit near the entrance and watch the young boys scamper by, urging their sheep homeward with homemade wooden staffs. They looked like extras on a Hollywood movie lot.

The Temple of the Sun God stood on a lonely hillside facing the shores of Lake Titicaca. I stifled another pang of disappointment. Somehow I had expected something more spectacular from such a sacred place. We wandered slowly back, past women driving flocks of sheep along the narrow footpaths and carrying newborn lambs in their knotted shawls. Thatched houses perched among the grassy hillsides like scattered grains of rice. Footpaths meandered through the rolling landscape. There were no cars; the island had no roads. The birthplace of the Inca. I tried to imagine what it would be like to know exactly where your Eden lies.

I watched the distant farmers inch across their fields, sowing corn as they had a thousand years ago. The island exuded serenity. At last, I began to understand. A truly sacred place didn't need elaborate stone monuments. Whether it was the birthplace of a mighty nation or just a quiet corner of the world—it was a sanctuary.

We spent that night with a local couple. He was 74 and she was 69. They spoke nothing but Aymara, the language of their pre-Inca ancestors. His face was a spiderweb of wrinkles, creasing skin as dark and shiny as mahogany. She had twisted, driftwood hands and fingers that held a lifetime of handmade memories. Their home looked like the inside of a baker's oven—blackened walls and windowless, and no larger than a horse's stall. The door was narrower than my shoulders, and I had to get down on my knees to crawl inside.

Stalactites of tarry cobwebs collected smoky residue from the cooking fire. The few battered pots were still seasoned with the crust of last week's meals. The old woman and I found a common language in my spinning and her stew, taking turns at the spindle and with the stirring spoon. Her face took on the warm glow of the fire whenever she looked at the two-year-old clinging tightly to her husband's thigh. No, it wasn't their granddaughter, she told me. They had not been blessed with children. She was his nephew's daughter, sent to take care of them as they grew old. At first it seemed like a callous act, but as I watched the old man carefully ladle out the little girl's meal, adjust her hat, and rest a wrinkled hand upon her head, I changed my mind. There was a school just down the road, they told me in gestures and drawings in the dirt. She would go there once she was old enough. In the meantime there were chickens to be chased and sheep to herd and two pigs in the pen, and an entire island to explore without the slightest fear of strangers, cars, or trucks or drugs or even dirty magazines.

I slept in one of the storage huts, under sheaves of hanging corn and piles of alpaca blankets still burred with seeds and hay. The old man came over with his lantern to make sure that all was well. The little girl wrapped herself around his leg and peered at me with huge brown eyes. Once more his leathery hand dropped gently on her head in a feather touch as old as time itself.

A sacred place.[9]

At the end of her book, Muller remarks that the Inca Empire was never really conquered. The fine palaces and temples of the nobility were ravaged and often destroyed; thousands of people became slaves or died from exotic diseases; much of Inca material culture vanished rapidly in the face of European iron tools. But the ancient religious beliefs of the people of the highland Andes survived—astronomical knowledge used to time the planting and harvesting of crops, shamanism and the use of hallucinogenic substances to allow people's minds to travel to the supernatural world, the close-knit ties of kin and reciprocal obligations. With quiet deftness, the Inca melded their traditional religious beliefs, the sun god Viracocha, and other deities and rituals into Catholic ceremony and worship. Over five centuries, Inca society adapted to radically new and often traumatic circumstances, its roots still deep in Andean soil. Many of its traditional institutions and family rituals survive to this day.

From Stonehenge to Samarkand—our ongoing fascination with ruins, with the remains of the past, thrives unabated, even if the character of our travel has shifted from adventure and discovery to what one could, I suppose, call packaged enjoyment. Such packaging is inevitable, for cultural tourism has become a huge growth industry, and archaeological sites have become assets that contribute large sums to many national economies. This is one reason why UNESCO has developed a program of World Heritage Sites, prized locations such as Stonehenge and the Parthenon that transcend the petty nationalisms of individual nations and societies. We live in an era of global economies, an era in which daily life is evermore commoditized, in which travel and, for that matter, visits to archaeological sites are packaged, bought, and sold like items in a supermarket.

On the plus side, this means that even people of relatively modest means can visit the past in all corners of the world as conveniently as they take a train to a nearby city. The same packaging also gives access to the past to a far wider audience than merely the wealthy and the archaeologically inclined.

Where once archaeology and visiting archaeological sites were a luxury accessible to the few, they are now part of both popular culture and modern industrial society. Package tours lure many people to experience the past, but there are hazards, too—relentless tourist traffic that wears away ancient stairways, the warmth of visitors' bodies that raises the humidity in arid Egyptian tombs, the patina of innumerable human hands massaging the bas-reliefs at Angkor Wat. As a result, the International Monuments Fund, a private organization, has dedicated itself to assist in the conservation of archaeological sites in many parts of the world. Our generation and future generations face extraordinary challenges in preserving what remains of the past for the future. If there is one benefit from the mass archaeological tourism of today, it is that public concern about preserving the past for the future will intensify. Should we lose our past, with all the lessons, precedents, and insights it offers, then we have forfeited the very essence of human identity, positioned as it is between past and future.

The figurative price we pay for packaging is a loss of individuality and fewer opportunities to experience the past at leisure and alone. Fortunately, however, as long as there is archaeology, and as long as archaeological sites welcome visitors, there will always be people with curiosity and persistence, whose enjoyment of the past will wander far beyond the arcane details of chronologies, ancient cults, and architectural niceties. They will not be content to remain in the crowd and to digest a potted version of the past from a hurried hour. Their sense of exploration and inquiry will take them far from the major sites and the commonplace locations. Such travelers are like their kin of an earlier time, people who crave more—who crave a chance to linger, to experience, and to explore. Over five centuries ago, William Camden called archaeological travel "a backward-looking curiosity." Nothing has changed about this unique curiosity, a curiosity that makes leisurely archaeological travel a profoundly satisfying adventure. To experience the past rather than merely to visit its remains is one of the great and, alas, now rarer pleasures for the discerning traveler.

Notes

Introduction

1. Excerpt from an 1846 letter by Gustave Flaubert, quoted in Christopher Woodward's *In Ruins* (New York: Pantheon, 2001), page 72.
2. For the purposes of this book, the terms "archaeological site" and "ruin" are considered interchangeable—although, of course, archaeological sites often comprise far more standing walls than ruins do. Evocative attitudes toward both of them are normally similar.
3. Woodward, *In Ruins*, page 69.
4. Excerpt from *The Genius of Christianity* by François René, Vicomte de Chateaubriand, quoted in Woodward, *In Ruins*, page 89.
5. Southwell quotation from Robert Bowdler, "A Sad Prospect for the Soul" (2001); quoted in Woodward, *In Ruins*, page 94.
6. Letter from Rose Macaulay to Constance Babington Smith, in Macaulay's *Letters to a Friend, 1950–1952* (London: Collins, 1961), page 112.

Chapter 1

1. Rose Macaulay, *The Pleasure of Ruins* (London: Thames and Hudson, 1977), page 26.
2. Macaulay, *Pleasure*, page 26.
3. Austen Henry Layard, *Nineveh and Its Remains* (London: John Murray, 1849), page 112.
4. Quoted in Macaulay, *Pleasure*, page 27.
5. Zephaniah 13:15.
6. *Herodotus: The Histories*, translated by Robin Waterfield (Oxford: Oxford University Press, 1998), book 2, pages 78–82.
7. Macaulay, *Pleasure*, page 28.
8. Waterfield, *Herodotus*, book 2, pages 146–148. In my text, I have used the most common pharaonic spellings; those in the extract are no longer commonly used.

9. For a brief summary of early tourism along the Nile, see Brian Fagan, *The Rape of the Nile* (revised edition, Boulder, Colo.: Westview Press, 2004).
10. Pliny the Elder, *Natural History*, XXIII.
11. Pliny, *Natural History*, XXIII.
12. Translated by E. L. Bowie; http://www.liminalityland.com/memnon.htm.
13. Quoted in Fagan, *Rape*, page 24.
14. *Hesiod: Works and Days*, translated by Dorothea Wender (Baltimore: Pelican Books, 1973), pages 62–64.
15. Lucretius, *De Rerum Natura*, II, 75; http://classics.mit.edu/Carus/nature_things.html.

Chapter 2

1. William Stukeley, *Itinerarium Curiosum* (London: Printed for the author, 1724), page 76.
2. Sir Thomas Browne, *Religio Medici* (written and not intended for publication, 1643).
3. Quoted in Christopher Chippindale, *Stonehenge Complete* (third edition, London: Thames and Hudson, 2004), page 20.
4. Chippindale, *Stonehenge*, pages 22ff., describes Geoffrey of Monmouth and his history.
5. William Caxton, *Rerum Anglicarum* (Westminster, 1480); quoted in Chippindale, *Stonehenge*, page 25.
6. Quoted in Chippindale, *Stonehenge*, page 28.
7. Quoted in Glyn Daniel, *The Origins and Growth of Archaeology* (Harmondsworth, U.K.: Penguin, 1967), page 24.
8. William Camden, *Britannia* (London: William Aspley, 1637), page 234; English translation by Philemon Holland.
9. Quoted in Daniel, *Origins*, page 6.
10. Caroline Malone, *Avebury* (London: English Heritage, 1989), summarizes research on Silbury.
11. Camden, *Britannia*; quoted in Daniel, *Origins*, page 25.
12. Camden, *Britannia*; quoted in Daniel, *Origins*, pages 25–26.
13. Camden, *Britannia*, page 729. Sir John Cotton (1571–1631) was a pupil of Camden's and a well-known antiquarian.
14. Quoted in Malone, *Avebury*, page 21.
15. Quoted in Malone, *Avebury*, page 21.
16. Quoted in Malone, *Avebury*, page 21.
17. John Aubrey, *An Essay towards the Description of the North Division of Wiltshire* (1659–1670); quoted in Daniel, *Origins*, pages 26–27.
18. Edward Llwyd, "Letter to Dr. Tancred Robinson," *Philosophical Transactions of the Royal Society*, 1713, page 97.
19. Stukeley, *Itinerarium Curiosum*, page 76. There are several biographies of Stukeley; Stuart Piggott's *William Stukeley: An Eighteenth-Century Antiquary*

(Oxford: Clarendon Press, 1950; revised edition, London: Thames and Hudson, 1985) gives an archaeologist's perspective.

20. Quoted in Chippindale, *Stonehenge*, page 71.
21. William Stukeley, *Stonehenge: A Temple Restored to the British Druids* (London: Innys and Manby, 1740), pages 10, 11, and 19.
22. Stukeley, *Stonehenge*, page 19.
23. Stukeley, *Stonehenge*, page 5.
24. Chippindale, *Stonehenge*, page 86.
25. Stukeley, *Itinerarium Curiosum*, page 138.

Chapter 3

1. Edward Gibbon in a letter dated June 20, 1764; quoted in Christopher Hibbert's *The Grand Tour* (New York: Putnam, 1969), page 165.
2. Quoted in Hibbert, *Grand Tour*, page 10.
3. Quoted in Hibbert, *Grand Tour*, page 10.
4. Quoted in Hibbert, *Grand Tour*, pages 16–17.
5. Quoted in Melissa Calaresu, "Looking for Virgil's Tomb: The End of the Grand Tour and the Cosmopolitan Ideal in Europe," in *Voyages and Visions*, edited by Jas Elsner and Joan-Pau Rubiés (London: Reaktion Books, 1999), pages 138–161. The quotation from Pietro Napoli-Signorelli is on page 139.
6. John Evelyn (1620–1706) was a diarist and garden designer, famous for his descriptions of Italian Renaissance gardens. The quotations in this paragraph are in Hibbert, *Grand Tour*, page 25.
7. Quoted in Calaresu, "Looking," page 152.
8. John Wilkes (1720–1798) was a wealthy country squire with political ambitions, and was also a notorious rake. The quotation is in Hibbert, *Grand Tour*, page 140.
9. The Baltimore family was prominent in the early settlement of Newfoundland and Maryland; their wealth came from Maryland. Quoted in Hibbert, *Grand Tour*, page 140.
10. Edward Gibbon (1734–1794), the son of a country gentleman, became a historian. His *History of the Decline and Fall of the Roman Empire* was published between 1776 and 1787. Quoted in Hibbert, *Grand Tour*, pages 141–142.
11. John Chetwode Eustace (1762–1815) was a prominent Catholic priest who traveled widely in Italy. His *A Classical Tour through Italy* was published in 1813 and enjoyed wide readership. The quotations are from the seventh edition (London: Thomas Tegg, 1841), volume 1, pages 265 and 268.
12. Johann Wolfgang von Goethe, *Italienische Reise* (Berlin: Hempel, n.d.), page 44. (See *Goethe: Italian Journey*, translated by Robert R. Heitner [Princeton, N.J.: Princeton University Press, 1994].)
13. Hippolyte Adolphe Taine (1828–1893) was a French critic and historian whose studies of the ancien régime fostered the idea that history should be concerned with the entire social life of a nation. His work inspired scholars in philosophy

and the social sciences. The extract is from Taine's *Italy, Rome, and Naples*, translated by J. Durand (New York: Leypold and Holt, 1970), pages 48–51.

14. Quoted in Hibbert, *Grand Tour*, page 222.
15. Quoted in Hibbert, *Grand Tour*, page 231.

Chapter 4

1. George Gordon, Lord Byron (1788–1824), *Don Juan*, canto III, stanza 16.
2. Richard Chandler, *Travels in Greece* (Oxford: Clarendon Press, 1776), pages 294–295.
3. Quoted in C. P. Bracken, *Antiquities Acquired* (North Pomfret, Vt.: David and Charles, 1975), page 17. This work is a useful summary of early travelers.
4. Amir Sobati's *The Parthenon Marbles and Lord Elgin* (London: Amir Sobati, 2002) and William St. Clair's *Lord Elgin and the Marbles* (Oxford: Oxford University Press, 1984) are useful accounts of the long-drawn-out controversy.
5. Extract from William Otter, *The Life and Remains of the Reverend Edward Daniel Clarke* (London: G. Cowie, 1824), volume 4, pages 618–621. Clarke's description of the statue appears in his *Greek Marbles Brought from the Shores of the Euxine, Archipelago, and Mediterranean, and Deposited in the Vestibule of the Public Library of the University of Cambridge* (Cambridge, U.K.: Cambridge University Press, 1809).
6. Samuel Pepys Cockerell, *Travels in Southern Europe and the Levant* (London: Longmans, 1903).
7. Quoted in Bracken, *Antiquities*, page 94.

Chapter 5

1. A. W. Kinglake, *Eothen* (New York: Putnam, 1847), page 47.
2. Vivant Denon, *Travels in Upper and Lower Egypt* (London: Longman and Rees, 1803), volume 1, page 145.
3. For a biography of Giovanni Belzoni, see Stanley Mayes, *The Great Belzoni* (London: Tauris Parke Paperbacks, 2003).
4. The pharaoh Rameses II built Abu Simbel as a shrine to the gods Amun and Re-Horakhy, as well as to himself. Abu Simbel is famous for its façade of huge seated figures of the pharaoh. UNESCO moved the temple to higher ground in 1968, at a cost of $40 million, to avoid flooding by the rising waters of Lake Nasser, formed by the Aswan Dam.
5. Burkhardt letter, quoted in Mayes, *The Great Belzoni*, page 142.
6. Letter by Champollion to his brother Jacques-Joseph. Quoted in Niccolo Rosselini, *Monumenti dell'Egito e della Nubia* (Pisa, Italy: University of Pisa, 1832), page 254.
7. John Lloyd Stephens, *Incidents of Travel in Egypt, Arabia Petraea, and the Holy Land* (New York: Harper, 1837). The extracts here are from pages 68–69 and 109–112.

8. Stephen Olin, *Travels in Egypt, Arabia Petraea, and the Holy Land* (New York: Harper, 1846), pages 112–114.
9. William Holman Hunt was an artist who remained faithful to Pre-Raphaelite ideas, painting moralistic and religious works with extreme detail and brightness. The extract comes from Hunt's *Pre-Raphaelitism and the Pre-Raphaelite Brotherhood* (New York: Macmillan, 1905), pages 210–213.
10. David Millard (1794–1873) was a Presbyterian minister and religious writer. The extract is from his *A Journal of Travels in Egypt, Arabia Petraea, and the Holy Land* (New York: Sheldon, Lamport and Blakeman, 1855), pages 244–246.
11. Quoted in *Flaubert in Egypt*, edited and translated by Francis Steegmuller (London: Bodley Head, 1972), page 56. Gustave Flaubert (1821–1880) was a French realist novelist, and his masterpiece *Madame Bovary* was published in 1856. *Madame Bovary*, about the frustrations and love affairs of a provincial doctor's wife, caused Flaubert to be prosecuted on moral grounds, but he won his case. He visited Egypt in 1849, ostensibly to study antiquities with the photographer Maxim du Camp, but was soon seduced by the sensuality of the place.

Chapter 6

1. William Kennet Loftus, *Travels and Researches in Chaldea and Susiana* (London: Nisbet, 1857), page 111.
2. Zephaniah 6:14.
3. Quoted in Eric Schmidt, *Persepolis I: Structures, Reliefs, Inscriptions* (Chicago: Oriental Institute of the University of Chicago, 1963), page 63.
4. Claudius James Rich, *Narrative of a Journey to the Site of Babylon in 1811* (London: Duncan and Malcolm, 1839), page 45.
5. Rich, *Narrative*, page 46.
6. Rich, *Narrative*, page 50.
7. Rich, *Narrative*, page 49.
8. Robert Ker Porter, *Travels in Georgia, Persia, Armenia, and Ancient Babylon* (2 volumes; London: Longmans, 1821), volume 1, page 177.
9. Porter, *Travels*, volume 2, page 274.
10. Porter, *Travels*, volume 2, pages 306–309.
11. Porter, *Travels*, volume 2, page 319.
12. Porter, *Travels*, volume 2, page 387.
13. Porter, *Travels*, volume 2, pages 338–339.
14. Porter, *Travels*, volume 2, pages 363–364.
15. Porter, *Travels*, volume 2, pages 365–366.
16. Rich, *Narrative*, pages 232–236.
17. Porter, *Travels*, volume 2, page 585.
18. Robert Byron, *The Road to Oxiana* (New York: Oxford University Press, 1982), page 167 (originally published, London: Jonathan Cape, 1937).

Chapter 7

1. Constantin-François Volney, *The Ruins; or, Meditation on the Revolutions of Empires and the Law of Nature* (New York: William A. Davis, 1796), page 1.
2. William Henry Bartlett (1809–1859) was a well-known book illustrator who became a successful travel author with his *Forty Days in the Desert: In the Tracks of the Israelites* (London: Arthur Hall, Virtue and Co., 1848). The quotation is from page 165.
3. C. F. Volney, *The Ruins*, Chapters 1 and 2.
4. P. V. N. Myers, *Remains of Lost Empires* (New York: Harpers, 1875), pages 29–30.
5. Jeremiah 49:16, 17.
6. John Lloyd Stephens, *Incidents of Travel in Egypt, Arabia Petraea, and the Holy Land* (New York: Harper, 1837. University of Oklahoma Press, 1970), pages 249–257.
7. John Lloyd Stephens, *Incidents of Travel in Egypt, Arabia Petraea, and the Holy Land* (reprint, Norman: University of Oklahoma Press, 1970), page 264.
8. Stephens, *Incidents,* pages 264–265.

Chapter 8

1. Hardwicke D. Rawnsley, *Notes for the Nile* (London: Heinemann, 1892), page 310.
2. Quoted from a letter by Wilkinson to the artist Robert Hay; see Brian Fagan, *The Rape of the Nile* (revised edition, Boulder, Colo.: Westview Press, 2004), page 177.
3. Douglas Sladen, *Egypt and the English* (London: Hurst and Blackett, 1908).
4. Mark Twain, *Innocents Abroad* (Hartford, Conn.: American Publishing Company, 1871).
5. Amelia Edwards, *A Thousand Miles up the Nile* (New York: Scribners, 1877), page 112.
6. Amelia Edwards, *A Thousand Miles up the Nile* (London: Longmans Green, 1877).
7. John Lloyd Stephens, *Incidents of Travel in Egypt, Arabia Petraea, and the Holy Land* (New York: Harper, 1837. Norman: University of Oklahoma Press, 1970), pages 117–118.

Chapter 9

1. The quotations are in *Relación de las Cosas de Yucatan*, translated by Alfred M. Tozzer (Cambridge, Mass.: Peabody Museum of American Archaeology and Ethnology, 1941), pages 14–15.
2. Jean Frédéric Waldeck, *Voyage pittoresque et archéologique dans . . . Yucatan* (Paris: B. Dufor, 1838), pages 77–78.

3. John Lloyd Stephens, *Incidents of Travel in Central America &c* (Harper, 1841. University of Oklahoma Press, 1983), pages 79ff.
4. John Lloyd Stephens, *Incidents of Travel in Central America &c* (Harper, 1841. University of Oklahoma Press, 1983), pages 297ff.
5. William Prescott, *The History of the Conquest of Peru* (New York: Harper, 1847), page 125.
6. Bernabe Cobo's 1653 *Historia del Nuevo Mundo*, translated by Roland Hamilton as *History of the Inca Empire* (Austin: University of Texas Press, 1979), page 56.
7. Ephraim George Squier, *Incidents of Travel and Exploration in the Land of the Incas.* (New York: AMS Press, 1973), pages 544ff.
8. Hiram Bingham, *Lost City of the Incas* (New York: Duell, Sloan, and Pearce, 1962), pages 212–214.

Chapter 10

1. *Narratives of the Coronado Expedition, 1540–1542*, edited by George P. Hammond (Albuquerque: University of New Mexico Press, 1940), page 222.
2. *J. H. Simpson: Journal of a Military Reconnaissance from Santa Fe, New Mexico, to the Navajo Country, Made in 1849*, edited by Frank McNitt (Norman: University of Oklahoma Press, 1964), page 36.
3. McNitt, *Journal*, page 48.
4. William Henry Jackson, *Time Exposure* (New York: G. P. Putnam's Sons, 1940), pages 231–234.
5. *Zuñi: Selected Writings of Frank Hamilton Cushing*, edited by Jesse Green (Lincoln: University of Nebraska Press, 1979), pages 47–48. The extracts quoted in this chapter come from "My Adventures in Zuñi," which Frank Cushing published in the *Century Illustrated Monthly Magazine* 25 (1882): 191–207 and 500–511, and 26 (1883): 28–47. The articles have been reprinted in books at least four times.
6. Green, *Zuñi*, pages 50–53.
7. Green, *Zuñi*, page 55.
8. Green, *Zuñi*, pages 55–58.
9. Green, *Zuñi*, pages 69–74.
10. Lilian Whiting, *The Land of Enchantment: From Pike's Peak to the Pacific* (Boston: Little Brown, 1906), extracted from pages 183–266.
11. James Faris, *The Nightway: A History and Documentation of a Navajo Ceremonial* (Albuquerque: University of New Mexico Press, 1990), extracted from pages 50–54.
12. Harvey Fergusson, *Footloose McGarnigal* (New York: Knopf, 1930), extracted from pages 103 and 107.
13. Brian Fagan, *Chaco Canyon: Archaeologists Explore the Lives of an Ancient Society* (New York: Oxford University Press, 2005), pages 3–4.

Chapter 11

1. Quoted in Sven Hedin, *My Life as an Explorer* (New York: Garden City Publishing Company, 1925), page 186.
2. Hedin, *My Life*, page 188.
3. Letter from Stein to his friend Percy Allen, March 17, 1901; quoted in Jeanette Mirsky, *Sir Aurel Stein: Archaeological Explorer* (Chicago: University of Chicago Press, 1977), page 255.
4. Extracts by Stein in this chapter are from his *Ruins of Desert Cathay* (London: Macmillan, 1912), pages 28–31.
5. Quoted in Mirsky, *Sir Aurel Stein*, page 443.

Chapter 12

1. Quotations in this paragraph are from Ella K. Maillart's *Forbidden Journey* (London: Heinemann, 1937; reprint, London: Century Publishing, 1983), page 3.
2. Peter Fleming, *News from Tartary* (London: Jonathan Cape, 1936), page 11.
3. Fleming, *Tartary*, pages 166–167.
4. Fleming, *Tartary*, pages 87–88.
5. Paul Fussell, *Abroad: British Literary Travelling between the Wars* (Oxford: Oxford University Press, 1980), page 73.
6. Evelyn Waugh, *When the Going Was Good* (London: Duckworth, 1946), page 11.
7. Quoted in Paul Fussell's "Introduction" in his edition of Robert Byron's *The Road to Oxiana* (New York: Oxford University Press, 1982), page vi. (*The Road to Oxiana* was originally published in 1937 by Jonathan Cape, London.)
8. Quoted in Fussell, "Introduction," pages vi–vii.
9. Quoted in Fussell, "Introduction," page viii.
10. Quoted in Fussell, "Introduction," page viii.
11. Byron, *Road to Oxiana*, page 42.
12. Byron, *Road to Oxiana*, page 43.
13. Byron, *Road to Oxiana*, page 78.
14. Byron, *Road to Oxiana*, page 80.
15. Byron, *Road to Oxiana*, pages 93–98.
16. Bryon, *Road to Oxiana*, pages 122–123.
17. Byron, *Road to Oxiana*, pages 209–213.
18. Byron, *Road to Oxiana*, pages 168–169. Ernst Herzfeld was a German archaeologist who led an American expedition at Persepolis in 1931–1935.
19. Byron, *Road to Oxiana*, pages 175–178.
20. Byron, *Road to Oxiana*, pages 198–201.
21. Byron, *Road to Oxiana*, page 286.

Chapter 13

1. Paul Theroux, *Riding the Iron Rooster* (New York: Random House, 1990), page 222.

2. Paul Theroux, *Dark Star Safari* (Boston: Houghton Mifflin, 2003), pages 38–48.
3. Brian Fagan, "The Wanderer's Lament," *Archaeology* 52 (1999): 9–22.
4. David Atherton, "Facing Ghosts of the Past atop the Great Wall," *Los Angeles Times*, March 9, 2002.
5. Tom Bissell, *Chasing the Sea: Lost among the Ghosts of Empire in Central Asia* (New York: Pantheon, 2003), pages 163–178.
6. Bissell, *Chasing the Sea*, pages 219–220 and 236–241.
7. Hugh Thomson, *The White Rock* (New York: Overlook Press, 2003), page 44.
8. Thomson, *The White Rock*, pages 182–188.
9. Karin Muller, *Along the Inca Road* (Washington, D.C.: National Geographic Society, 2001), pages 239–242.

Guide to Further Reading

The literature of adventure, archaeological discovery, and archaeological travel is enormous, often repetitive, and frequently, alas, dull. The suggestions for further reading that follow are some of the more interesting references and accounts, which offer a good start for the reader anxious to delve further into this diverse genre.

Chapter 1: Beginnings

First, some general works that should be on the reading list of anyone interested in archaeological travel. Rose Macaulay's *The Pleasure of Ruins* first appeared in 1953, but I would recommend the 1964 edition, which features excerpts from the original book chosen by Constance Babington-Smith and evocative photographs by Roloff Beny (London: Thames and Hudson, 1964). Macaulay's is an emotional, literary work, but nevertheless captures the essence of ruins. So does Christopher Woodward's *In Ruins* (New York: Pantheon, 2001), which offers an art historian's perspective. Woodward has a particularly useful bibliography. *Eyewitness to Discovery*, edited by Brian Fagan (New York: Oxford University Press, 1996), is an earlier companion to the present book, *From Stonehenge to Samarkand.*

One of the best translations of Herodotus is by Robin Waterfield, *Herodotus: The Histories* (Oxford: Oxford University Press, 1998). For the early history of Egyptology, see Brian Fagan, *The Rape of the Nile* (revised edition, Boulder, Colo.: Westview Press, 2004).

Chapter 2: The Antiquarians

Christopher Chippindale's *Stonehenge Complete* (revised edition, London: Thames and Hudson, 2004) is the definitive account of visits to Stonehenge, and Caroline Malone's *Avebury* (London: English Heritage,

1989) is the definitive account of visits to Avebury. On antiquaries generally, see Stuart Piggott, *Ruins in a Landscape: Essays in Antiquarianism* (Edinburgh: Edinburgh University Press, 1976), and T. D. Kendrick, *British Antiquity* (London: Methuen, 1949). Piggott also wrote an excellent biography of Stukeley: *William Stukeley: An Eighteenth-Century Antiquary* (revised edition, London: Thames and Hudson, 1985). See also David Boyd Haycock, *William Stukeley: Science, Religion, and Archaeology in Eighteenth-Century England* (London: Boydell Press, 2002).

Chapter 3: The Grand Tour

Jeremy Black, *The British Abroad: The Grand Tour in the Eighteenth Century* (Gloucester, U.K.: Sutton, 2003), and the same author's *Italy and the Grand Tour* (New Haven, Conn.: Yale University Press, 2003) are authoritative. See also Brian Dolan, *Ladies of the Grand Tour: British Women in Pursuit of Enlightenment and Adventure in Eighteenth-Century Europe* (New York: Harper Collins, 2001). Christopher Hibbert, *The Grand Tour* (New York: Putnam, 1969), is another excellent popular summary. See also Melissa Calaresu's perceptive article, "Looking for Virgil's Tomb: The End of the Grand Tour and the Cosmopolitan Ideal in Europe," in *Voyages and Visions: Towards a Cultural History of Travel*, edited by Jas Elsner and Joan-Pau Rubiés (London: Reaktion Books, 1999), pages 138–161. An academic study of early travel writing is Nigel Leask's *Curiosity and the Aesthetics of Travel Writing, 1770–1840* (New York: Oxford University Press, 2002).

Chapter 4: Greece Bespoiled

Robert Eisner's *Travelers to an Antique Land* (Ann Arbor: University of Michigan Press, 1991) is a comprehensive study of travelers to Greece and includes excellent coverage of archaeological sites. The book contains an extensive bibliography. C. P. Bracken, *Antiquities Acquired: The Spoliation of Greece* (North Pomfret, Vt.: David and Charles, 1975), is a popular account. See also Fani-Maria Tsigakou, *The Rediscovery of Greece* (London: Thames and Hudson, 1981), and David Constantine, *Early Greek Travelers and the Hellenic Ideal* (Cambridge, U.K.: Cambridge University Press, 1984).

Chapter 5: Pharaohs and Pyramids

Brian Fagan, *The Rape of the Nile* (revised edition, Boulder, Colo.: Westview Press, 2004), is a popular survey of the people and events in this chapter, and also has comprehensive references to biographies and other materials. A useful anthology of Egyptian travelers is *Egypt: A Traveller's Anthology*, edited by Christopher Pick (London: John Murray, 1991). Peter Clayton's *Chronicle of the Pharaohs* (London: Thames and Hudson, 1994) is an excellent account of Egypt's kings for the beginner. F. Gladstone Bratton, *A History of Egyptian Archaeology* (London: Hale, 1967), is particularly informative about the early Greek authors and early tourists.

Robin Feddon's *Egypt: Land of the Valley* (London: John Murray, 1965) is a wonderfully evocative essay on ancient and mid-twentieth-century Egypt. For Napoleon in Egypt, see Christopher Herold, *Bonaparte in Egypt* (New York: Harper and Row, 1962).

Chapter 6: From Babylon to Persepolis

Seton Lloyd, *Foundations in the Dust* (revised edition, London: Thames and Hudson, 1980), is a classic account of early archaeology in Mesopotamia. A more technical comprehensive study of the same subject, with excellent readable historical information, is Mogens Trolle Larsen's *The Conquest of Assyria* (London: Routledge, 1996). See also Brian Fagan, *Return to Babylon* (revised edition, Boulder: University of Colorado Press, 2007).

Chapter 7: Palmyra and Petra

John Lloyd Stephens, *Incidents of Travel in Egypt, Arabia Petraea, and the Holy Land* (Norman: University of Oklahoma Press, 1970), was originally published in 1837 and is still an entertaining, evocative read. The same sites are well covered by Rose Macaulay in her *Pleasure of Ruins* (London: Thames and Hudson, 1964). Jane Taylor, *Petra and the Lost Kingdom of the Nabateans* (Cambridge, Mass.: Harvard University Press, 2005), offers excellent coverage of this spectacular site. See also Maria Giulia Amadasi and Eugenia Equini Schneider, *Petra*, translated by Lydia G. Cochrane (Chicago: University of Chicago Press, 2002). For Palmyra, try Richard Stoneman, *Palmyra and Its Empire: Zenobia's Revolt against Rome* (Ann Arbor: University of Michigan Press, 1995).

Chapter 8: Tourists Along the Nile

The general books cited for Chapter 5 are also relevant here. Amelia Edwards's *A Thousand Miles up the Nile* (New York: Scribners, 1877) is a deserved Victorian classic and well worth reading, and an important biography is Joan Rees's *Amelia Edwards: Traveler, Novelist, and Egyptologist* (London: Rubicon Press, 1998). *Lucie Duff-Gordon, Letters from Egypt, 1862–1869*, edited by Gordon Waterfield (New York: Praeger, 1969), is a deeply moving, vivid account of life in Egypt in the 1860s. Do not miss *Amelia Peabody's Egypt*, edited by Elizabeth Peters et al. (New York: William Morrow, 2003), a serious companion for Peters's wonderful detective stories featuring the fictional Egyptologist Amelia Peabody. If you have not read Peters's stories, you have missed a delicious treat. Piers Brandon's *Thomas Cook: 150 Years of Popular Tourism* (London: Secker and Warburg, 1991) is a useful biography of this pioneer travel agent. John Pemble, *The Mediterranean Passion: Victorians and Edwardians in the South* (Oxford: Clarendon Press, 1987), is an academic study of this enormous topic.

Chapter 9: Maya and Inca

The Conquest of Mexico (Baltimore: Pelican Books, 1963) offers J. H. Cohen's definitive translation of Bernal Diaz's account of the Spanish conquest of Mexico. The classics are John Lloyd Stephens, *Incidents of Travel in Central America, Chiapas, and Yucatan* (New York: Harpers, 1841; reprint, Washington, D.C.: Smithsonian Institution Press, 1993), and *Incidents of Travel in Yucatan* (New York: Harpers, 1843; reprint, Washington, D.C.: Smithsonian Books, 1996). They are as entertaining today as they were when they were first published. Robert L. Brunhouse, *In Search of the Maya* (Albuquerque: University of New Mexico Press, 1973), provides an excellent study of early Maya explorers and travelers. For the history of both Maya and Inca archaeology, see Gordon R. Willey and Jeremy A. Sabloff, *A History of American Archaeology* (third edition, New York: W. H. Freeman, 1993). Ephraim Squier, *Incidents of Travel and Exploration in the Land of the Incas* (reprint, Cambridge, Mass.: Peabody Museum of Archaeology and Ethnology, 1972), is well worth reading to gain insights into conditions in the late nineteenth century.

Chapter 10: The World of the Pueblos

A huge literature surrounds the southwestern pueblos. A good starting point is Don D. Fowler, *A Laboratory for Anthropology: Science and Romanticism in the American Southwest* (Albuquerque: University of New Mexico Press, 2000). James E. Snead, *The Making of Southwest Archaeology* (Tucson: University of Arizona Press, 2001), is another excellent, more technical, but readable study. No one should miss Frank Cushing's stirring adventures: *Zuñi: Selected Writings of Frank Hamilton Cushing*, edited by Jesse Green (Lincoln: University of Nebraska Press, 1979), is an accessible and well-edited collection of Cushing's work. For more on Chaco Canyon, read Brian Fagan, *Chaco Canyon: Archaeologists Explore the Lives of an Ancient Society* (New York: Oxford University Press, 2005).

Chapter 11: To Desert and Steppe

Two traveler-explorers dominate this chapter, Sven Hedin and Sir Aurel Stein. Hedin loved to boast of his travels, and an impression of them can be found in his own *My Life as an Explorer* (New York: Garden City Publishing Company, 1925). For a biographical account, try George Kish, *To the Heart of Asia: The Life of Sven Hedin* (Ann Arbor: University of Michigan Press, 1984). Aurel Stein was not a fluent writer, and was a boring lecturer. You are better off following his life and publications through two excellent biographies: Jeanette Mirsky, *Sir Aurel Stein: Archaeological Explorer* (Chicago: University of Chicago Press, 1977), and Annabel Walker, *Aurel Stein: Pioneer of the Silk Road* (Seattle: University of Washington Press, 1999). See also Susan Whitfield, *Aurel Stein on the Silk Road* (Chicago: Serindia Publications, 2004). Christoph Baumer, *Southern Silk Road: In the Footsteps of Sir Aurel Stein and Sven Hedin* (Hong Kong: Orchid Press, 2000), provides a lavishly illustrated, up-to-date look at the archaeology of numerous Silk Road sites.

Chapter 12: Individualists

The archaeological (and other) travelers of the first half of the last century have generated a considerable amount of academic literature, which is surveyed in *Tourists with Typewriters*, edited by Patrick Holland and Graham Huggan (Ann Arbor: University of Michigan Press, 1998). Much of the discussion in these pages is arcane in the extreme for general readers. Paul Fussell, *Abroad: British Literary Travelling between the World Wars* (Oxford: Oxford University Press, 1980), is a widely quoted study of these travelers. Ella Maillart, *Forbidden Journey* (London: Heinemann, 1937; reprint, London: Marlboro Press, 2003), is a classic and should be read alongside her companion's book, Peter Fleming's *News from Tartary* (London: Jonathan Cape, 1936; reprint, London: Marlboro Press, 1999). These books give an unrivaled picture of what it was like to travel in central Asia three-quarters of a century ago. Many travel-writing aficionados regard Robert Byron's *The Road to Oxiana* (London: Jonathan Cape, 1937) as another classic, but it is an eccentric book without a very strong story line. (See also Paul Fussell's edition of Byron's book, New York: Oxford University Press, 1982.) In "From Herat to Kabul: Retracing Robert Byron's Road to Oxiana," *Asian Affairs* 27.1 (1966): 3–12, the travel journalist Jonathan Ford attempts to follow Byron's route.

Chapter 13: Travel as Commodity

You only have to read the travel sections of major newspapers to realize how commodified travel has become. Stories about travel to archaeological sites are surprisingly rare, however. *The Cambridge Companion to Travel Writing*, edited by Peter Hulme and Tim Young (Cambridge, U.K.: Cambridge University Press, 2002), is useful, as are annual volumes in the *Best Travel Writing* series, published by Travelers' Tales Guides. Paul Theroux's writings are excellent examples of contemporary travel writing, for he is a perceptive observer.

Archaeological travel articles appear in *Archaeology Magazine,* as well as in London-based *Current World Archaeology* and Albuquerque-based *American Archaeology*. *National Geographic Magazine* is also a major source of travel stories that combine adventure and archaeology, or sometimes treat of archaeology alone. For modern examples of the genre, see Tom Bissell, *Chasing the Sea: Lost among the Ghosts of Empire in Central Asia* (New York: Pantheon, 2003), and Hugh Thomson, *The White Rock* (New York: Overlook Press, 2003). See also Robert McGhee, *The Last Imaginary Place* (New York: Oxford University Press, 2005), which weaves anthropology, archaeology, history, and travel into an account of the Arctic past.

Acknowledgments

From Stonehenge to Samarkand was long in gestation, and involved reading an enormous number of archaeological writings, many of them, I must admit at once, extremely dull. I am grateful to Casper Grathwohl of Oxford University Press for commissioning this book in the first place, and also for his patience with my dilatoriness in completing the project. This book owes a great deal to the editorial skills of Ben Keene, who also has shown exemplary patience with me. His suggestions have been invaluable. Finally, grateful thanks to Katie Henderson for her sterling work on the illustrations and permissions and to Georgia Maas, who expertly navigated the mauscript through the rapids of production.

This book is a loosely drawn sequel to an earlier anthology, *Eyewitness to Discovery*, a series of firsthand accounts of archaeological discoveries published by Oxford University Press in 1996. There are some inevitable, and unavoidable, overlaps between the two books, but I am unapologetic, for adventure, discovery, and travel overlap. After all, who can compile an anthology of travel writing without including John Lloyd Stephens's account of Copán?

Every reasonable effort has been made to acquire the necessary permissions to reproduce the writings in this volume. Inquiries regarding copyright should be addressed to the publisher.

Credits

While every effort has been made to secure permission, we apologize if in any case we have failed to trace the copyright holder.

Texts

Pages 105–108 *Incidents of Travel in Egypt, Arabia, Petraea, and the Holy Land* by John Lloyd Stephens. Reprinted with permission of University of Oklahoma Press.

Pages 109–110 *Incidents of Travel in Egypt, Arabia, Petraea, and the Holy Land* by John Lloyd Stephens. Reprinted with permission of University of Oklahoma Press.

Pages 127–128 *Incidents of Travel in Egypt, Arabia, Petraea, and the Holy Land* by John Lloyd Stephens. Reprinted with permission of University of Oklahoma Press.

Pages 135–137 *Incidents of Travel in Yucatan* by John Lloyd Stephens. Reprinted with permission of University of Oklahoma Press.

Pages 138–141 *Incidents of Travel in Yucatan* by John Lloyd Stephens. Reprinted with permission of University of Oklahoma Press.

Pages 141–142 *Incidents of Travel in Yucatan* by John Lloyd Stephens. Reprinted with permission of University of Oklahoma Press.

Pages 150–155 *Lost City of the Incas* by Hiram Bingham. Reprinted with permission of Orion Publishing Group.

Pages 166–168 Reprinted from *Zuñi: Selected Writings of Frank Hamilton Cushing* edited, with an introduction, by Jesse Green with permission of the University of Nebraska Press. Copyright © 1979 by the University of Nebraska Press.

Pages 169–170 Reprinted from *Zuñi: Selected Writings of Frank Hamilton Cushing* edited, with an introduction, by Jesse Green with permission of the University of Nebraska Press. Copyright © 1979 by the University of Nebraska Press.

Pages 170–172 Reprinted from *Zuñi: Selected Writings of Frank Hamilton Cushing* edited, with an introduction, by Jesse Green with per-

	mission of the University of Nebraska Press. Copyright © 1979 by the University of Nebraska Press.
Pages 172–175	Reprinted from *Zuñi: Selected Writings of Frank Hamilton Cushing* edited, with an introduction, by Jesse Green with permission of the University of Nebraska Press. Copyright © 1979 by the University of Nebraska Press.
Pages 185–186	*My Life as an Explorer* by Sven Hedin. Reprinted with permission of Asian Educational Services.
Pages 227–233	Excerpts from *Dark Star Safari: Overland from Cairo to Cape Town* by Paul Theroux. Copyright © 2003 by Paul Theroux. Reprintedby permission of Houghton Mifflin Company. All rights reserved.
Pages 239–242	"Facing Ghosts of the Past atop the Great wall" by David Atherton. Reprinted with permission of the author, © 2002 by David Atherton
Pages 242–246	From *Chasing the Sea* by Tom Bissell, copyright © 2003 by Thomas Carlisle Bissell. Used by permission of Pantheon Books, a division of Random House, Inc.
Pages 246–251	From *Chasing the Sea* by Tom Bissell, copyright © 2003 by Thomas Carlisle Bissell. Used by permission of Pantheon Books, a division of Random House, Inc.
Pages 251–255	*The White Rock* by Hugh Thompson. Reprinted with permission of Overlook Press.
Pages 255–257	From the book *Along the Inca Road* by Karin Muller. Copyright © 2000 Karin Muller. Reprinted with permission of the National Geographic Society.

Illustrations

2-1	Copyright Allan T. Kohl/Art Images for College Teaching
2-2	© National Portrait Gallery, London
3-1	Fine Art Photographic Library, London/Art Resource, NY
4-1	Copyright Allan T. Kohl/Art Images for College Teaching
4-2	Erich Lessing/Art Resource, NY
4-3	Foto Marburg/Art Resource, NY
5-1	Victoria & Albert Museum, London/Art Resource, NY
6-1	Giraudon/Art Resource, NY
6-2	SEF/Art Resource, NY
7-1	Photo by Galen R Frysinger, www.galenfrysinger.com
8-1	Erich Lessing /Art Resource, NY
8-2	Courtesy of the Mark Twain Project, Bancroft Library, University of California, Berkeley
10-1	Northern Arizona University, Cline Library
10-2	Courtesy of L. Tom Perry Special Collections at the Harold B. Lee Library, Brigham Young University

10-3 © The J. Paul Getty Trust, [1993]. All rights reserved.
10-4 Courtesy of Filter Press
11-2 Bildarchiv Preussischer Kulturbesitz/Art Resource, NY
12-1 Borromeo/Art Resource, NY
12-2 Courtesy of Musée de l'Elysée
13-1 Erich Lessing/Art Resource, NY
13-2 Erich Lessing/Art Resource, NY
13-3 Erich Lessing/Art Resource, NY

Index